ETHICAL CAPITALISM

Shibusawa Eiichi and Business Leadership in Global Perspective

T0341446

Shibusawa Eiichi (1840–1931) was a Japanese banker and industrialist who spearheaded the modernization of Japanese industry and finance during the Meiji Restoration. He founded the first modern bank in Japan, and his reforms introduced double-entry accounting and joint-stock corporations to the Japanese economy. Today, he is known as the "father of Japanese capitalism."

Ethical Capitalism is a volume of essays that explores the thought, work, and legacy of Shibusawa Eiichi and offers international comparisons with the Japanese experience. Shibusawa advocated for *gappon-shugi*, a principle that emphasized developing the right business, with the right people, in service to the public good. The contributors build a historical perspective on morality and ethics in the business world that, unlike corporate social responsibility, concentrates on the morality inside firms, industries, and private-public partnerships. *Ethical Capitalism* is not only a timely work; it is a necessary work, in a rapidly globalizing world where deregulation and lack of oversight risk repeating the financial, environmental, and social catastrophes of the past.

(Japan and Global Society)

PATRICK FRIDENSON is a professor of international business history in the Centre de Recherches Historique at L'Ecole des Hautes Etudes en Science Sociales in Paris.

KIKKAWA TAKEO is a professor in the Graduate School of Innovation Studies, Tokyo University of Science.

JAPAN AND GLOBAL SOCIETY

Editors: IRIYE AKIRA, *Harvard University*; KIMURA MASATO, *Shibusawa Eiichi Memorial Foundation*; DAVID A. WELCH, *Balsillie School of International Affairs, University of Waterloo*

How has Japan shaped, and been shaped by, globalization – politically, economically, socially, and culturally? How has its identity, and how have its objectives, changed? *Japan and Global Society* explores Japan's past, present, and future interactions with the Asia Pacific and the world from a wide variety of disciplinary and interdisciplinary per-spectives and through diverse paradigmatic lenses. Titles in this series are intended to showcase international scholarship on Japan and its regional neighbours that will appeal to scholars in disciplines both in the humanities and the social sciences.

Japan and Global Society is supported by generous grants from the Shi-busawa Eiichi Memorial Foundation and the University of Missouri–St Louis.

Editorial Advisory Board

Frederick R. Dickinson, University of Pennsylvania
Michael Donnelly, University of Toronto
Joel Glassman, University of Missouri–St Louis
Izumi Koide, Graduate School of University of Tokyo
Gil Latz, Indiana University–Purdue University Indianapolis
Michael A. Schneider, Knox College
Patricia G. Steinhoff, University of Hawaii at Manoa
Patricia Wetzel, Portland State University

For a list of books published in the series, see page 216.

Ethical Capitalism

Shibusawa Eiichi and Business Leadership in Global Perspective

EDITED BY PATRICK FRIDENSON
AND KIKKAWA TAKEO

UNIVERSITY OF TORONTO PRESS
Toronto   Buffalo   London

© University of Toronto Press 2017
Toronto Buffalo London
www.utppublishing.com
Printed and bound by CPI Group (UK) Ltd, Croydon, CR0 4YY

Reprinted in paperback 2017

ISBN 978-1-4875-0106-8 (cloth)   ISBN 978-1-4875-2296-4 (paper)

♾ Printed on acid-free, 100% post-consumer recycled paper.

First published as *Gurōbaru shihonshugi no naka no Shibusawa Eiichi: Gappon kyapitarizumu to moraru* by Tokyo: Toyo Keizai, 2014.

Library and Archives Canada Cataloguing in Publication

Ethical capitalism : Shibusawa Eiichi and business leadership in global perspective / edited by Patrick Fridenson and Kikkawa Takeo.

(Japan and global society)
Includes bibliographical references.
ISBN 978-1-4875-0106-8 (cloth).   ISBN 978-1-4875-2296-4 (softcover)

1. Shibusawa, Eiichi, 1840–1931.   2. Capitalism – Moral and ethical aspects.   3. Capitalism – Japan.   I. Fridenson, Patrick, 1944–, author, editor II. Kikkawa, Takeo, 1951–, author, editor   III. Series: Japan and global society

HB501.E85 2017   306.3′42   C2016-907698-9

University of Toronto Press acknowledges the financial assistance to its publishing program of the Canada Council for the Arts and the Ontario Arts Council, an agency of the Government of Ontario.

Canada Council   Conseil des Arts
for the Arts   du Canada

ONTARIO ARTS COUNCIL
CONSEIL DES ARTS DE L'ONTARIO
an Ontario government agency
un organisme du gouvernement de l'Ontario

Funded by the   Financé par le
Government   gouvernement
of Canada   du Canada

Canadä

Contents

Foreword

University of Toronto Press, in cooperation with the University of Missouri–St Louis and the Shibusawa Eiichi Memorial Foundation of Tokyo, has launched an ambitious new series, "Japan and Global Society." The volumes in the series explore how Japan has defined its identities and objectives in the larger region of Asia and the Pacific and, at the same time, how the global community has been shaped by Japan and its interactions with other countries.

The dual focus on Japan and on global society reflects the series editors' and publishers' commitment to globalizing national studies. Scholars and readers have become increasingly aware that it makes little sense to treat a country in isolation. All countries are interdependent and shaped by cross-national forces so that mono-national studies, those that examine a country's past and present in isolation, are never satisfactory. Such awareness has grown during the past few decades when global, transnational phenomena and forces have gained prominence. In the age of globalization, no country retains complete autonomy or freedom of action. Yet nations continue to act in pursuit of their respective national interests, which frequently results in international tensions. Financial, social, and educational policies continue to be defined domestically, with national communities as units. But transnational economic, environmental, and cultural forces always infringe upon national entities, transforming them in subtle and sometimes even violent ways. Global society, consisting of billions of individuals and their organizations, evolves and shapes national communities even as the latter contribute to defining the overall human community.

Japan provides a particularly pertinent instance of such interaction, but this series is not limited to studies of that country alone. Indeed, the books published in the series will show that there is little unique about Japan, whose history has been shaped by interactions with China, Korea, the United States, and many other countries. For this reason, forthcoming volumes will deal with countries in the Asia-Pacific region and compare their respective developments and shared destinies. At the same time, some studies in the series will transcend national frameworks and discuss more transnational themes, such as humanitarianism, migration, and diseases, documenting how these phenomena affect Japan and other countries and how, at the same time, they contribute to the making of a more interdependent global society.

Lastly, we hope these studies will help to promote an understanding of non-national entities, such as regions, religions, and civilizations. Modern history continues to be examined in terms of nations as the key units of analysis, and yet these other entities have their own vibrant histories, which do not necessarily coincide with nation-centred narratives. To look at Japan, or for that matter any other country, and to examine its past and present in these alternative frameworks will enrich our understanding of modern world history and of the contemporary global civilization.

Iriye Akira

Preface

Today business, public opinion, media and social networks, academia, governments, and international organizations bustle with discussions on economy and morality.[1] Is economy congruent with morality? Is morality congruent with economy? What are the possible relations between discourse on business ethics and actual practices? The message of this book is that looking at ideas, networks, or rules developed in Japan from the late nineteenth century onwards is relevant and important for today: to better understand how and why the motivation to "do good" might emerge, how to strengthen it, what difficulties might arise, and what role there might be for ethical capitalism in Japan, as Shibusawa Eiichi, recognizing that wealth is not enough, first exemplified it.

Markets under modern capitalism do not rely simply on finance or competition. Markets need rules in order to function, and whereas earlier markets were related to the political and fiscal power of the nobility, later market rules usually have been elicited either by enterprises themselves or by other types of institutions (local, national, or international). Morality can be one dimension of such rules, and it can be a matter of conflict between national actors or, as quite early on, between national and foreign actors. Religion also contributes to shape discussions on economic morality, as research has confirmed[2] – indeed, this book stresses that religion matters. Yet religious belief is not the only source of inspiration for actors. Economic morality is also connected to secular discussions among entrepreneurs, academics, in the media, and in the public sphere. Furthermore, as this book outlines, the ways these discussions could extend to relations between employers and wage-earners, between producers and consumers, and between business and nature lead to the theme of corporate social responsibility. It is no surprise that views and actions in favour of ethical capitalism – which Shibusawa pioneered in Asia – have been the exception, not the norm. I simply note here that minorities matter: their views or strategies have often much later become the bases for new convergences.

Historically, what is morality in business? In a recent book of historical sociology about business ethics in the United States from the 1850s to the 1930s, Gabriel Abend suggests that morality consists of three levels: "moral and immoral behavior, or the behavioral level; moral understandings and norms, or the normative level; and the moral background, which includes what moral concepts exist in a society, what moral methods can be used, what reasons can be given, and what objects can be morally evaluated at all. This background underlies the behavioral and normative levels; it supports, facilitates, and enables them." Through this perspective, Abend examines for the United States the work of numerous business ethicists and organizations – such as Protestant ministers, business associations, and business schools – and identifies two types of moral background. "Standards of practice" is characterized by its scientific worldview, moral relativism, and emphasis on individuals' actions and decisions. The "Christian merchant" type is characterized by its Christian worldview, moral objectivism, and conception of a person's life as a unity.[3] Such analysis can be extended to other ethical views: in early nineteenth-century France, Henri de Saint-Simon created a type of utopian socialism that he called the "new Christianity" to combine industrialization and ethics, and this can be extended to other religions, such as Catholicism or those of India (and what about Islam?). A striking feature of this book is how it reveals that Shibusawa reinterpreted the ancient views of Confucius to organize morality in Meiji Japan in a dynamic perspective. In our own time the People's Republic of China has used neo-Confucianism to become a major economic power.

What was at stake for the three Western historians who joined the Japanese research project dealing with a notion – *gapponshugi* – totally unknown to them and whose contributions are presented in this volume? Let me explain my own viewpoint as a Frenchman. As I was eager to understand Japanese economic growth and civilization, I first visited Japan in 1964, when I was twenty. I became a business historian, and have remained in contact with my Japanese counterparts since 1973; I have been going to Japan to do comparative research since 1992. In a nutshell this experience over all these years has convinced me that it would be short-sighted to analyse modern Japanese economic life only in terms of catching up with the West – that it is more important to understand how the Japanese have been able to create another way to be modern.

When in spring 2011 the Shibusawa Eiichi Memorial Foundation in Tokyo asked three Western historians – from the London School of Economics, the Harvard Business School, and the École des hautes études en sciences sociales, respectively – to join its new research project on *gapponshugi*, we accepted for three more reasons.

One was the importance of the core topic of the project: building a historical perspective on morality and ethics in world business, themes that had been relatively neglected by the social sciences, including history. There has been a flurry of studies on corporate social responsibility since the 1950s,[4] and particularly since the 1990s, but they have emphasized either business attitudes to the environment or the continuity between corporate social responsibility and paternalism. But morality inside firms, among firms, and between firms and governments, and public integrity as components of globalization, although closely related, were in need of further research. This was also true of the links between morality and the contemporary concern for governance, as is evidenced in the case of public sector integrity:

> Integrity is the corner stone of good governance. Fostering integrity and preventing corruption in the public sector support a level playing field for businesses and is essential to maintaining trust in government. "Integrity" refers to the application of values, principles and norms in the daily operations of public sector organizations. Governments are under growing pressure from the public to use information, resources and authority for intended purposes. Achieving a culture of integrity requires coherent efforts to update standards, provide guidance, and monitor and enforce them in daily practice. It also requires countries to anticipate risks and apply tailored countermeasures.[5]

The second reason we Westerners accepted the invitation to join the *gapponshugi* project was the view of capitalism that the leading Japanese banker and industrialist Shibusawa Eiichi developed in the course of Japan's economic modernization. We wanted to know more about the origins and content of the unusual and intriguing ideal of "harmony of morality and economy" that this pioneering entrepreneur advocated and practised throughout his long life. To these questions the book gives two main answers. The first is that three types of business leaders exist in Japan: owners, salaried managers, and investor managers; as the creator of some five hundred companies and a supporter of a type of shareholders' capitalism (*gapponshugi*), Shibusawa belongs to the third category. A second element is related to the shifting frontier between public and private. In Japan, Shibusawa argued in favour of private business, and thought that the state's role should only be to support private business – indeed, his championing of ethical capitalism was linked to this primacy of the private. Today this debate has taken new forms: whereas a number of academics have argued that firms are not equipped to be social institutions, others have stressed the broadening of the responsibility of firms as a consequence of capitalist growth. Shibusawa's views also led the authors of this book to ask if ethical profit-making is not a contradiction in terms. Furthermore, were Adam Smith and Confucius "in full agreement with one another" as to the possible compatibility between "the life of virtue and the life of business"?[6] We understood Shibusawa's notion of *gapponshugi* as the idea that a free market needs rules, that such rules should include ethics, and that simply copying Western rules and practices was not necessarily the best way for other countries to reach the difficult goal of combining business, economic growth, and morality. We also came to understand that this was an issue not only for Japan in the Meiji and Taisho eras (1868–1926), but that it remains a challenge today and for all nations. Indeed, the world financial crisis of 2008 posed many ethical questions, and stressed "the critical differences between compliance and ethics."[7]

The third reason was the unique opportunity this project has given Western historians to interact with Japanese scholars in different fields (history, philosophy, and sociology) over a period of three years. The book before your eyes thus brings together Western and Japanese scholarship. It argues that there is more than one way to do capitalism. It explains how and why, in Japan in the last third of the nineteenth century, a major business leader, Shibusawa Eiichi, expressed the view that business enterprise could and should earn profits and enhance the public good simultaneously. It asks whether the solutions Shibusawa suggested are relevant today for the business community – and a parallel might be drawn with *The Book of Five Rings*, written in 1645 by the Japanese swordsman Miyamoto Musashi, which appealed to world businessmen in the 1980s for its discussion of conflict and taking the advantage. It considers that regulation and moral behaviour are not necessarily alternatives, and that the building of public trust is essential.

It explains that bankers, industrialists, merchants, and distributors must confront multiple ethical issues and look for workable solutions. Ethical capitalism is one of them. The book aims at understanding both the Asian and Western origins of ethical capitalism, mapping the evolving arguments about the responsibility of business and the changing practices of firms, surveying the shifting relationship between public and private, and debating the relationship between morality and economy for globalized economies and societies from the perspective of sustainable growth.

By stressing that ethics is an important move in this direction, but that it is not enough, and by adding that the congruence between economy and morality partly depends on developing the motivation among businesspeople themselves to do good, Shibusawa still speaks to our contemporary debate.

Patrick Fridenson

NOTES

1 My thanks to those who gave papers at session 15 of the World Economic History Congress, Kyoto, 5 August 2015 and to the anonymous referees at the University of Toronto Press.
2 Françoise Bayard, Patrick Fridenson, and Albert Rigaudière, eds., *Genèse des marchés* (Paris: Comité pour l'histoire économique et financière de la France, 2015).
3 Gabriel Abend, *The Moral Background: An Inquiry into the History of Business Ethics* (Princeton, NJ: Princeton University Press, 2014), 16, 18, 25–7, 32.
4 Aurélien Acquier, Jean-Pascal Gond, and Jean Pasquero, "Rediscovering Howard R. Bowen's Legacy: The Unachieved Agenda and Continuing Relevance of *Social Responsibilities of the Businessman," Business & Society* 50, no. 4 (2011): 607–46.
5 See Organisation for Economic Co-operation and Development, "Public Sector Integrity Reviews" (Paris: OECD, 2000), available online at http://www.oecd.org/corruption/ethics/publicsectorintegrityreviews.htm.
6 Melissa S. Williams, "Moral Foundations of Politics and the Harmony of Ideas," in *Rediscovering Shibusawa Eiichi in the 21st Century*, ed. Gil Latz (Tokyo: Shibusawa Eiichi Memorial Foundation, 2014), 250–2.
7 John Reynolds, *Ethics in Investment Banking*, with Edmund Newell (Basingstoke, UK: Palgrave Macmillan, 2011).

Acknowledgments

The contents of this book are based on a three-year research project (2011–13) on Shibusawa Eiichi's Confucian-inspired concept of *gapponshugi*, which insists that capitalism can be, and has a responsibility to be, ethical, and the historical development of this concept among businesspeople in Japan and elsewhere. We would like to take this opportunity to express our deepest gratitude to those who have continuously extended their strong support for this project. First, we recognize the Shibusawa Eiichi Memorial Foundation, without whose generous financial and logistical support this project would not have gotten off the ground in the first place. Second, we extend our sincere thanks to the University of Missouri–St Louis for its generous financial support of the series Japan and Global Society, published by the University of Toronto Press. In particular, we would like to give our thanks to Mr Shibusawa Masahide, president of the Shibusawa Eiichi Memorial Foundation, and to Dr Joel Glassman, associate provost and director of international studies, University of Missouri–St Louis. Third, we express our gratitude to: Osaka University; Bunkyo Gakuin University; the London School of Economics; the Harvard Business School; the Organisation for Economic Co-operation and Development; the Japan Cultural Institute in Paris (The Japan Foundation, France); the École des hautes études en sciences sociales, Paris; and the Business History Society of Japan for their kind support for our symposia and numerous brainstorming sessions during this project.

Many people offered helpful comments and suggestions. Two anonymous readers, who read the entire manuscript thoroughly, provided constructive criticism. Reflecting on these comments during the revision process has made the volume much better in the end. Among many scholars who gave us comments and suggestions, we would like to give special mention to Professors Yui Tsunehiko, Kagono Tadao, and Gil Latz.

Finally, at the publication stage, special mention must be made of Daniel Quinlan at the University of Toronto Press for his support, wisdom, and expertise. We also thank our freelance copy editor, Barry Norris.

We should note that we have adopted the traditional Japanese practice of putting family or surnames first, except for individuals who regularly use the Western name format or who are better known in the West by that format.

We would like to close with the standard disclaimer that the opinions expressed in this volume, and any errors, are the sole responsibility of the authors alone and not those of the organizations or individuals who have supported our work. As editors, we are of course keen to learn of any errors the volume might contain, so that we can address them in any future revisions.

Patrick Fridenson and Kikkawa Takeo

ETHICAL CAPITALISM

Shibusawa Eiichi and Business Leadership
in Global Perspective

Introduction

KIKKAWA TAKEO

Modern capitalism has contributed immensely to human material wealth in the modern era. Wealth, however, is not an unalloyed good, and its distribution is far from equal across the globe, as present-day socio-economic disparities confirm both within countries and between regions of the world. Pursuit of larger profits can lead to reckless behaviour. For example, bubble economies can occur that, upon bursting, bring worldwide financial crises such as the Great Depression caused by the stock market crash in 1929 and the bankruptcy of Lehman Brothers in 2008. The root of these crises is the failure to regulate the excesses of capitalist behaviour. One of the most important and stimulating challenges of our time is how to re-establish global capitalism based on well-defined ethical principles that govern entrepreneurial business activities such that the benefits of such economic behaviour are accentuated and the limitations carefully considered and managed. Both the public and private sectors are tackling this challenge, but it is one that is represented, nonetheless, by a conundrum: is morality necessary for economic success, or is economic success independent of moral considerations?

This book aims to explore new possibilities for global capitalism in the twenty-first century through an analysis of *gapponshugi*, a nineteenth- and early twentieth-century principle of capitalism infused with moral values, and that here is defined as the principle of developing a business by assembling the best possible people and funding to achieve the mission and aim of pursuing the public good. One of the most important advocates of *gapponshugi* was Shibusawa Eiichi (1840–1931), well known as an entrepreneur who played a leadership role in establishing modern Japan during the late nineteenth and early twentieth centuries.

To understand the relationship between *gapponshugi* and Shibusawa's thinking and contributions to Japanese society, I begin by offering a brief review of his life.

Shibusawa Eiichi was born in Chiaraijima (now Fukaya, Saitama Prefecture), during the First Opium War between Britain and China. His father, Shibusawa Ichiroemon, had a distinguished talent for commerce and financial management. Through promoting the sale of indigo and silk, the Shibusawas became a wealthy farming family in Chiaraijima, enabling Eiichi to learn the structure of commerce and acquire financial skills through conducting businesses with his father.

As a youth, Shibusawa studied both Chinese and Japanese classics, including the Analects of Confucius, with his cousin Odaka Junchū, whose younger sister Chiyo became Eiichi's first wife in 1858. Shibusawa's values were shaped by the tumultuous events surrounding the end of Japanese feudalism in the middle of the nineteenth century, and by Confucianism, the basic principle of the samurai class, who were the ruling elite of the Tokugawa era and later became the main actors responsible for inaugurating the Meiji Restoration. A prime example is his relationship with Odaka, who was not only his tutor but also a master swordsman. Through him, Shibusawa met loyalists of the emperor who believed in the notion of *sonnō jōi* (revere the emperor, expel the barbarians). In 1863, as a result of this influence, Shibusawa absconded with weapons from Takasaki Castle that were to be used in cooperation with forces from the feudal Chōshū region to topple the Tokugawa government. In a subsequent meeting with Chōshū leaders, he came to understand that their plan was reckless, and he left his home for Kyoto, then the centre of a radical political movement. There, he was hired by Hitotsubashi Yoshinobu, a brilliant feudal lord who deeply respected the emperor. Through several remarkable achievements in domestic trade and financial management, Shibusawa gradually changed his notion of *jōi* (expel the barbarians), and became interested more broadly in world affairs. When Hitotsubashi became the fifteenth and last Tokugawa shogun in 1865, Shibusawa became one of the Tokugawa government's officers, a two-year period that heralded his pending contributions to Japan's modernization.

Shibusawa's career took several sharp turns, from serving the Tokugawa regime to an unexpected assignment to travel to Europe, which resulted in a year of work and study in Paris between 1867 and 1868. Upon returning to Japan, he held a significant role in the new Meiji government as a senior bureaucrat in the Ministry of Finance.

He participated in crafting a number of important laws and rules that shaped the Japanese economy and prepared Japan to become a modern state. In 1873, he moved to the private sector, becoming an entrepreneur working to develop the Japanese economy. When the Meiji government introduced a new banking system to Japan, Shibusawa had the opportunity to study both US and European examples. In his position as head of Dai-Ichi Kokuritsu Ginko (First National Bank), the country's first Western-style banking institution, from its establishment in 1873 until his retirement in 1917, Shibusawa was involved in funding and managing some five hundred mostly newly established companies covering the entire spectrum of Japan's emerging modern economy.

Shibusawa was quite strategic in the way he introduced to Meiji Japan the key concepts around which Western civilization was organized. Abandoning the doctrine of *jōi*, he introduced and implemented various aspects of the Western world, including its philosophy, modes of organization, technology, and the notion of capital in order to modernize Japan. To achieve this goal, Shibusawa had to carry out a reform of the feudal characteristics of the Tokugawa system relating to economic thought, business habits, and consciousness. He was, in short, at the forefront of Japan's modernization, which required the establishment of new and better forms of government and governance in Meiji Japan. To that end, Shibusawa first tried to change Japanese leaders' ideas about the concept of the "public" and the nature of the economy. Shibusawa felt strongly that Japan's leaders needed to understand the meaning and implications of the drastic reforms required to modernize the state.[1] Through his activities, Shibusawa continuously strove for harmony between the economy and morality, using the Analects of Confucius as a philosophical basis for economic behaviour. He often said: "I want people who are engaged in commerce not to misunderstand its meaning, and to look for private gain in a way that also benefits the public. Before long this will not only bring about prosperity for oneself and one's family but, at the same time, it will also enrich the nation and, therefore, will make possible a peaceful society."[2]

Shibusawa's economic thought was unique in two ways. First, although it was based on Confucianism, which had provided parents and children or lords and vassals with behavioural norms, Shibusawa broadened its ethical scope to the level of the nation. Second, he stressed that the economic activities of those engaged in commerce and industry should be based on Confucian principles and aimed at creating an ethic for commercial behaviour that included rendering services to the public and the state. In this way, Shibusawa made clear the ethical grounds for those involved in commerce and industry in a modern nation. Astonished by the economic vitality and prosperity of the West, Shibusawa zealously embraced its rational form of organization and technology. Nevertheless, the Analects continued to form the basis of his thought, which was rooted in the education he received in childhood. Notwithstanding his contact with various value systems during his adult life, this never changed: despite his striving to understand Western liberalism, democracy, and Christianity, and the high value he set on them, the Analects remained the foundation of his thinking.

Shibusawa's leadership had three dimensions: *shusshisha keieisha* (investment manager),[3] social entrepreneur, and cosmopolitan business leader.

Investment manager

Generally speaking, there are two types of managers: capitalists and professional managers. Shimada Masakazu argues, however, that Shibusawa's business practices also included investment in, as well as management of, new companies.[4] Shibusawa thought that both the investor and the investment should serve the national interest. As a risk-taking venture capitalist, he exercised shrewd judgment and benefited from a number of decisions he made in the stock market. Perhaps most important, Shibusawa's activities were based on a broader philosophical desire to cultivate responsible capitalism. He did not support laissez-faire capitalism, for example; rather, he urged a variety of constraints on capitalist forces, and suggested that business leaders serve the broader public interest, not only for Japan, but also in support of world development.[5]

Social entrepreneur

From a contemporary point of view, Shibusawa Eiichi's thinking was based on three principles:[6]

- he advocated that business leaders should take the initiative in creating wealth for society through the establishment of good conditions for their economic activities in cooperation with the public sector;

- he attached importance to disclosing information to the public about the concepts and the mechanisms shaping private enterprise; and
- he thought of Japan both as a part of and in terms of its responsibilities to international society, and he advocated the importance of respecting one's fellow human beings as a precondition for successful business activities.[7]

Shibusawa was impressed by the relationship between constitutional monarchs and business leaders he witnessed in Europe in 1867–68. He observed that business leaders were on an equal footing with both the monarch and government officials in discussing economic and financial problems. Based on these travel experiences, Shibusawa endeavoured to pursue several important goals to improve conditions for the Japanese business community after his return to Japan. As a starting point, he sought to change public attitudes towards business activities. He advocated that business activities should be supported by the same Confucian principles that served as the foundation of samurai ethics in the Edo era, arguing that the pursuit of fair business dealings was consistent with Confucianism. In this line of reasoning, he incorporated the imagery of the abacus (representing economic activities), observing that it was not at odds with the teaching of the Analects. In any system, if wealth is not proper, it will not last long, a view expressed by the famous Scottish economist Adam Smith in his *An Inquiry to the Nature and Causes of the Wealth of Nations*. Indeed, Shibusawa was cognizant of the relationship between his thinking and Smith's.

Beyond his remarkable and revolutionary reconsideration of Confucianism, Shibusawa advocated competition and opposed monopoly. When Iwasaki Yatarō, the founder of the Mitsubishi (Three Diamonds) Group, asked Shibusawa to cooperate with the Yūbin Kisen Mitsubishi Kaisha (the group's main company in the early Meiji era) to monopolize Japan's merchant marine, Shibusawa rejected the proposal. Although he did not place perfect confidence in competition, Shibusawa held that it was essential for the Japanese business community to maintain conditions in which each corporation would compete fairly.

Shibusawa made every effort to improve the social status of business in Japanese society. He believed that the higher the status of business, the stronger its power and, commensurately, the stricter should be its ethics. Based on this principle, he resigned from the Finance Ministry in 1873, along with his sponsor, Inoue Kaoru, and continued to work as a private business leader until his death in 1931. His goal was to establish *jitsugyō-kai* (the business world) as a power centre whose goal was to change and improve Japanese society, equivalent to the roles played by politicians and the bureaucracy. Previously, during the Edo era, Japan's strict class system had relegated those involved in business to the lowest class. Shibusawa understood intuitively that the then-ruling samurai class underestimated the importance of business activities, But his insight went deeper, for he was also aware that most merchants, despite their interest in political economy trends, were not interested in the policy-making process.

As Shibusawa's business philosophy matured, he concluded that it was necessary for the public to understand the structure and systems of new economic organization, such as corporations, stock markets, and financial institutions. He proceeded to introduce these concepts to Japan based on his experience and study of developed Western countries. Many government officials initially strongly opposed the reform of Japan's economic organization, but Shibusawa reasoned that, to cultivate *gappon* capitalism, it was necessary not just for businessmen, but for all Japanese, including politicians, government officials, and academicians, to understand these Western systems and their concepts and to take an interest in them. To this end Shibusawa took many initiatives to promote greater public awareness of them. He established the modern banking system in Japan and hundreds of companies in various fields. Typically, once these companies had achieved a degree of success, he moved on to new opportunities, leaving the companies to other talented managers, many of whom he mentored. He founded and managed hundreds of new business associations,[8] and became the first president of the Tokyo Chamber of Commerce, the Tokyo Bank Association, and the Tokyo Stock Exchange. Through those business groups, corporations and businessmen were able to exchange information and perspectives, as well as submit their proposals to such public organs as the central government.

Cosmopolitan business leader

Shibusawa had a unique perspective on "global thinking." When confronted with an issue intertwining Japan and the world, he offered insight as a business leader about what role Japan could play. Shibusawa argued, for example, that Japanese business leaders and companies should aim at improving relationships with Western countries, encouraging the development of Asian countries – China in particular – and settling disputes peacefully.

Shibusawa was also aware of the importance of Japan's image in international society. He did much not only to modify misunderstandings about Japan in foreign countries, but also to create real and good images of the nation. He cooperated with the establishment of Japanese news agencies such as *Kokusai Tsūshinsha* (International News Agency) because he knew that those who manage information also can manage many other issues facing modern countries and their economies. He encouraged communication with foreign correspondents so as to improve the accuracy of stories they transmitted about Japanese society and to express his ideas concerning the appropriate role for Japan in international society. His basic policy for public relations followed three rules: simplicity, speed, and sincerity presented with humour. Today, ironically, his policy is at odds with that of most Japanese corporations, which are consistently criticized for being "faceless" – for not presenting their thoughts and vision clearly, and for shying away from engaging the public in discussions about the issues of the day.

Shibusawa's warnings to Japanese business leaders and companies, particularly during the 1910s and 1920s, were prophetic. As a consequence of the First World War, Japan became the strongest country in East Asia in terms of military and economic power. But as wealth accumulated, many Japanese companies and business leaders were unable to maintain high moral principles. The *Ishii Sadahichi* Incident, which occurred at the beginning of the 1920s, is a typical example. During the economic boom brought about by the First World War, Ishii became a so-called *sensō narikin* (war profiteer) by trading lumber and stocks. When the post-war economic bubble burst, Ishii's company ran short of funds and suddenly went bankrupt, leaving behind a tremendous amount of debt. Such business activities took little account of the kind of company-specific stewardship principles that Shibusawa advocated, and the negative repercussions rippled far beyond the company's problems, in the eyes of the public at large at that time.

After retiring from the business world in 1917 at the age of seventy-seven, Shibusawa devoted himself to playing an active role in other important fields, such as *kokumin gaikō* (non-governmental diplomacy), international exchange, social welfare, and education. As a result of these activities, Shibusawa is generally referred to as "the father of modern Japanese capitalism." His motivation was based on his lifelong study of Confucianism and on his understanding of the role banks play in creating a rich, prosperous, and peaceful society, a conclusion he arrived at as a result of his experiences in Europe in 1867–68. Shibusawa was a unique social entrepreneur and business leader whose values and notion of the public good cultivated the modern Japanese economy and society in ways both similar to – and yet in important respects different from – contemporary US business leaders such as Rockefeller, Carnegie, and Morgan.

With this review of Shibusawa Eiichi's life and work as background, one can now turn to a brief overview of the book's contents.

In Chapter 1, Shimada Masakazu describes Shibusawa's importance in economic circles, based on empirical data such as appointments to corporate positions, assets, and shareholder equity ratios. Shimada then compares the Shibusawa model, which introduced to Japan the Western system of stock corporations as collective organizations, with closed models such as those of Mitsui and Mitsubishi, which are closer to a homegrown conglomerate. He concludes that Shibusawa's greatest achievement was the development in Japan of a market-type economic model that both funds and human resources may enter or exit freely.

In Chapter 2, Tanaka Kazuhiro rethinks the Analects of Confucius as the basis of Shibusawa's principles: the union of economy and morality, as found in his *Rongo to soroban* (The Analects and the abacus). Adam Smith, in *The Theory of Moral Sentiments*, the philosophical foundation for his *Wealth of Nations*,[9] explains the mechanism of a competitive market in which, as long as one's business stays true to justice, the "invisible hand of God" will help maintain a proper balance between supply and demand even if one places a priority on the pursuit of one's personal interests. For Shibusawa, however, prioritizing the public interest – as *gapponshugi* does – rather than one's own, was a more important way to do business.

In Chapter 3, Patrick Fridenson explores the question of the ideal relationship in society between public and private organizations – one that has attracted a great deal of attention in all eras and places – by analysing the Shibusawa case in the broader context of world history. He also introduces the thinking of the famous French philosopher and economist, Henri de Saint-Simon, on the role of the entrepreneur in society – ideas thought to have influenced Shibusawa during his stay in Paris in 1867–68.

In Chapter 4, Miyamoto Matao discusses *gapponshugi* as "a type of capitalism in which its players can easily be identified," and attributes Shibusawa's historic role to his facilitating the rapid extension in Japan of the stock corporation system and, as a financial figure, in developing and leading Japanese economic circles. Miyamoto also adds insight into how Shibusawa's principles and actions should be considered in the modern history of the nineteenth-century Japanese economy.

Janet Hunter in Chapter 5 depicts the characteristics of Shibusawa's business morality as seen in articles in Japanese and British newspapers of the day, which included harsh criticism of Japanese business activities by overseas observers, especially in Britain. What made Shibusawa's views on business morality so unique? How did his contemporaries, both within and without Japan, see them? How did Shibusawa respond to these perspectives?

This last question is taken up in Chapter 6 by Kimura Masato, who analyses Shibusawa's response to criticisms from outside Japan. He posits that Shibusawa was uniquely devoted to the improvement of business morality through proactive activities – domestic and international – that transcended the economy, in parallel with similar trends in global society.

In Chapter 7, Geoffrey Jones highlights the characteristics of *gapponshugi* and its basis in the ethical prescriptions found in the Analects of Confucius by citing examples of enterprises and entrepreneurs around the world in the nineteenth century and later who assumed an ethical responsibility for their commercial activities. This leads Jones to observe that today's capitalistic world might be open to accepting the principles of *gapponshugi*.

In the final chapter, I discuss the significance of *gapponshugi* in terms of current efforts to overcome the difficulties capitalism has faced since the collapse of Lehman Brothers in 2008 and the need to build a new moral framework for global capitalism. Citing Ronald Dore's writing on financial capitalism, I compare so-called Anglo-Saxon capitalism with Japanese-German capitalism, identify problems, and propose the principle of *gapponshugi* as a potential solution to these problems.

This book is based on the results of three years of research through The *Gapponshugi* Project, led by the Shibusawa Eiichi Memorial Foundation's Research Department and composed of eight researchers from Japan, Britain, and France. Following a kickoff meeting in Osaka in July 2011, brainstorming continued in London, Boston, Paris, Tokyo, and other cities with discussion of *gapponshugi* from numerous perspectives. The researchers grappled with many challenges regarding the meaning of *gapponshugi* and the background necessary to understand it. As a result of these extended and, at times, heated discussions, thinking distilled first into a Japanese publication and now its English translation and publication by the University of Toronto Press.[10]

In September 2012 the first joint panel of the Business History Society of Japan and the European Business History Association took place in Paris, where Shibusawa Eiichi first developed the idea of *gapponshugi* nearly 150 years ago. On 25–26 November 2013 a public symposium was held at the headquarters of the Organisation for Economic Co-operation and Development (OECD) and the Maison de la culture du Japon à Paris. These gatherings aimed to present through public discussion the results of the research project. It is impressive that economic officials, businesspeople, business history researchers, and many others, including OECD ambassadors from several European countries, showed much greater interest in the project than had been expected. With this English-language publication, our hope is that many more entrepreneurs, businesspeople, economic and business historians, and other interested readers will learn about the concept of *gapponshugi*. Shibusawa's achievements date back more than a century, but his principles deal with universal issues of morality and the economy. They remain highly relevant today.

NOTES

1 See Gil Latz, ed., *Rediscovering Shibusawa Eiichi in the 21st Century* (Tokyo: Shibusawa Eiichi Memorial Foundation, 2014), 2–19; see also idem, "Back to the Future: The Intellectual Themes of the Second Shibusawa Seminar on Japanese Studies," in *Challenges for Japan: Democracy, Business, and Aging* (Tokyo: International House of Japan, 2001), 5–28; and idem, "Introduction to Shibusawa Eiichi's Legacy," in *Challenges for Japan: Democracy, Finance, International Relations, Gender*, ed. Gil Latz and Koide Izumi, vi–xi (Tokyo: International House of Japan, 2003).

2 Shibusawa Eiichi, *Rongo to soroban* [The Analects and the abacus] (Tokyo: Kokusho Kankōkai, [1916] 1985), 85.

3 Shimada Masakazu defines the characteristic of Shibusawa's management as *shusshisha keieisha* in his *Shibusawa Eiichi no kigyōsha katsudō no kenkyū* [The entrepreneurial activities of Shibusawa Eiichi: The creation of a joint-stock company system in the pre-war period and the role of the investor-executive] (Tokyo: Nihon Keizai Hyoronsha, 2007).

4 Ibid.

5 Shimada Masakazu, "Eiichi Shibusawa, Industrialist, as Viewed through the Financial Documents of the Shibusawa Family," *Bunkyo Women's University Keiei Ronshū* 7, no. 1 (1997): 19–40. See also Oshima Kiyoshi, Katō

Toshihiko, and Ōuchi Tsutomu, *Jinbutsu – Nihon shihonsyugi 3: Meiji shoki no kigyōka* [Personalities in Japanese capitalism – 3: Entrepreneurs of the early Meiji period] (Tokyo: University of Tokyo Press, 1976): 291–333.

6 Almost all of Shibusawa's materials are included in Ryūmonsha, ed., *Shibusawa Eiichi denki shiryō* [Shibusawa Eiichi biographical materials], 68 v. (Tokyo: Shibusawa Eiichi denki shiryō kankōkai, 1955–71).

7 See the mission statement of the Shibusawa Eiichi Memorial Foundation, available online at http://www.shibusawa.or.jp/english/outline/index.html.

8 For the number of companies that Shibusawa was involved in establishing, see the index of Ryūmonsha, *Shibusawa Eiichi denki shiryō*, and the opening chapter of Latz, *Rediscovering Shibusawa Eiichi*, 5–9.

9 Adam Smith, *The Theory of Moral Sentiments* (Indianapolis, IN: Liberty Fund, [1790] 1982); and idem, *An Inquiry into the Nature and Causes of the Wealth of Nations* (New York: Modern Library, [1776] 1937).

10 The Japanese version is Kikkawa Takeo and Patrick Fridenson, eds., *Gurōbaru shihonshugi no naka no Shibusawa Eiichi: Gappon kyapitarizumu to moraru* [*Gappon* capitalism: The economic and moral ideology of Shibusawa Eiichi in global perspective] (Tokyo: Toyo Keizai, 2014).

1 Tensions between the Open Market Model and the Closed *Zaibatsu* Model

SHIMADA MASAKAZU

Shibusawa Eiichi (1840–1931) is the entrepreneur who best embodies the spirit of modern Japan. He established a wide range of companies and banks, steered the operations of the business world, and set the standard for entrepreneurial social action; he also popularized the joint-stock company system under the banner of *gappon* capitalism (*gappon-shugi*). He was the catalyst behind numerous companies, making his own investments to lead the way towards their establishment. He also solicited investments from landowners, merchants, and other members of the wealthier classes in various joint-stock companies and even provided on-the-job training for many management personnel. Finally, he developed a management model for a market that would facilitate the circulation of large amounts of capital and human resources.

This chapter provides a detailed look at the joint-stock company system that Shibusawa championed as the ideal establishment for contemporary modern Japan, explores his reasons for fashioning the joint-stock company system in his vision, and examines the greater significance of the model that fuelled the growth of many Japanese industries and corporations.

Shibusawa Eiichi and the Importance of the Investor-Executive Role

For many years Japanese business historians have focused primarily on *zaibatsu*, exclusive diversified family business entities such as Mitsubishi and Mitsui. *Zaibatsu* indeed make for a compelling topic because they demonstrated astounding performance as large corporate structures, contributed to the creation of new industries and corporations, and churned out the executives of the future by actively recruiting exceptional university graduates and honing the skills of countless professional managers.

Work over the past ten years or so has shown, however, that the dominant corporate configuration in pre-war Japan was, in fact, of the non-*zaibatsu* variety and that major investors filled a considerable proportion of corporate management ranks; these revelations have made this particular realm of study a captivating one for researchers throughout the field.[1] Owner-executives, for example, accounted for 38.1 per cent of major corporation management, which procured the lion's share of their companies' required capital through stock. Corporations were able to minimize diffusion due to a relative scarcity of wealthy individuals, effectively grounding corporate governance, as researchers have illustrated, in consultation among shareholders. Scholars now argue that, as a result of these conditions, the economic system that pervaded the Meiji and Taisho periods was characterized by a "market-based system and the control of major shareholders."[2]

Shibusawa Eiichi in historical perspective

Shibusawa Eiichi was one of the most prominent owner-executives in the non-*zaibatsu* model, as Table 1.1 illustrates. In 1898 Shibusawa ranked eighteenth in overall income in the Tokyo/Yokohama area, twenty-fifth in a nationwide survey of major shareholders in 103 major corporations, and first in total number of board/director positions in corporations and other organizations, with thirty-one appointments.[3]

Many scholars also refer in particular to Shibusawa's close relationship with government using such terms as "the outstanding leader of private capitalism in this country,"[4] "the facilitator of the business world,"[5] "an ideologue of the bourgeoisie,"[6] "an organizer, a guide, an instructor, and a spokesman,"[7] and "a bridge between businessmen and the bureaucrats."[8] It is no doubt because so few others were performing these functions that particular attention was paid to Shibusawa's role as an organizer of the business world, to his nurturing of modern industry, extracting protection from the government, and to his contribution to the dissemination of economic ethics through such works as *Rongo to soroban* (The Analects and the abacus)[9] and *Dōtoku keizai gōitsu setsu* (The doctrine of inseparability of morality and economy).[10]

Meanwhile, Shibusawa's foundation of a large number of modern industries using the joint-stock company framework has also drawn

Table 1.1 High-Income Earners and Investors in Multiple Companies, Japan, 1898

Earner, investor	Location	Ranking in high-income earners list, Tokyo/ Yokohama	Ranking in list of major shareholders in 103 major companies	Number of directorships	Occupation, affiliation
Iwasaki Hisaya	Tokyo	1	3	*	
Mitsui Hachirōemon	Tokyo	2	4	*	
Sumitomo Kichiemon	Osaka	4	*	*	
Yasuda Zenjirō	Tokyo	6	7	9	
Ōkura Kihachirō	Tokyo	8	*	7	
Amamiya Keijirō	Tokyo	13	6	7	Head of Busō Chūō Railroad, nickel-silver trade
Nomoto Teijirō	Tokyo	*	10	*	
Wakao Family (Wakao Ikuzō)	Kanagawa	*	12	12	Raw silk merchant, head of Yokohama Wakao Bank
Tanaka Heihachi	Kanagawa	*	13	15	Raw silk merchant, president of l20th National Bank
Adachi Magoroku	Shizuoka	*	16	*	Agriculture, landlord
Toyama Shūzō	Osaka	*	18	12	President of Naniwa Bank, manager of Commercial Credit Agency
Tanaka Shinshichi	Kanagawa	*	19	*	
Matsumoto Jyūtarō	Osaka	14	30	28	Imported cloth merchant, president of 130th National Bank

Earner, investor	Location	Ranking in high-income earners list, Tokyo/Yokohama	Ranking in list of major shareholders in 103 major companies	Number of directorships	Occupation, affiliation
Moroto Seiroku	Mie	*	22	*	Forest management, cereal merchant
Hara Rokusuke	Tokyo	*	23	*	
Shibusawa Eiichi	Tokyo	18	25	31	
Abe Hikotarō	Osaka	19	21	19	Cereal merchant
Hara Zenzaburō	Yokohama	20	*	12	Merchant
Furukawa Ichibei	Tokyo	22	*	*	Ashio Copper Mine
Mogi Sōbei	Yokohama	23	*	*	Merchant, president of Daini Bank
Kōnoike Zen'emon	Osaka	25	*	*	Kōnoike Bank
Watanabe Fukuzaburō	Yokohama	26	*	9	Merchant, head of Yokohama International Warehouse
Kameda Kaijirō	Tokyo	*	29	*	
Fujita-gumi	Osaka	*	31	*	
Tsukamoto Partnership	Kyoto	*	32	*	

Note: The table lists only actual managers; it excludes figureheads such as members of the peerage.

Sources: Ishii Kanji, "Seiritsu-ki Nihon teikokushugi no ichi danmen" [One aspect of Japanese imperialism in its formative period – the accumulation of funds and the export of capital], *Rekishigaku Kenkyū*, no. 383 (1972); Takamura Naosuke, *Kaisha no tanjō* [The birth of the corporation] (Tokyo: Yoshikawa Kobunkan, 1996); Suzuki Tsuneo et al., "Meiji-ki no kaisha oyobi keieisha no kenkyū – Nihon zenkoku kaisha yakuinroku (Meiji 31-nenban) no bunseki" [Research on corporations and managers in the Meiji period – an analysis of the 1898 National List of Directors of Japanese companies], *Sangyo keizai Kenkyū kiyō* (Chubu University), 9 (1999); and Furubayashi K., ed., *Jitsugyōka jinmei jiten* [Biographical dictionary of businessmen] (Tokyo: Jitsugyō Tsūshin, 1911).

attention. Chō Yukio refers to the following two achievements of Shibusawa in this context: "(1) the joint-stock organization, and his introduction of a comprehensive range of modern industries, and (2) the eradication of the idea that the bureaucracy was superior to the private entrepreneur, which resulted in raising the social status of the businessman."[11] Further, Tsugai Yoshio notes the importance of his role as an "organizer of the industrial enterprise."[12] These scholars' evaluations of Shibusawa focus closely on his active promotion of the joint-stock form of company organization, carrying this through to the foundation of a large number of industrial enterprises.[13]

Most of the past research on Shibusawa has focused primarily on his brand of Confucian management ethics.[14] Showcased in many works, including *Rongo to soroban* and *Dōtoku keizai gōitsu setsu*, these tenets of Shibusawa's business perspective have long been cited as powerful influences on management ethics. This research, using a variety of approaches, has made great progress in clarifying the way in which Shibusawa tied Confucian morality – the traditional Japanese value system – to modern economic thought.

In Shibusawa's own view, however, he was not a "thinker" per se, but rather an "interpreter" of Confucius and his Analects, taking his own unique approach to the teachings therein. In this regard, Shibusawa strikes a contrast with Fukuzawa Yukichi, for example, who the general populace esteemed as an influential writer and journalist – a socially recognized man of thought. The remarkable popularity of Shibusawa's management ethics, then, should be attributed not to his influence as a respected intellectual, but to his impressive competence as an executive, a proven track record that effectively validated his management ethics as essential elements of success in business. The odd reality, however, is that, although Shibusawa created an extraordinary number of companies, managed them, and cultivated them into major corporations without fail, we still have very little insight into the actual management methods he employed. Shibusawa's ability to develop businesses without forming *zaibatsu* and his virtual deification over time as the "supreme leader of Japanese capitalism" have made it difficult to locate and identify his individual management strategies, which are now so deeply embedded in the various independent companies he brought to fruition.

In recent years, reflecting in part the need to reform business systems, there has been a renewal of interest in Japan in research on entrepreneurs and businesspeople as the protagonists of reform. This has prompted an evaluation of Shibusawa from a different perspective. Miyamoto Matao, for example, has focused afresh on entrepreneurial activity, with "a renewed appreciation of the strategic importance of the individual in economic phenomena." Concerning Shibusawa, Miyamoto says that "Shibusawa's most notable activity as an entrepreneur was his promotion of the foundation of corporations." Further, he points out that not only was this function exercised at the foundation stage, but "[Shibusawa] selected and directed the supervisory staff who in practice were to function as top management, and also had to take responsibility for the operation of the companies, reconciling conflicting interests by protecting supervisory staff who came under pressure from major shareholders."[15] He characterizes Shibusawa as representative of the innovative entrepreneur, possessed of an "animal spirit," and for the first time assigns a high value to Shibusawa's role as a manager of corporations after their initial foundation.

From a survey of previous research on Shibusawa, we can see that almost no empirical research has been carried out on his establishment and management of private sector enterprises. This surely should precede any judgment of his achievements. Over the course of my many years of research into these methods, I have been lucky enough to analyse the Shibusawa family's financial records – a valuable resource that no other researcher has yet referenced – to get a clearer picture of Shibusawa Eiichi's ownership activities as a major shareholder and his network of personal contacts at the top of the business sphere. The following section examines these unique systems in more detail.

A Profile of Shibusawa Eiichi

Shibusawa Eiichi was born in 1840 in a small village about eighty kilometres outside Tokyo in what is now Fukaya City, Saitama Prefecture. His father was a progressive, wealthy farmer who carried on a big business in farming and the processing and selling of indigo dyestuffs, and who consequently assumed the status of a leader in the community. In his youth, Shibusawa learned the rudiments of the Chinese classics from an older male cousin who was a Sinologist, and in this way he acquired a better-than-average cultural training. Still, he sensed the contradictions in the class society that existed during the Edo period, a time when everyone had to submit without objection to the sometimes outrageous demands of the warrior class, and he took part in the political movements that bubbled over after Commodore Matthew

Perry's visit to Japan in 1853. He would go so far as to plan such direct action against the foreigners as taking over castles controlled by the shogunate and torching the open port in Yokohama, but just before the plan was initiated he realized how reckless it was and abruptly called it off. He went into hiding in Kyoto to escape the shogunate's search for the plotters. He entered the services of Hitotsubashi Yoshinobu, a man of whom people had high expectations as being the "most enlightened person in the shogunate" (and the man who would later become the fifteenth shogun), and for his services Shibusawa acquired the status of a warrior. After Yoshinobu became shogun, the government sent an envoy to the Paris Exposition, and Shibusawa was chosen to accompany the group. This enabled him to see with his own eyes the advanced world of Western Europe.

During his absence, the shogunate fell. Upon his return to Japan, Shibusawa had an opportunity, albeit a very short one, to experiment with modern business in Shizuoka Prefecture, where Yoshinobu was living in seclusion. Later, Shibusawa was promoted to a position in the government: in the Ministry of Finance, he was engaged in enlightening businessmen and in other activities aimed at smoothing the way for the introduction of banks and companies into Japan. Caught up in political manoeuvrings, he resigned his government post and became president of Dai-Ichi Kokuritsu Ginko (First National Bank), an establishment for which he had been lobbying Mitsui and other wealthy merchants while working for the government.

With a foothold at Dai-Ichi Kokuritsu Ginko, Shibusawa then went on to become involved in a whole host of companies. He acted as the chairman of the board of Tokyo Gas; Nihon Renga Seizō K.K. (Nihon Bricks Corporation); Tokyo Rope; Kyoto Orimono; Tokyo Jinzō o Hiryō (Tokyo Artificial Fertilizer); Tokyo Ishikawajima Shipbuilding; the Imperial Hotel; Oji Paper; Iwaki Tankō K.K. (Iwaki Coal Mining); Hiroshima Suiryoku Denki K.K. (Hiroshima Hydro Electricity); and the Sapporo Beer Company, among others. He also provided financial assistance for the establishment of several of Japan's largest companies, such as Osaka Bōseki Kaisha (Osaka Mill); Nihon Railway; the Tokyo Marine and Fire Insurance Co., Ltd.; and Nihon Yūsen Kaisha; and served as an executive at each of these companies.

In 1909, on the occasion of his sixty-ninth birthday, he resigned from almost all these positions, remaining only as president of Dai-Ichi Bank. In 1916, at the age of seventy-six, he also gave up that position, the base of all his business activities, and withdrew completely from the frontlines of the business world. He remained active, however, promoting private sector diplomacy, spreading dedication to business virtues, and encouraging new ways to handle labour problems. In 1931, his long life came to an end when he passed away at the age of ninety-one.

Shibusawa's Joint-Stock Company System

Shibusawa's role and his personal network in his companies

We can identify the following four characteristics of companies in which Shibusawa was involved.[16] First, naturally enough, an extremely large number of them were in industries that introduced completely new Western knowledge or technology that hitherto had not existed in Japan. Second, many, such as railroads, ports, and coal mines, were industries that can be regarded as the infrastructure of a modern economy. Third, when he took on a major function as a director, he restricted himself to a single company in each industry. We can also see (what has until now passed almost unnoticed) that, in cases where he did take up posts in more than one company in the same industry – railroads or coal mines, for example – he made it a principle that there should be no geographical overlap between them.

When we look at the composition of the management of companies in which Shibusawa was involved, we find that the number of managers involved in several Shibusawa-connected companies was not particularly large; in other words, he operated these enterprises in collaboration with a huge number of different managers. The small number of managers who did share multiple management posts with Shibusawa in the *zaibatsu* companies were restricted to key persons such as Takashi Masuda of Mitsui and Shōda Heigorō of Mitsubishi. Others who stand out are Asano Sōichirō, with seven company directorships, and Ōkura Kihachirō, with six. Multiple directorships were also held by many directors of Shibusawa's key bank, Dai-Ichi Kokuritsu Ginko, such as Saionji Kiminari and Odaka Jirō.

Concerning share ownership, I also explored the extent of Shibusawa's involvement in terms of both ownership and financing of companies. If I consider companies where he had an ongoing presence, including a continuing position as chairman, his share of the companies' stock was quite high, between 10 and 30 per cent. In companies where he was simply a director or auditor, or chairman for a brief period, his shareholding rarely exceeded a few per cent; in many cases, his name does not appear on the list of major shareholders. Even where he held the post of chairman or director, he owned only enough stock to enable him to exercise his management power authority without hindrance.

As far as his involvement at the startup stage of a company is concerned, Shibusawa almost always played an important role in authorizing the appointment of directors at the inaugural shareholders' meeting. Shareholders held more authority in companies of the Meiji period than in enterprises after the Second World War, but from the inaugural shareholders' meetings it was necessary to reconcile the interests of both large and small shareholders. In this context, Shibusawa as an investor-manager made sure that the intentions of the company's promoters were put into practice.

Shibusawa's involvement with companies after their establishment continued in a variety of forms; at shareholders' meetings, in particular, he played a vital role in important decisions concerning the long-term direction of the company, such as its continuance, dissolution, or merger with other firms. General meetings of company shareholders in pre-war Japan, unlike those in the post-war era, were often drawn-out affairs that sometimes lasted six hours or more. On occasion, Shibusawa would fill in for an ill company president and act as chair, working to navigate the morass of divergent interests between different shareholders. Instead of attempting to steer discussions with a unilateral approach, he listened patiently to all the parties involved and waited for one side to broach the possibility of a compromise. Through this process, parties with different interests eventually recognized certain common ground, making the company more of a public entity with shared long-term interests. Essentially, companies became "public" areas within the "private" sphere.

Before and after shareholders' meetings, Shibusawa would attend a variety of gatherings both within and outside the company, attempting to solve problems by reconciling opposing interests, or acting as arbitrator or intermediary. Since mergers caused changes in the composition of shareholdings, the selection of a new management team would be left to Shibusawa, who was regarded as able to make judgments that took into account both the interests of shareholders and the need for stable management. If conflict arose within a company, Shibusawa would be given the task of selecting a manager to sort matters out.

One characteristic of Shibusawa's entrepreneurial activities and top management methods was the great importance he attached to information. What is not often recognized about his information-gathering behaviour is that it was based on personal interviews. He regarded this face-to-face contact as important for several reasons. First, such interviews included the whole process of gathering, disseminating, and acting on information. Second, they made possible the gathering, dissemination, and sharing of information at the implicit level, where non-verbal information, nuances, and feelings came into play. Shibusawa gathered and exchanged information through meetings with a wide variety of people outside his companies, such as managers, investors, and members of the government. His decision-making process involved the use of the information gathered in this way in a repeated series of intimate discussions and meetings with selected members of his top management; proposals for action would result from this process of knowledge creation.

I also researched the other managers in firms where Shibusawa acted as chairman or director. For Shibusawa to be able to engage simultaneously in a large number of undertakings, an essential requirement was a group of investor-executives who agreed with his approach, could act with him, and, where necessary, deputize for him. It appears that the role of these investor-executives was particularly important in the groundbreaking days when a company was first established. Among the people who undertook these tasks were Asano Sōichirō, the Masuda brothers Takashi and Katsunori, Magoshi Kyōhei, and Saionji Kiminari and Kusaka Yoshio of Dai-Ichi Bank.

Once a company had been established, there was a need for supporting actors who could check and monitor its operations on a day-to-day basis. This task was undertaken by young managers selected and trained by Shibusawa, such as Uemura Chōzaburō, Ōkawa Heizaburō, and Umeura Seiichi, or managers trained in Dai-Ichi Bank, such as Sudō Tokizaburō and Toki Hiroshi. When Shibusawa was faced with consolidating a company that had overextended itself, or rebuilding a company that was having problems because of mistakes by previous managers, he often undertook bold restructuring measures, including mergers of two or more companies. It was precisely because Shibusawa was surrounded by managers on whom he could rely that it was possible for him to adopt measures that involved remoulding the structure of the enterprises.

Non-*zaibatsu* firms had to find their own sources of finance and managerial talent. Shibusawa's non-*zaibatsu* companies therefore obtained funding from wealthy members of the nobility and from merchants and landlords. Because these investors tended to be interested in short-term profits, Shibusawa needed to fill his top management posts with investor-managers, who could persuade them of the importance of securing long-term, stable profits. In the last decades of the nineteenth century, the country still had produced only a handful graduates, but Shibusawa had to find human resources capable of filling the posts of executive director or general manager – people entrusted with day-to-day management. Shibusawa found these people through a variety of channels, and trained specialist managers by having them accumulate practical on-the job experience. The existence of this talented and diverse group of allied managers enabled Shibusawa to engage in a wide range of entrepreneurial activities.

Finance and investment

I was fortunate to be the first to be granted access to the *Shibusawa-ke monjo* (Shibusawa family records), fragments of disconnected memos that are thought to have been jotted down by Shibasaki Kakujirō, a secretary in charge of keeping the accounts of the Shibusawa family; and the *Shibusawa dōzokukai kaigiroku*, records of meetings of the Shibusawa family, held monthly from 1891 on, at which reports were presented to Shibusawa Eiichi and the families of his sons and daughters in regard to all the fluctuations in their assets These important resources allowed me to analyse the flow of Shibusawa's finances in his activities as investor and manager.[17] The *Shibusawa-ke monjo* provides an idea of the funds available to the Shibusawa family and how its assets moved in 1891. From the *Shibusawa dōzokukai kaigiroku* it is possible to see long-term trends in the movement of funds and assets held by the Shibusawa family from 1891 on.

From the household accounts of the Shibusawa family for 1891, I uncovered the following:

- The household accounts of the Shibusawa family were kept in written form and reported regularly at formal family meetings.
- Budgetary control was exercised over the household accounts, and the budget guidelines were, on the whole, followed.
- The account records were of two types: a "profit and loss ledger" and a "balance of funds ledger." The expenses of the family were managed overall based on the profit and loss account, while the balance of funds account was managed independently.

- Slightly over 60 per cent of Shibusawa's own income came from dividends from shares; only about 10 per cent was derived from fees for the directorships he held in various companies.
- The Shibusawa family's living and maintenance expenses came to less than 20 per cent of its total income. According to the regulations, the balance was either deposited in a joint fund or distributed as dividends to branches of the family.
- Investments in anonymous partnerships exceeded those in joint-stock companies, and there was a considerable volume of loans to individuals, approaching the proportion devoted to investments.
- It appears there was a conscious effort to keep the balance in the balance of funds account steady over a single year. There was a rough balance between the purchase and the sale of shares, and between loans repaid by individuals and fresh loans to others.

Shibusawa's asset management was structured to keep income and expenditures (mainly through the sale of his stockholdings) in balance. It was clear that profits, mainly from dividend income, were not directly connected to new investments, including additional subscriptions of shares already in his possession. Shibusawa's profit and loss account did, of course, contain many revenue sources that were available as resources for the management of his assets. These included transferred profits, the family's joint fund, and the portion of family profits transferred to Shibusawa himself. These resources were essential for Shibusawa as hedges against the risks entailed in his investments in company startups and unlimited liability investments in anonymous partnerships, as well as the large loans he actively furnished individuals. He experienced any number of company failures, and in such cases drew on the family's joint funds to discharge his financial responsibilities.

It is thus clear that Shibusawa's high-risk investments in new companies in the early stage of industrial development were only possible because of the high returns the investments offered.

I next turned my attention to the forty-year period between 1891 and 1931 (the year of Shibusawa's death) and analysed the companies in which he was involved. The companies in which he invested differed widely, from anonymous partnerships to joint-stock companies, and my analysis revealed a different image of Shibusawa from the popular perception of a promoter and nurturer of joint-stock companies. For companies with a strong public utility character, requiring large amounts of capital, he used the joint-stock company structure; for high-risk, high-return ventures, he set up limited partnerships; and small individual businesses were established as ordinary partnerships.

Limited partnership companies were made up of two types of investors: those with unlimited liability and those with limited liability. In the former, all investors held the authority to manage the business, and all were "active"; all jointly bore unlimited liability, which meant that, should the company have an external debt and be unable to repay it out of its capital, the debt would have to be repaid by all the investors even if they had to use their own private assets.[18] In the latter, in contrast, investors had no more liability than the amount of money they had invested in the company because they did not have the right to manage the business.

Limited and unlimited partnerships are forms of company organization that many people are generally familiar with, but the dormant partnership is not so well known. The very few studies that have considered dormant partnerships usually define them in terms of a form of joint investment business operation made up of "limited liability" investment by "silent" partners, with management of the operations by those running the business. In this sense, dormant partnerships resemble limited partnerships, but only those running the business appear to the outside world as bearers of rights and obligations, while the names of those who are investing partners remain unknown (secret) to outsiders.[19] Researchers thus have cast dormant partnerships as prototypes of the company organization originating in the Edo period as a kind of *commenda*, an anonymous association or guild.

Until now, dormant partnership companies have been categorized as very similar to limited partnership companies because they specified two types of members: unlimited liability members and limited liability members. Among the many companies Shibusawa was involved in are many examples of dormant partnerships used in combination with unlimited partnerships. Shibusawa was approached with requests to invest in mining, agricultural, marine, and other businesses that essentially are individual business operations or businesses with high risks. In such cases, he apparently tried to secure a limited liability after his investments by concluding dormant partnership contracts; after all, direct investment in an unlimited partnership would mean he would have to assume unlimited liability. In particular, when establishing ordinary partnerships, he combined them with anonymous partnerships – whose origins can be traced back to the Tokugawa period – making it easier for outside investors to participate, since there was a limit to the risks they bore. Thus, rather than considering the joint-stock company as the only appropriate business form, Shibusawa chose the appropriate form of organization depending on the scale and goals of the enterprise. This is an important point, which has hitherto received no attention whatsoever.

Concerning Shibusawa's sale of shares, I was able to confirm that, to raise funds for new investment, he cleverly combined dealings on the stock exchange with dealings on the outside spot market (a financial market where financial instruments such as securities and bonds are traded immediately), and even in companies of which he was a director, he would invest and then actively sell off shares when the conditions were somewhat advantageous. It is clear that, rather than strengthen his control over the companies he had established, he gave priority to raising capital to establish new companies.

I also explored Shibusawa's share purchases, his investment in a variety of businesses, and the wide range of movements of funds and shares into and out of his possession. Shibusawa had a "fixed-term loan facility" of about JY20,000 from Dai-Ichi Bank, but for borrowings greater than this amount, he put up collateral and specified the purpose of the loan. Shibusawa's purchase of new shares was financed by the sale of shares on the market and elsewhere – not, in principle, by bank loans using his shareholdings as collateral.

Funding for his operations was necessary not only during the establishment of a new enterprise, but also when massive investments were needed to increase capitalization. There were, of course, occasions when it was not possible to go to existing shareholders for further investment – when funding was suddenly required for operating expenses, for example, or for additional investment to meet an unexpected contingency outside the established business plan. Since access to funding at low interest rates was difficult, Shibusawa sometimes loaned the money directly in such cases, or provided funds and credit in a variety of ways by lending his own shares as collateral for a loan from a financial institution or by acting as the joint guarantor of a loan.

On occasion, Shibusawa provided such funds by taking out a personal loan, and the evidence clearly shows that he was not always able to recover the funds provided in this way. In fact, the opposite was the case: in many instances, the funds provided were non-recoverable. One could say that, by not only investing, but also by providing businesses with funding and credit in a variety of forms, Shibusawa tried to create stability for the long term by establishing businesses in the unstable and uncertain conditions of the mid-Meiji period. The end result was that this was supported by the effective donation of a considerable quantity of his personal assets.

Summary

The pre-war Japanese economic system that Shibusawa shaped not only featured a diverse network of personal contacts and funding methods; it also ensured relatively stable operations with a variety of safety nets despite its unmistakably market-competition-oriented character. The characteristics of the system and its safety net mechanism are summarized in Table 1.2.

Table 1.2 Shibusawa's Pre-war Joint-Stock Company System

Features of system		Safety net
Establishment	Nurturing investor-managers and establishing their status	The importance of investor-managers in reconciling conflicts of interest between shareholders and managers
Operations	Importance of information	Quick detection of and response to operational problems
Training	Training managers outside the university graduate system	Dissemination of the system and rapid response to problems by use of a wide range of human resources
Investment	Use of different forms of company organization plus anonymous partnerships	Choice of organization appropriate to level of risk
	System of circulation of funds by sale and purchase of shares	Demonstrating merits of joint-stock system to investors
Finance	Individual loans and credit guarantees	Provision of short-term funds, supplementing investment system safety valve
		Sharing risk by providing personal credit guarantees for large-scale loans
Banking(Dai-Ichi Bank)	Creating firm foundation through profits from colonial bank operations	Avoiding long- and short-term risks due to weakness of financial foundation

Taking the lead in establishing his system, Shibusawa trained and developed the full-time administrators responsible for company operations as well as groups of investor-executives who would serve as key investment partners, using information-oriented top management methods to correct course on poor business performance trends and faulty business models. In terms of raising capital, he used both the joint-stock company system and anonymous partnerships in establishing a structure that simultaneously drove business development on various levels.

Providing businesses with valuable investment, funding, and credit in a variety of forms, Shibusawa worked to create stability for the long term by establishing businesses amidst the unstable and uncertain conditions of the mid-Meiji period. This system represented a marked departure from those implemented by *zaibatsu* such as Mitsui, Mitsubishi, and Sumitomo. During the Meiji period, *zaibatsu* remained private, generally owned by a closed family circle of owners, and operated by a specific leader and a group of college graduate administrators. Shibusawa's system, meanwhile, stood in stark contrast: it advocated collecting capital from a broad range of sources and drawing from a broad palette of human resources.

Shibusawa's *Gappon* Capitalism

The question that follows naturally, then, is why did Shibusawa introduce this joint-stock company system, replete with his own innovations, to Japan? His personal background and writings offer several insights.

Shibusawa spent 1867 and 1868 in Paris and elsewhere in Europe as an attendant to Tokugawa Akitake, the younger brother of Tokugawa Yoshinobu, the fifteenth and last shogun of the Tokugawa government during the Edo period. After returning to Japan in 1869, Shibusawa worked as a high government official in the Meiji government's Ministry of Finance for approximately four years. In 1871, during his post at the ministry, he condensed many of his experiences in Europe into *Rikkai ryakusoku* (The elements of company formation), a monograph that explains his views on implementing corporate organizations. Although Shibusawa emphasizes the importance of a private organization in saying that "company directors must be chosen from major shareholders," he also writes that "the company must benefit and provide for those involved but, as a distributor of goods and materials, must also

consider the public good of the entire country," underlining the central-
ity of the public interest in corporate organizational strategies.[20]

Shibusawa continued to refer to *gappon* capitalism in a variety of different settings, but the fundamental themes remained constant. Several
quotes might better delineate his vision of *gappon* capitalism. Explain-
ing his reasons for believing *gappon* capitalism to be such a crucial system, Shibusawa says, "A single wealthy individual does not make the
country more prosperous. To elevate the low status of people engaged
in commerce and industry, we must make improvements to the whole
by helping the joint-stock company organizations take root." This passage shows that, to Shibusawa, the best way for Japan to overcome
its late start in the march towards modernization was to enhance the
often-disparaged profile of those in commerce and industry by adopting the *gappon* (joint-stock company) method.[21]

Shibusawa also addresses corporate organization, likening it to "a
form of republicanism, with shareholders as the citizens." For Shibusawa, corporate organizations, which comprised many members and
a wide breadth of viewpoints, required management standards that
were "governed by reason rooted in the Analects of Confucius."[22] In the
same passage, he goes on to clarify his views on the Analects: "The idea
of energizing commerce and industry and enriching the country by first
improving the status of commercial and industrial men does not come
directly from the Analects. Rather, I drew on the Analects as a corner-
stone to fortify my own approach to management." Shibusawa used
the Analects because it was an accepted discourse on logic and reason
that represented a common ground for members of the company.[23]

In a famous radio address that also included references to Adam
Smith's *The Theory of Moral Sentiments*, Shibusawa continued to adhere
to the line of thought discussed above, saying: "To make the nation
truly prosperous, we must enrich the country; to enrich the country, we
must make scientific progress and help commerce and industry thrive;
to help commerce and industry thrive, we must establish joint-stock
corporate organizations that draw on the investment contributions of
many different individuals; and to operate companies under the joint-
stock system, managers must conform to steadfast reason and logic."[24]

Conclusion: Shibusawa's Conception of Capitalism

The *gappon* capitalism Shibusawa envisioned operated within a European model framework, but it also bore elements of its designer's belief

that, at its core, a joint-stock company should be a "public" entity. By positioning and operating joint-stock companies in the market model to prevent them from being controlled by specific individuals, Shibusawa called for the creation of "public property" in the private sector. Designed to help destroy the notion of honouring government personnel while slighting ordinary citizens, and to infuse the official, governmental world with the power of the private sector, Shibusawa's management model emphasized morals that supported this "public function in private sector" arrangement, and reinforced the importance of entrusting the duties of operation to recipients of modern education.[25] As this arrangement required a fusion of various layers both old and new, Shibusawa ventured – purposely, in fact – to use the traditional Confucian Analects as the common factor in his commentaries on morality.

In addition to Shibusawa's establishment of a wide range of companies and banks and his leadership in the business world, he also popularized the joint-stock company system according to his vision of *gappon* capitalism. To mediate successfully between management and major shareholders with different interests and to stabilize operations at market-based joint-stock companies, unique changes and innovations were necessary. The methods Shibusawa devised based on his own collection of personal experiences included methods for choosing company formats optimal for business and generating capital through credit-creating functions.

In Meiji-period Japan, *zaibatsu* held enormous sway in terms of both capital and organizational might. They served as powerful engines of modernization by recruiting elite college graduates who had studied in the West and absorbed the advantages of modern education. Company startup capital was supplied by the *zaibatsu* and their respective families – never through general funding. At first glance, Shibusawa's market-based model and the *zaibatsu* model, which kept both capital and the organization closed, appear to be completely incompatible – and, in fact, they were formidable rivals in various industries. A closer look reveals, however, that many *zaibatsu* executives took part in Shibusawa's market-based model, while Shibusawa himself served as an administrator in *zaibatsu* organizations. The two models thus had some common elements in terms of both capital and the people involved.

Market-based companies during the Meiji period experienced a considerable amount of friction both among stockholders with divergent interests and among executives with different backbones. Companies established policies to sift through these tangled webs of interests to identify common elements, a process that gradually helped formulate each company's long-term vision. These basic stances on long-term interests, propagated by executives who were familiar with both models, began to take on increasingly similar traits. In many ways, these visions boosted Japan's national interests in its quest to modernize; even more significantly, they established a foundation of common interests among major stockholders.

NOTES

1 Okazaki Tetsuji and Okuno Masahiro, eds., *Gendai nihon keizai shisutemu no genryū* [The Japanese economic system and its historical origins] (Tokyo: Nihon Keizai Shimbun Shuppansha, 1993).

2 Teranishi Jyūrō, *Nihon no keizai shisutemu* [The Japanese economic system] (Tokyo: Iwanami Shoten, 2003).

3 According to Ishii Kanji, Shibusawa ranked seventeenth on the list of high-income earners in 1898; see Ishii Kanji, "Seiritsu-ki Nihon teikokushugi no ichi danmen – shikin chikuseki to shihon yushutsu" [One aspect of Japanese imperialism in its formative period – the accumulation of funds and the export of capital], *Rekishigaku Kenkyū*, no. 383 (1972). Further, an analysis of the major shareholders of 103 of the largest companies in Japan by Takamura Naosuke shows Shibusawa in twenty-fifth position: *Kaisha no tanjō* [The birth of the corporation] (Tokyo: Yoshikawa Kobunkan, 1996). Research shows that total capital of the thirty-one companies of which Shibusawa was a director in 1898 amounted to ¥126 million, far surpassing any other, being one and a half times the figure for the next highest on the list: Tanaka Ichibei, whose twenty-one companies had a total capitalization of ¥84 million; see Suzuki Tsuneo, Kobayakawa Yōichi, and Wada Kazuo, *Kigyōka nettowaku no keisei to tenkai: Detabesu karamita Nihon no chiiki Keizai* [The formation and development of business networks: A database study of regional economics in modern Japan] (Aichi: University of Nagoya Press, 2009); and Suzuki Tsuneo et al., "Meiji-ki no kaisha oyobi keieisha no kenkyū – Nihon zenkoku kaisha yakuinroku (Meiji 31-nenban) no bunseki" [Research on corporations and managers in the Meiji period – an analysis of the 1898 National List of Directors of Japanese companies], *Sangyō keizai kenkyū kiyō* (Chubu University), 9 (1999).

4 Tsuchiya Takao, *Nihon shjhonsyugi-jō no shidōsyatachi* [Leaders in the history of Japanese capitalism] (Tokyo: Iwanami Shoten, 1939).

5 Ōshima Kiyoshi, Katō Toshihiko, and Ōuchi Tsutomu, *Jinbutsu – Nihon shi-honsyugi 3: Meiji shoki no kigyōka* [Personalities in Japanese capitalism – 3: Entrepreneurs of the early Meiji period] (Tokyo: University of Tokyo Press, 1976).

6 Ibid.

7 Morikawa H., "Shibusawa Eiichi – Nihon kabushiki kaisha no sōritsusha" [Shibusawa Eiichi – Founder of the joint-stock company in Japan], in *Nihon no kigyō to kokka* [Enterprises and the state in Japan], Nihon rekishi kōza 4 (Tokyo: Nihon Keizai Shimbunsha, 1976).

8 J. Hirschmeier, *Nihon ni okeru kigyōka seishin no keisei* (Tokyo: Toyo Keizai Shinposha, 1965). Translation by Tsuchiya T. and Yui T. of *The Origins of Entrepreneurship in Meiji Japan* (Cambridge, MA: Harvard University Press, 1964). Apart from Tsuchiya's work, there has been remarkably little systematic research on Shibusawa. He is almost always referred to, however, in research on other entrepreneurs and businessmen of the pre-war period, and these references to him nearly all agree in regarding him as the leader of Japanese capitalism and of the Japanese business world.

9 Shibusawa Eiichi, *Rongo to soroban* [The Analects and the abacus] (Tokyo: Kokusho Kankō Kai, [1916] 1985).

10 Shibusawa Eiichi, "Dōtoku keizai gōitsu setsu" [The doctrine of inseparability of morality and economy] (radio broadcast, 13 June 1923), in *Seien-sensei enzetsu senshū* (Tokyo: Tokyo Ryūmonsha, 1937).

11 Shibusawa Eiichi, *Amayogatari: Shibusawa Eiichi jiden* [The autobiography of Shibusawa Eiichi], annotated by Chō Yukio (Tokyo: Iwanami Shoten, 1984).

12 Tsugai Yoshio, *Nihon shihonsyugi no gunzō* [Figures in Japanese capitalism] (Tokyo: Kyōikusha, 1980).

13 See also Abe E., "Shibusawa, Eiichi," in *International Encyclopedia of Business and Management*, ed. M. Warner (London; New York: Routledge, 1996).

14 See, for example, Seoka M., "Shibusawa Eiichi niokeru ideorogi to kakushinsei" [Shibusawa Eiichi's ideology and progressiveness], *Osaka daigaku keizaigaku* 26 (1–2, 1976); idem, "Shibusawa Eiichi niokeru kakush-insei no keiseikatei" [The formation of Shibusawa Eiichi's progressive thought], *Osaka daigaku kejzajgaku* 26 (3–4, 1977); Asano S., *Nihon no kin-daika to keiei rinen* [Japanese modernization and management philosophy] (Tokyo: Nihon Keizai Hyoronsha, 1991); Oh Kaka, "Shibusawa Eiichi no *Rongo soroban* setsu to *Nihonteki na shihonshugi no seishin*" [Shibusawa Eiichi's The Analects and the abacus and the Japanese spirit of capitalism], in *Shibusawa kenkyū* 7, ed. Shibusawa Kenkyūkai (Tokyo: Shibusawa Memorial Museum, 1994); Umezu J., "Shijō no rinritreki kiso wo

motomete – Fukuzawa Yukichi to Shibusawa Eiichi" [Toward an ethical basis for the market economy – Yukichi Fukuzawa and Shibusawa Eiichi], in *Jiyū keizai to rinri* [The liberal economy and ethics], ed. Katō Hirotaka (Tokyo: Seibundo, 1995); Matsukawa K., "Kōdō no shishin toshite no Rongo" [The Analects of Confucius as a guide for action], in *Shinjidai no Sōzō Kōeki no Tsuikyūsha Shibusawa Eiichi* [Creation of the new era: Shibusawa Eiichi – Proponent of the public good], ed. Shibusawa Kenkyūkai (Tokyo: Yamakawa Shuppansha, 1999); Sakamoto Shinichi, *Shibusawa Eiichi no kesei saimin shisō* [Confucian politico-economic thought of Shibusawa Eiichi] (Tokyo: Nihon Keizai Hyoronsha, 2002).

15 Miyamoto Matao, *Nihon no kindai 11: Kigyōkatachi no chōsen* [Modern Japan 11: The challenge of the entrepreneurs] (Tokyo: Chuo Koronsha, 1999), 288.

16 Shimada Masakazu, "How Shibusawa Eiichi Offered Models of Investment and Management to Introduce Modern Business Practice into Japan," *Japanese Yearbook on Business History* 19 (2002): 9–31; idem, *Shibusawa Eiichi no kigyōsha katsudō no kenkyū* [The entrepreneurial activities of Shibusawa Eiichi]; idem, "The Entrepreneurial Activities of Shibusawa Eiichi: The Creation of a Joint Stock Company System in the Prewar Period and the Role of the Investor-Executive," *Japanese Research in Business History* 25 (2008): 93–114; and idem, *Shibusawa Eiichi: Shakai kigyōka no senkusha* [Shibusawa Eiichi: The pioneer of the social enterprise] (Tokyo: Iwanami Shoten, 2011).

17 Both the Shibusawa family records and Records of meetings of the Shibusawa family are kept in the Shibusawa Archives established by the Shibusawa Eiichi Memorial Foundation.

18 Takamura, *Kaisha no tanjyō*, 13–14.

19 Ibid., 19–20.

20 Shibusawa Eiichi, *Rikkai ryakusoku* [The elements of company formation] (Tokyo: Ministry of Finance, 1871).

21 Shibusawa Eiichi, "Seien-sensei kungen" [The precepts of Dr. Seien], *Ryūmon Zasshi* 249 (1909).

22 Ibid.

23 Ibid.

24 Shibusawa, "Dōtoku keizai gōitsu setsu."

25 Shimada Masakazu, "Senzenki nihon no shōgyō kyōiku seido no hatten: Tokyo no shiritsu shōgyō gakkō to Shibusawa Eiichi" [The development of the commercial school system in pre-war Japan: The support from Shibusawa Eiichi to the private commercial school in Tokyo], *Business Review Faculty of Business Administration* 19, no. 1 (2009).

2 Harmony between Morality and Economy

TANAKA KAZUHIRO

"Harmony between morality and economy" is one of the common translations of and *Dōtoku keizai gōitsu*, the hallmark philosophy of the entrepreneur Shibusawa Eiichi. Although the general understanding is that morality and economy tend to be mutually contradictory, Shibusawa insisted that they were consistent with each other and that it was definitely possible to unite morality with production and profit-making. He himself referred to this approach as *Rongo to soroban* (The Analects and the abacus), where the Analects represent morality and the abacus stands for economy.

Shibusawa's career as an entrepreneur was suffused with the idea of harmony between morality and economy. It began when he resigned from the Ministry of Finance and attempted to pursue economic activities in the private sector as the founder of Dai-Ichi Kokuritsu Ginko (First National Bank). Tamano Seiri, a close colleague in the civil service, criticized his approach of turning to the private sector to become a merchant. Drawing on the Analects and other Confucian literature Shibusawa refuted Tamano's criticism, saying that no nation would be formed by scorning money, that the work of civil servants was not the only valuable work, and that valuable work which a person should undertake was to be found everywhere; he then declared, "I will devote my life to the Analects."[1] This was in May 1873. At that time, Shibusawa decided to devote his life to business, with the teachings of the Analects as the touchstone, and from that time on he pursued business activities based on the conviction that "morality and economy are compatible."[2]

Shibusawa not only practised that doctrine; he also proactively advocated it. Whether one is an entrepreneur, a politician, or any other kind of person, those who put their own convictions into practice are not always proactive advocates of such convictions. Some say absolutely nothing about their own beliefs, while others put them into words if asked. Shibusawa, however, took the initiative, communicating his conviction of harmony between morality and economy to people working in business as well as to the public at large.

Was it because Shibusawa craved the limelight? One could hardly say so. As a leader in Japanese economic circles of his day, he believed it was absolutely necessary to propagate the idea that morality and economy are consistent, even as he busily engaged in setting up and managing companies in order to encourage the sound development of the Japanese economy and to make the nation wealthy.

What then is the significance of this harmony? What does it mean that morality and economy are compatible? Shibusawa himself left behind a vast number of speeches on the doctrine, but as he was an entrepreneur, not an academic, he did not present the principles in a systematic way. Even today there seems to be entirely correct and shared understanding of the doctrine. This chapter aims to clarify the overall picture of Shibusawa's doctrine of harmony between morality and economy and to present a platform for a common understanding of it.

I begin with an overview of the philosophy after clarifying the meaning of "morality," "economy," and "harmony." Of the three terms, an accurate understanding of harmony is especially important. The doctrine of harmony between morality and economy consists of two assertions that I explore – namely, that "economy is congruent with morality" and that "morality is congruent with economy." Next, I clarify the implications of this doctrine for businesspeople in today's market economy, and compare it with the theories of Adam Smith. I conclude by considering the relationship between the doctrine of harmony between morality and economy and Shibusawa's *gapponshugi*, the principle of capitalism infused with moral values.

Overview of Harmony between Morality and Economy

The meaning of "economy" in Shibusawa's doctrine is twofold: profit/ wealth, and business activities that generate profit and wealth. A manufacturing industry, for example, contributes to people's daily lives by the production and sale of goods from raw materials; such "business activities" bring manufacturers profit and wealth. The former are the root cause; the latter are the result. The same applies to the financial industry, the services industry, and a range of other businesses.

The meaning of "morality" is also twofold. The morality that prohibits a person from undertaking certain acts – for example, that one should not deceive another person – is referred to as "passive morality," and is what first comes to mind when we hear the term morality. There is, however, another aspect to morality: the "active morality" that urges a person to do what should be done, such as helping someone in trouble who is immediately in front of one. Urging or instructing another person to undertake such an act is also an aspect of active morality. Both aspects of morality are essential for an accurate understanding of Shibusawa's doctrine of harmony between morality and economy.

Morality is demanded of all human beings, not just those engaged in economic activities. The teachings of Confucianism, which are the foundation of Shibusawa's doctrine of morality, also include righteousness as a human being. Shibusawa, however, focused on the relation between morality and economy in his doctrine of harmony. He emphasized morality as the righteous way of those engaged in economic activities. In general, the two are believed to be contradictory, or at least unrelated. Yet, as a leading economic figure of his time, Shibusawa thought the economy and people engaged in economic activities were in particular need of a moral base.

Economy is congruent with morality and morality is congruent with economy

The doctrine of harmony between morality and economy consists of two assertions. The first is that economy is congruent or consistent with, and essential for, morality. With this assertion, Shibusawa morally justified economy. Profit, wealth, and the business activities that generate them are never morally evil as long as they are pursued through justifiable methods. Moreover, conducting business activities and generating profit and wealth are essential for realizing morality, and therefore represent the moral righteousness that those engaged in economic activities should proactively pursue. The emphasis here is obviously on active morality.

The second assertion is that morality is congruent or consistent with, and essential for, economy. Here, I refer to passive morality. When describing the morality demanded of merchants, Shibusawa used the term "commercial morality," a common expression at the time. Shibusawa produced many speeches and writings on commercial morality, the essence of which can be summarized as follows: one should not lie, and one should not put personal profit first. Morality's congruence with economy asserts that, by following commercial morality, economy will not be hindered; indeed, it will function well. Shibusawa maintained that morality is essential for the stability and continuous development of economy.

The theoretical structure of harmony between morality and economy

The doctrine of harmony between morality and economy that Shibusawa propounded is supported by two subdoctrines: economy is congruent with morality, and morality is congruent with economy. Stated more accurately, harmony between morality and economy asserts that the two subdoctrines are like two sides of a coin; thus, morality and economy are inseparable. In a lecture on harmony between morality and economy delivered in January 1919 at the Tokyo Commercial School, Shibusawa stated: "If lacking morality, a dispute is certain to arise even if economic development is attained. The economy will be ruined as a result of the dispute … If merely emphasizing morality and adhering to conventional morality is not accompanied by material wealth and its power, such morality will not be effective even if it is replete with good intentions. This will not enable the world and its people to be saved … Therefore, the two must be congruent with each other."[3] It is obvious that the first part corresponds to "morality is congruent with economy" and the second part to "economy is congruent with morality." When the two are combined, they are congruent, as noted in the third part. This is the theoretical structure of harmony between them.

This type of logic is frequently seen in Shibusawa's other lectures and writings. For example, in the preface to his famous book, *Rongo to soroban*, appears a statement that replaces "morality and economy" with "the Analects and the abacus" for simplification: "The abacus is made of the Analects … [T]he Analects activate true wealth with the abacus … [T]herefore, it has always been said that the Analects and the abacus are at the same time infinitely remote and infinitely close."[4] The theoretical structure is identical with the above. Economy is congruent with morality, and morality is congruent with economy, therefore morality and economy are inseparable.

Inseparable instead of balancing

"Harmony" between morality and economy is also commonly described as "balancing" morality with economy and vice versa. It is certain that Shibusawa objected to both economic and moral extremes: he warned both against profit-seeking activities that ignored ethics and against conventional morality that considered economic activities to be vulgar. But there is a risk of losing sight of the essence of his doctrine if one uses the term "balancing." The idea of balancing between the two is based on the premise that morality and economy are essentially different; balance between the two is required precisely because they are of a different nature. In everyday life, we regard morality and economy as different phenomena. This is why we tend to suppose that Shibusawa emphasized "balancing" morality and economy. However, Shibusawa thought that morality and economy are not two different things – the two are inseparable, and neither will hold without the other. Shibusawa admitted that morality and economy are generally regarded as contradictory in nature, but said nonetheless that the two "must be one and the same": "Few people come to realize that there exists harmony between the *Analects* [morality] and the *abacus* [economy] … [However,] I have been firmly convinced for a long time that the Analects and the abacus must be one and the same."[5]

Morality and production and profit-making are thus compatible, according to Shibusawa, and can be implemented simultaneously.[6] He did not claim, however, that morality and economy agree in every case: he said neither that "greed is good" nor that "we should behave ethically because ethics pays," to put it in contemporary terms. Rather, "genuine morality" and "genuine economy" are inseparable, and "morality that does not seek profit is not genuine, and perfect wealth and justifiable money-making are consequent on morality."[7] The Confucian scholar and contemporary of Shibusawa, Mishima Chūshū, put this in more pithy terms: "Morality that does not make profit is not genuine morality. Profit that is not based on morality is not genuine profit."[8] Mishima and Shibusawa were on friendly terms as two peers who advocated the doctrine: Mishima from the perspective of a Confucian classics specialist, and Shibusawa from the perspective of an entrepreneur.

"Genuine morality" is achieved by attaining economic results, while "genuine economy" is achieved by practising morality. For this purpose, effort, both to achieve economic results and to practise morality, is required of those engaged in economic activities. As Shibusawa said: "It would not be possible for plants named morality and economy to bloom on the water and the two to harmonize perfectly as a pistil and a stamen blowing in the wind and coming into union. Therefore, in order to harmonize morality and economy, a person who harmonizes them, a firm resolution by the person to do so, and carefulness in daily life are required."[9]

Although such efforts are required of people, harmony between morality and economy clearly indicates that the two aspects are essentially congruent, even though they appear contradictory in nature. This point is extremely important for those engaged in economic activities. If morality and economy are contradictory in nature, the best one can expect is a balance between the two, meaning that neither can be pursued in its entirety. Some might be sceptical about whether balance can really be attained between two things that are contradictory in nature, but they appear in a completely different light if the essential congruence between them is stated clearly. One can pursue both morality and economy with full force to attain the practical target of achieving harmony between them, because one can be confident that such an effort will be rewarded.

The best example of an economic person who endeavoured with conviction to achieve such harmony is Shibusawa Eiichi himself. Yet it was only after around 1910, when Shibusawa was seventy, that he incorporated into his theoretical structure the idea that morality and economy must be one and the same and began to assert the doctrine of harmony between the two. As such, this terminology should be used only with respect to statements he made around this time and later. No such rigour is required here, however. The two subdoctrines – that economy is congruent with morality, and that morality is congruent with economy – were already frequently stated in the years when Shibusawa was active at the forefront of economic development, advocating *gapponshugi*, although Shibusawa did not then consciously integrate the two ideas into his statements. Still, the essence of the doctrine of harmony between morality and economy, as it came to be noted in later years, can be understood fully from each of the subdoctrines. For this reason, in the remainder of the chapter, I focus on the first of the two subdoctrines – that economy is congruent with morality – to examine this concept in more detail.

Economy Is Congruent with Morality

The idea that economy is congruent with morality means that economy is compatible with, and essential for, morality. As noted, economy consists of two elements: commercial, industrial, and other business activities; and the profit and wealth generated by such activities. Generally, profit and wealth are thought of as contradicting morality; thus, business activities that generate profit and wealth are viewed as morally suspect. Shibusawa claimed, however, that profit and wealth in themselves are not contrary to morality – that business activities are not "the root of evil," but instead are morally justifiable: in short, that profit and wealth and business activities are compatible with morality.

Shibusawa, however, took another step away from such passive justification to assert the moral legitimacy of business activities. He believed that the most important morality was to make people wealthy, and he asserted that business activities are essential for realizing that ultimate morality. He further stated that, for such activities to be fully implemented, it was also essential for those involved to attain profit and wealth. In other words, business activities and profit and wealth are not just compatible with, but *essential for*, morality.

Profit and wealth and business activities are compatible with morality

Every moral system and religion, to a greater or lesser degree, is sceptical of placing value on wealth and fame, regarding them as things that should be shunned or, at best, as necessary evils to be met with reluctant approval. The same holds true for the neo-Confucianism that dominated East Asian thinking from the fourteenth century onward, which regarded economic wealth and the desire for it as moral evils, and contentment with poverty as a moral good.

Because the Tokugawa shogunate had treated neo-Confucianism as the only legitimate school of thought, Edo-period Japan regarded profit and commerce as vulgar. In the early Meiji period, when Shibusawa launched his business activities, the scorn for commerce and profit was still pervasive. Shibusawa confronted this way of thinking head on, however, advocating that the pursuit of profit should not be rejected, but affirmed on moral grounds.

Shibusawa said that neither wealth itself nor a person's pursuit of wealth was morally bad, and often presented arguments along the following lines: Wherever one looks in the Analects – one of the most important books of Confucianism – Confucius (and his disciples) never said that wealth, or its pursuit, is bad. Here and there one does indeed see words that warn against obtaining wealth. However, if the words are interpreted carefully and with an unbiased eye, none goes beyond an admonishment against obtaining wealth *dishonestly*. The Analects (Chapter III) state, for example: "The Master said, 'Wealth and honour are what people want, but if they are the consequence of deviating from the *dao* [the way], I will have no part in them.'"[10] Shibusawa argued that the statement "does not regard wealth and honour as vulgar, but only warns people not to obtain them dishonestly."[11] He criticized the conventional view among scholars that "more than a few construe 'people' of this chapter as evil people, and believe that evil people desire gain of wealth and honour, which require dishonest means to obtain. As such, wise people try to avoid wealth and honour, and cast them away even if they cross their path."[12] He also said, "Wealth and honour gained through righteous means are never to be regarded as vulgar and abandoned,"[13] and that a man of virtue is not embarrassed by profit that is consistent with righteousness.[14] Even Confucius said, "It is a disgrace to remain poor and without rank when the way prevails in the world."[15]

As long as profit and wealth are morally suspect, the business activities that generate them will be targeted for moral criticism as "the source of evil." If, however, profit and wealth are not evil, the business activities that create them also escape moral transgression.[16] By vigorously asserting the moral legitimacy of profit and wealth, Shibusawa also advocated the moral legitimacy of business activities. In doing so, he took aim at the contempt for business – especially among society's leading classes – that was a major obstacle to its development in Japan in the early Meiji period.

It was not only by morally vindicating profit and wealth, however, that Shibusawa asserted the legitimacy of business activities; he also strongly advocated for the moral value of such activities.

Business activities and profit and wealth are essential for morality

Shibusawa thought that freeing people's daily lives from financial worries and making them wealthy reflected the essence of Confucian morality – which is extremely important for a correct understanding of his doctrine. In this view, contrary to the conventional (and mistaken) interpretation, activities that increase people's affluence, far from being vulgar, are in fact honourable and even morally important. To show how Confucius emphasized this, Shibusawa often quoted the following exchange between Confucius and his disciple Tsze-kung from the Analects: "Tsze-kung said, 'Suppose the case of a man extensively conferring benefits on the people and able to assist all, what would you say of him? Might he be called perfectly virtuous?' The Master said,

'Why speak only of virtue in connection with him? Must he not have the qualities of a sage?'"[17]

Confucius thus extolled the act of making people affluent as the ultimate human good (possibly even beyond human).

In his *Rongo kōgi* (Lectures on the Analects), Shibusawa praised this as "part and parcel of the Analects."[18] He also said, "The trifling charities, kindnesses, and sympathies that take place between individuals are a small virtue [*shōjin*]. Politics and acts based on the kind of virtue that extends affection to many people and comes to the aid of people who are suffering, is a great virtue [*taijin*]."[19] Shibusawa also cited other parts of canons of Confucianism (in addition to the Analects) specifically to demonstrate that Confucius taught that "It is a wise man's duty to support and enrich people's lives."[20] Mainstream Confucian scholars, however, have presumed to ignore these teachings, arguing that economic activity is contrary to the teachings of Confucius, a position that Shibusawa never ceased to criticize. In a speech given in his eighties, he stated, "It was a fallacy for scholars lecturing on the Analects to have separated morality from production and profit-making. They are absolutely compatible."[21] In Shibusawa's view, to make people better off through economic activity is to practise the ultimate virtue. Confucius, though, expected statesmen, not merchants and manufacturers, to provide public welfare for the people. Commerce and industry were regarded not as providers, but as recipients of public welfare. Everybody in Japan thought along these lines – that it was the task of government, not of the private sector, to improve people's lives. Shibusawa thought, however, that, in the modern age, private sector commerce and industry could, and should, also take a stand for the good of the nation and society through individual work and business activity – indeed, he thought the private sector should play the *leading* role.[22]

Shibusawa believed that business activities by the private sector are essential for making people affluent. He also thought profit and wealth from business activities are essential for such activities to be pursued thoroughly and, thus, that individuals' profit and wealth are essential for morality. Only when people can expect to obtain profit and wealth for themselves will they patiently and enthusiastically strive for the moral good of working for the public welfare: "What if a particular work has no relation to your own profit? You will not put your heart and soul into the work if it is clear that the success of the work earns others a fortune but not yourself or that the failure of it costs others a fortune but not yourself. However, if it is your own [profit-related] work, you would wish to develop it, and it is a plain fact that you actually will develop it."[23] Shibusawa even said, "Self-interest can generate public good. A public good is fragile unless it is based on self-interest."[24] For the public good to be rock solid, the person striving for the public good must be able to see a profit.

An important point here is that Shibusawa never thought that self-interest should be completely sacrificed for ultimate morality. He never brought up the "virtue of upright poverty" that people tend to associate with the term "morality." He deliberated on morality based on natural human emotions. As long as they are obtained by legitimate means, profit and wealth as moral evils are not only repudiated; they promote moral good, and can be pursued fair and square: economy is congruent with morality. This does not mean, however, that people who engage in economic activities should be motivated first (shōjin) by the pursuit of self-interest. So let us now take a look at the other aspect of harmony between morality and economy: morality is congruent with economy.

Morality Is Congruent with Economy

In arguing that morality is congruent with economy, Shibusawa meant by "morality" the passive morality that prohibits people from doing what should not be done. More specifically, it is commercial morality, which prohibits telling lies and putting self-interest first in the course of making profit and wealth through business.

Not telling lies is the same as acting in good faith. And not putting self-interest first means primarily seeking profit for others. These aspects of morality tend to be regarded as a hindrance to business activities and the gaining of profit and wealth. Shibusawa held, however, that both are consistent with economy and essential for it.

Acting in good faith is consistent with business activities

"Do not act in bad faith" is a central pillar of the morality Shibusawa advocated. In Japan of the Edo period, the idea that one should work with integrity, in good faith, and without fraud or dishonesty when engaging in business activities was, of course, prevalent. The *Sekimon Shingaku* school of ethics, founded in the early eighteenth century by Ishida Baigan, is well known for advocating such teachings. Nonetheless, among the merchants of the time, the dominant way of thinking was completely the opposite. For example, there was the proverb, "lies also count for capital." According to this proverb, money is not the only capital for business activities; the ability to lie skilfully to customers and suppliers when conducting business also constitutes capital. It suggests that, with this kind of capital, one can operate one's business smoothly, and on this basis make a good profit.[25]

By Shibusawa's time, such attitudes had faded compared to the old days, "when things were so desperate that merchants hardly ever needed to think about truth and morals." But Shibusawa expressed his concern that, even in the Meiji society of his own time, "the idea that indifference to the principles of truth is acceptable has spread in commercial and industrial circles to this very day."[26] He criticized the shallow moral awareness in Japanese business circles of the time, and advocated ethical conduct in business activities with honesty and good faith. In an 1893 speech entitled "The Duties of Businessmen," Shibusawa severely criticized the notion that "lies also count for capital," saying, "this is truly a great mistake. It is so shameful it brings tears to the eyes."[27] He also asked the audience whether manufacturers and merchants alike could do business if they do not demonstrate trustworthiness, and he emphasized that trust and sincerity are the foundation of business.[28]

It seems quite obvious that honesty is essential for business activities. No customer will buy from a merchant who tells lies, and no supplier will sell to such a merchant. Banks hardly lend money twice to debtors who act in bad faith. That honesty is the best policy ought to be common currency everywhere in the business world. Why, then, are many people sceptical about the validity of this argument, saying instead that acting in good faith is *not* consistent with business activities in practice? Shibusawa had two main answers to this question.

The first answer is that people confuse tactics, which are essential for business, with lies, which are not necessary for it, and tend to regard tactics as lies.[29] For example, in business it stands to reason that the merchant does not tell the customer the cost price of a product. If the merchant were open about the cost price and all else in the name of honesty, the customer would drive a hard bargain and the merchant would not be able to make a profit – and if he cannot make a profit, he will not be able to continue trading or to provide products to customers. Nevertheless, people are apt to regard even these kinds of reasonable tactics as "lies" or "secrets." Therefore, before you know it, the rational idea that *tactics* are necessary for business turns into the irrational idea that *dishonesty* is necessary for business. In contrast, if the merchant knows, for example, that a product in his stock is defective and he conceals this fact to sell the product to customers, this is not a tactic but nothing short of an underhanded lie. The merchant can hardly claim that he cannot do business unless he tells such lies.

Shibusawa's second answer to the claim that acting in good faith is not consistent with business activities is that the profit earned by means of dishonest conduct might increase, but only temporarily: "It is easy to act contrary to morality because the idea that extra profit is always desirable takes precedence in profit-making."[30] For example, if a merchant knows that a product is defective and conceals that fact to sell it, he will probably make a profit at first, but when the truth is discovered, he will likely bear a loss that is higher than the profit earned. Shibusawa repeatedly warned that wealth obtained by dishonest means will not last long. In reality, of course, profit might continue for a long time if the dishonesty remains undiscovered. As an entrepreneur, Shibusawa was not so naive as to deny this possibility.

The important point here is that because it might be possible to earn a profit (even if temporarily, or unexpectedly over the long term) by acting in bad faith, it does not follow that one cannot earn a profit unless one acts in bad faith – that is to say, acting in good faith is still consistent with business activities. It is possible to earn an adequate profit, to say the least, even if one acts in *good* faith – indeed, profit obtained in this way will last a long time. If such is the case, good faith on the one hand and business activities on the other hand are clearly consistent. In this sense, morality is congruent with economy. That was Shibusawa's way of thinking.

Having said that, the possibility remains that one will earn even more profit (even if temporarily) by acting in bad faith. Then we have to admit that the temptation to act in bad faith to make a greater profit is constantly present. Honesty and business profit are consistent in essence, but it is perhaps due to this temptation that some people engage in business activities that contradict the virtue of honesty in practice. That is precisely why Shibusawa repeatedly raised the importance of moral edification with everyone engaged in business activities.

The idea that extra profit is always desirable prompts people not only to act in bad faith, but also to give precedence to their own profit over the profit of others. In the capitalist world, it is totally acceptable to pursue *primarily* one's own self-interest as long as one acts in accordance with rules and regulations. Shibusawa would not agree with that, however. Let us investigate further in the next section.

Primarily seeking others' profit is consistent with earning
profit for oneself

I have already stated that Shibusawa did not deny the pursuit of self-interest; rather, it was something that should be approved and recommended. He insisted, however, that the pursuit of self-interest should not be the *primary* motive. According to Shibusawa, seeking profit primarily for others is consistent with obtaining profit for yourself. Primarily seeking profits for others *will not hinder conducting business activities smoothly and gaining profits from them; it is even essential for this purpose.* This is the second meaning of the phrase, "morality is congruent with economy."

By way of explanation, Shibusawa frequently quoted this phrase from the Analects: "Authoritative persons establish others [first] in seeking to establish themselves and promote others [first] in seeking to get there themselves."[31] These words by Confucius express what Shibusawa wanted to say in a concise and finely nuanced, accurate way. The phrase advocates trying to fulfil the wishes of other people before fulfilling one's own; it does not, however, negate the achievement of one's own wishes. It does not say that one must not think about achieving one's own purpose just because it helps to achieve someone else's purpose. Instead it argues that one may achieve one's own purpose as long as one helps others achieve theirs first. Here exists no taste of selfless devotion that people easily associate with moral teachings.

Although this teaching is pragmatic enough to agree with the pursuit of one's own desires, people might still criticize it as idealistic, arguing that, by taking this lesson at face value, one ends up yielding to others and, in the end, not achieving one's own wishes. Shibusawa would have refuted that contention, instead warning that if one prioritizes self-interest, one will have trouble achieving it. For example, if everybody scrambles to be first at the railway ticket gate, everyone will be packed in together and in the end nobody can pass through. In this way, if individuals have a sense of "caring only for themselves," in the end nobody will be able to obtain profit for himself or herself.[32]

Do not monopolize one's profit

Should one keep as much profit as one wants for oneself, so long as one has made that profit without taking precedence over that of others? Shibusawa would have said "no." In addition to seeking profit for others in the *process* of profit-generating business activities, he demanded that the profit gained as a *result* of such activities be used to seek profit for others – in the form of a donation, for example. He argued that the profit one earns becomes morally wrong if one monopolizes it, and that only when individuals return some part of the profit to society will they become wealthier. In this he took a long-term, dynamic view of the relationship between the wealth of individuals and that of society.

Shibusawa demanded that the wealthy classes return to society the wealth they earn.[33] To put these ideas into practice, Shibusawa personally donated a significant share of the income he earned from his work in the business world to welfare facilities and schools, among other things. He praised Andrew Carnegie, who was an enthusiastic philanthropist, as a model entrepreneur practicing the doctrine of the harmony between morality and economy. In contrast, in a lecture given at Ryūmonsha in 1906, Shibusawa criticized John D. Rockefeller for conspicuously monopolizing his wealth; only in 1913 did Rockefeller establish the Rockefeller Foundation.[34] Gaining profit, then, is not morally evil per se, but even profit that is earned without dishonest conduct becomes morally evil if it is conspicuously monopolized.

The Characteristics of the Doctrine of Harmony between Morality and Economy

"The gentleman is alert to what is right."

To sum up the idea that "morality is congruent with economy," one will earn sufficient profit even if one deals honestly in business, and the profit one earns in this way will be long lasting. Those who primarily seek profit for others will find it easier to earn profit for themselves. And if one does not monopolize one's wealth, but instead returns it to society, in the end return it will return to one and become one's own profit.

Today this immediately calls to mind the phrase, "ethics pays." The logic of those who trot out this slogan when exhorting corporations to be ethical is obvious: one should be ethical because it pays to be ethical. This was not, however, the logic of Shibusawa. His basic position was that one should be ethical because a human should be ethical, that one should be honest in business because business should be done with honesty, and that one should prioritize the profit of others because it is right to do so. In Shibusawa's view, one who heeds morality merely because it pays will no longer do so if that person encounters a situation where profit can be made *without* observing morality. For example, in *Rongo to soroban*, he states: "If one wishes to dedicate himself to a company or a bank but his wish stems only from the self-interest in the form of seeking his own profits, or if he gives out greater dividends only because he is also a shareholder and hopes to further fill his own cashbox, then there is a problem. If this person encounters a situation where he will profit more by forcing the company or the bank to go bankrupt and to levy damage on the shareholders, it will be doubtful if he can resist the temptation."[35]

Profit is not the cause but the effect of observing morality. Shibusawa favoured the following aphorism from the Analects: "The gentleman is alert to what is right. The petty man is alert to what is profitable."[36] The gentleman or virtuous person acts with morality as the criterion for judgment; by so doing, he also gains profit for himself. In other words, morality is the objective, and by meeting the objective one earns profit as a by-product. For example, in reference to the previously mentioned saying of Confucius that "Authoritative persons establish others [first] in seeking to establish themselves and promote others [first] in seeking to get there themselves," Shibusawa said, "[If you put it this way] it can also be read as reluctantly giving priority to others in order to meet your own desires, but I am sure that the true intention of Confucius was never anything so mean … The true intention of Confucius was simply to teach that the virtuous person should follow this sequence."[37] The virtuous person prioritizes others because he believes he should prioritize them. As a result, he earns profit not only for others, but also himself. Such is the sequence.

In his doctrine, Shibusawa expounded on the economic nature of morality not because he wanted to show businesspeople how to make profit by exploiting morality for opportunistic purposes, but because, through resolving the misunderstanding that morality does *not* pay, he wanted to show them the definite possibility of achieving morality and making profit concurrently. The main point of the argument for the economic nature of morality is morality, not economy.

It is natural, however, that being convinced of the economic nature of morality is not enough for businesspeople to behave morally. That is why Shibusawa repeatedly emphasized the *importance* of morality as well as the economic nature of it. It was Shibusawa's long-standing desire that the moral standard of Japanese business circles should be improved through these discourses – and that business circles would make society affluent.

Comparison with the philosophy of Adam Smith

Many people find commonality with Shibusawa's harmony between morality and economy and the philosophy of Adam Smith. Shibusawa himself recognized the common features. In an audio-recorded speech given in 1923, Shibusawa stated as follows:

> From what I have heard, Great Britain's Adam Smith, who is the father of economics, was a professor of ethical philosophy at Glasgow University and established ethics based on sympathy, and then wrote the famous book *The Wealth of Nations* and established modern economics. This exemplifies that the teachings of a wise person of earlier years and those of a wise person of later years have the same origin and follow the same path. I believe that harmonization between morality and economy is an eternal principle accepted both in Asia and the West.[38]

There are indeed noteworthy common features in the philosophies of the two men. First, they regarded the self-interest of human beings positively, and emphasized that the pursuit of self-interest by individuals plays an important role in bringing prosperity to society at large. Shibusawa thought that, in order for people to work with enthusiasm and patience to realize the ultimate goal of making society affluent, it is essential that they should be able to look forward to profit from the undertaking. Smith asserted that, if individuals engaged in economic activities sought their own wealth and social status, the invisible hand ultimately would bring prosperity and harmony to society.[39]

Second, they did not approve of unlimited self-interest, but supported self-interest restricted by morality. Shibusawa always said, "do not behave dishonestly," and "do not place self-interest first"; he never approved of the pursuit of self-interest at the expense of commercial morality. He also believed that the fulfilment of self-interest through business activities is justified only when the activities also contribute to the economic well-being of the public. Shibusawa never recognized economic activities that bring profit only to oneself, without benefit to society, as proper. According to Shibusawa, the pursuit of self-interest needs to be underpinned both by passive morality (commercial morality) and by active morality. Smith approved of self-interest restricted by a "sense of duty,"[40] referring to awareness of general rules such as not breaching justice and bringing about beneficence when taking an action. Other people are angered if "justice" is breached; passive morality restricts and prohibits such acts. If beneficence is brought about, those who benefit will be happy; active morality promotes such acts. Therefore, Smith also demanded that the pursuit of self-interest be underpinned by both passive and active morality.

An important difference in the philosophies of Shibusawa and Smith comes into view, however, when one compares the two in more detail. Simply put, the difference is in whether the pursuit of public welfare is expected of entities engaged in economic activities. Shibusawa believed it was; Smith did not. For Shibusawa, the pursuit of public welfare to make people's lives more affluent was the "ultimate morality;" he therefore emphasized that those who engage in private sector economic activities should also take part in the effort, as discussed previously. This assertion is at the core of Shibusawa's harmony between morality and economy. Adam Smith, in contrast, does not seem to have expected that each entity engaged in economic activities would pursue public welfare. This point is clearly indicated in perhaps one of the most famous passages from *The Wealth of Nations*: "It is not from the benevolence of the butcher, the brewer, or the baker, that we expect our dinner, but from their regard to their own interest. We address ourselves, not to their humanity but to their self-love, and never talk to them of our own necessities but of their advantages."[41] Shibusawa would have expected the butcher and the baker to mind the needs of their customers, and to have a mindset of contributing to the betterment of public welfare in their own way.

Smith did mention beneficence, or active morality that urges people to do what should be done, in addition to passive morality that prohibits doing what should not be done. However, his emphasis was clearly on justice, not on beneficence: "[Beneficence] is the ornament which embellishes, not the foundation which supports the building, and which it was, therefore, sufficient to recommend, but by no means necessary to impose. Justice, on the contrary, is the main pillar that upholds the whole edifice."[42]

Businesspeople, Smith presumed, abide by the admonition "not to breach justice," and on that condition concentrate their efforts in pursuit of their own benefits. They attempt to expand their own wealth and raise their status, instead of bringing prosperity to society based on a sense of public morality: "[H]e intends only his own gain, and he is in this, as in many other cases, led by an invisible hand to promote an end which was no part of his intention."[43] Smith's position, in short, was that "public welfare follows private welfare."

Shibusawa's position, in contrast, can be described as "private welfare follows public welfare." Economic actors are expected not only not to breach justice, but also to bring about beneficence as a priority; in other words, to attempt consciously to practise the great virtue (*taijin*) of making people affluent. Needless to say, as a dedicated disciple of Confucianism, Shibusawa placed importance on the practice of benevolence, the virtue of the highest level of Confucianism. Shibusawa expected economic people to be benevolent, or gentlemen. A society is led to prosperity not unintentionally by the invisible hand, but by a series of efforts by each economic person to improve public welfare. They can also gain personal benefits in the process, and everyone can enjoy greater profit and wealth from a society that gains affluence. Shibusawa envisioned the relationship between individuals and society from such a long-term, dynamic perspective.

In the exposition at the end of the Iwanami-Bunko version of Shibusawa's *Amayogatari* (Oral autobiography), Chō Yukio points out the difference between the philosophies of Smith and Shibusawa: "A difference should be recognized between the ethos of civil society of Western Europe that advocates that public welfare follows private welfare, developed by Anthony Ashley Cooper, the third Earl of Shaftesbury, Francis Hutchinson, David Hume, and Adam Smith, and the ethos of communities of Japan that advocates private welfare follows public welfare."[44] This can be understood as the fundamental difference between Western and Asian philosophy. In the West, rights of individuals are given priority. In contrast, in East Asia – especially in Japan – it is traditionally a norm to think of one's obligations first, and rights to be enjoyed later. When pursued to the extreme, some tend to feel guilty about an individual's enjoying rights and benefits. Shibusawa denied such extreme thought, and supported the pursuit of private welfare. This does not mean, however, that he prioritized the pursuit of private welfare; rather, his assertion was that the pursuit of public welfare should come first.

The gentleman is alert to what is right, and the petty man is alert to what is profitable. Depending on where one begins – how to make money for oneself or discerning what is right for one to do – seems to make a big difference in the economic activities that follow. The crisis of global capitalism facing today's world does not seem unrelated to this point.

Conclusion: *Gapponshugi* and Harmony between Morality and Economy

Shibusawa Eiichi tried to make Japan affluent by promoting commerce and industry. *Gapponshugi* was the system he adopted for that purpose and that he endeavoured to disseminate: "If wishing for true prosperity of a nation, efforts must be taken to make the nation affluent. For making a nation affluent, science needs to be developed and commercial and industrial activities promoted. In order to promote commerce and industry, *gappon* organization is essential."[45] Simply put, a *gappon* organization is a joint-stock company. What Shibusawa hoped to emphasize by using the word *gappon*, however, was that, by conducting business with such an organization, many people will commit business resources to the extent possible with their respective abilities and gain returns commensurate with the commitment, instead of having only a specific person (the administrator of the business) commit business resources and monopolize the returns. It is important to note that the resources committed are not limited to cash. It is true that the purpose of a joint-stock company is to earn money, but for Shibusawa, the capital, or resources, also includes human resources.

To make a nation affluent through commerce and industry, a system is needed that combines diverse business resources possessed by many people to conduct businesses needed by society, while at the same time enabling each person engaged in the businesses to obtain personal benefit: "A nation will not be affluent if only one person gains wealth. It will not be strong. Especially today, the standing of the people engaged in commerce and industry in society is relatively low, and efforts need to be made to raise their standing. For this purpose, we need to think of a way to make the entire nation affluent. If we wish to do this, we have no choice but to resort to *gappon*. This is why I firmly decided to disseminate *gappon* organization, and this I have never forgotten."[46]

The Analects provided Shibusawa's foothold when he strove to disseminate *gappon* organization and run his companies, and Confucianism underpinned the doctrine of harmony between morality and economy, of which the representative text is the Analects. The Analects, however, were not where everything started: "It was not based on the Analects that I thought of raising the standing of people engaged in commerce and industry while promoting commerce and industry and expanding the nation's wealth. I decided to adopt such a policy for running businesses to suit my situations, but I thought it would be desirable to rely on the Analects as the standard for conducting businesses."[47] Shibusawa adopted the Analects and harmony between morality and economy as the "standard" after he had the idea that it is desirable to conduct businesses with *gappon* organization: "To manage a *gappon* organization company, one must rely on perfect and solid reasons and norms. So where should one find the standards to do this? There can be nothing but the Analects. Thus, I thought of managing businesses based on the Analects. It is an error that conventionally scholars of the Analects regard morality and production and profit-making as two separate things. The two can certainly be achieved at the same time. With this belief, I managed businesses for several decades. It is fortunate that I feel I made no great error in doing so."[48] The ideas that "morality and production and profit-making can be achieved at the same time" and that "morality and economy are congruent" represent harmony between morality and economy. These ideas provided a moral foundation when Shibusawa attempted to disseminate *gappon* organizations and conduct businesses himself based on such organizations.

"Economy is congruent with morality," first, recognizes the highest moral value in *making people affluent* through business activities or *promoting public welfare*; and, second, emphasizes that it is morally justifiable for those who engage in these business activities to obtain sufficient private benefit – indeed, it is essential to promote public welfare through business activities. According to Shibusawa, "bringing benefit widely to the people and helping the public" are acts "of a person who rules over the nation with the rule of Right," and "the rule of Right is never manifested if it deviates from efforts to make people's lives affluent by smoothly utilizing economic resources."[49] For Shibusawa, conducting businesses by *gappon* organization was, in fact, "ruling over the nation with the rule of Right":

> Adopting the basic policy of "aiming at prosperity of the nation and affluence for many people, without indulging in self-centeredness" when engaging in business and unfailingly conducting businesses in such a way can be described as the rule of Right in the business world. To the contrary, aiming only at profits of one's family and wealth for one's kin and striving to gain wealth at the cost of others can be described as the rule of Might in the business world … My sincere wish is that true businessmen will manage businesses with the rule of Right.[50]

What Shibusawa implied by the phrase "the rule of Might" probably refers to *dokuritsu-shugi* (independence) and the principle of personal business management practised by Iwasaki Yatarō. Shibusawa asserted that *gapponshugi*, which is the exact opposite way of conducting business, is the rule of Right in the business world.

It can be said that the subdoctrine "economy is congruent with morality" directly provided the grounds for promoting *gapponshugi* and disseminating joint-stock companies, which are *gappon* organizations. The active morality encouraged by the notion that "economy is congruent with morality" was the greatest pillar supporting *gapponshugi*. But that was not the only subdoctrine Shibusawa relied on when managing companies as *gappon* organizations. "Morality is congruent with economy" also played an important role.

Related to this doctrine is passive morality, which prohibits one from doing what should not be done. "Morality is congruent with economy" exhorts (1) that one should comply with commercial morality, such as not behaving unfaithfully and not putting one's self-interest first; and (2) that business activities and the securing of profit and wealth should not be contradictory to complying with commercial morality. Shibusawa recalled that he had never knowingly done what he should not do as a businessman: "[Since the time when I decided to manage businesses based on the Analects] I have engaged in business management with a firm and deep resolve that I must always act in a way that conforms to the norms. During these years, there must have been times when I was in error in what I thought of as fitting the norms. However, this is only because I lacked wisdom. I can declare that I have never made any action only because it brings profits, knowing that the act deviates from the norms and deceiving myself that I am not aware."[51] The "norms" from which Shibusawa never deviated include that one should not lie to benefit oneself, and that one should not conduct business by deceiving others.[52] Needless to say, these norms are extremely important as commercial morality, but they are not limited to business management based on *gapponshugi*. Unfaithful behaviour should be restricted and prohibited in all commercial undertakings, even with *dokuritsu-shugi* and the principle of personal business management.

The characteristic peculiar to *gapponshugi* is the other aspect of morality (passive morality) that advocates that self-interest should not be put first. It is a general understanding of the market economy that, as Smith also believed, one can give priority to the pursuit of self-interest as long as one conducts business without deceiving others and in a way consistent with justice. Shibusawa was not satisfied, however, only with "justice" that prohibits dishonest conduct; he emphasized "beneficence" that tries to bring benefits to others. For Shibusawa, not putting self-interest first was another norm to adhere to. He clearly stated this point "without indulging in self-centredness" when he tried to present the "rule of Right in the business world" or the appropriate way for *gapponshugi*. It is fine to pursue self-interest, but it should be done by placing benefits for others first. The way of conducting business based on such reasons and norms was indeed *gapponshugi*.

Shibusawa dedicated his life to developing commerce and industry based on *gapponshugi*, and thereby making the nation affluent. The moral ground that underpinned these efforts was the doctrine of harmony between morality and economy that comprises the two subdoctrines that economy is congruent with morality and morality is congruent with economy. His life, during which he developed numerous businesses based on the doctrine, was not only devoid of any great error. In an air of Asian modesty, Shibusawa noted, in expressing his pride in his achievements as a businessman: "Even though what I have achieved so far is very little, I believe I have proven the fact that the economic activities of mobilizing resources to achieve people's affluence on one hand and the moral practices of Confucian teachings on the other form a unity."[53] Shibusawa spent his lifetime demonstrating that business management based on *gapponshugi*, or harmony between morality and economy, can bring affluence to society, and that morality and economy can be achieved simultaneously.

NOTES

1 Shibusawa Eiichi, *Rongo to soroban* [The Analects and the abacus] (Tokyo: Kokusho Kankō Kai, [1916] 1985), 12.
2 Ibid.
3 Shibusawa Eiichi, *Seien hyakuwa* [Seien's 100 stories] (Tokyo: Kokumin Kyōiku Kai, [1913] 1926), 112. "Seien" is Shibusawa's pseudonym. See also Ryūmonsha, ed., "Shibusawa Eiichi's talk at Tokyo Commercial High School, March 1919," in *Shibusawa Eiichi denki shiryō* [Shibusawa Eiichi biographical materials], vol. 44 (Tokyo: Shibusawa Eiichi denki shiryō Kankō Kai, 1962), 270.
4 Shibusawa, *Rongo to soroban*, 1.
5 Shibusawa, *Seien hyakuwa*, 112.
6 Shibusawa Eiichi, "Dōtoku keizai gōitsu setsu" [The doctrine of inseparability of morality and economy] (radio broadcast, 13 June 1923), in *Seiensensei enzetsu senshū* (Tokyo: Ryūmonsha, 1937).

7 Shibusawa, *Seien Hyakuwa*, 138–9.
8 Mishima Chūshū, "Gi ri gōitsu ron" [On the inseparability of morality and profit], *Tokyo Gakushikaiin Zasshi* 8, no. 5 (1886): 54.
9 Ryūmonsha, ed., *Shibusawa Eiichi denki shiryō*, vol. 44, 212.
10 Confucius, "Analects, 4/5," trans. R.T. Ames and H. Rosemont, Jr., in *The Analects of Confucius: A Philosophical Translation* (New York: Ballantine Books, 1998).
11 Shibusawa, "Dōtoku keizai gōitsu setsu."
12 Shibusawa Eiichi, *Rongo kōgi* [Lectures on the Analects] (Tokyo: Meitoku Shuppan Sha, [1925] 1975), 150.
13 Ibid.
14 Shibusawa, "Dōtoku keizai gōitsu setsu."
15 Confucius, "Analects, 8/13," trans. B. Watson, in *The Analects of Confucius* (New York: Columbia University Press, 2007).
16 Even if wealth is not inherently bad, if profit is obtained through dishonest business activities in separate and specific situations, it can no longer be said that the specific profits and specific business activities are congruent with morality. I investigate this point in the next section.
17 Confucius, "Analects, 6/28," trans. J. Legge, in *Confucian Analects: The Great Learning and the Doctrine of the Mean* (New York: Dover Publications, [1893] 1971).
18 Shibusawa, *Rongo kōgi*, 284.
19 Ibid., 433.
20 Ibid.
21 Shibusawa, "Dōtoku keizai gōitsu setsu."
22 Sakamoto Shinichi, *Shibusawa Eiichi no kesei saimin shisō* [Confucian politico-economic thought of Shibusawa Eiichi] (Tokyo: Nihon Keizai Hyoronsha, 2002).
23 Shibusawa, *Rongo to soroban*, 87.
24 Shibusawa Eiichi, "Shōnin no hombun" [The duties of businessmen], in Ryūmonsha, *Shibusawa Eiichi denki shiryō*, vol. 26 (1959), 159.
25 Tsuchiya Takao, *Nihon keiei rinen shi* [The history of Japanese philosophy of management] (Tokyo: Reitaku Daigaku Shuppan Kai, 2002), 566.
26 Shibusawa, *Seien hyakuwa*, 138.
27 Shibusawa, "Shōnin no hombun," 160.
28 Ibid.
29 Shibusawa, *Rongo to soroban*, 184–5.
30 Shibusawa, *Seien hyakuwa*, 137.
31 Confucius, "Analects, 6/28."
32 Shibusawa, *Rongo to soroban*, 87.

33 Shibusawa did not demand that all businessmen should return all their profit to society. He did not tell the average businessman to donate to other people the sustenance earned through work, and to live in poverty.

34 Shibusawa Eiichi, "Kokusai keizai to shōgyō dōtoku" [International economy and business morals], in Ryūmonsha, *Shibusawa Eiichi denki shiryō*, vol. 26 (1959), 390.

35 Shibusawa, *Rongo to soroban*, 179; quoted by Moriya Atsushi, trans., "The Analects and the Abacus," in *Modern Japanese* (Tokyo: Chikumashobo, 2010), 209.

36 Confucius, "Analects, 8/13."

37 Shibusawa, *Rongo to soroban*, 122.

38 Shibusawa, "Dōtoku keizai gōitsu setsu," 307.

39 Adam Smith, *An Inquiry into the Nature and Causes of the Wealth of Nations* (New York: Modern Library, [1776] 1937), trans. Ōuchi Hyōe and Matsukawa Shichirō, vol. 1 (Tokyo: Iwanami Shoten, 1959).

40 Adam Smith, The *Theory of Moral Sentiments* (Indianapolis, IN: Liberty Fund [1790] 1982).

41 Smith, *Wealth of Nations*, 14 (Ohuchi and Matsukawa, vol. 1, 118).

42 Smith, *Theory of Moral Sentiments*, 86.

43 Smith, *Wealth of Nations*, 423 (Ohuchi and Matsukawa, vol. 3, 56).

44 Chō Yukio, "Exposition," in Shibusawa Eiichi, *Amayogatari: Shibusawa Eiichi jiden* [The autobiography of Shibusawa Eiichi], annotated by Chō Yukio (Tokyo: Iwanami Shoten, 1984), 330.

45 Shibusawa, "Dōtoku keizai gōitsu setsu," 308.

46 Shibusawa Eiichi, "Seien sensei kungen" [Instructions and lessons by Master Seien], in Ryūmonsha, *Shibusawa Eiichi denki shiryō*, vol. 26, 447.

47 Ibid., 448.

48 Shibusawa, "Dōtoku keizai gōitsu setsu," 308.

49 Shibusawa, "Seien sensei kungen," 449.

50 Shibusawa Eiichi, Speech at autumn meeting of Ryūmonsha, 1907, in Ryūmonsha, *Shibusawa Eiichi denki shiryō*, vol. 26, 1959 406.

51 Shibusawa, "Seien sensei kungen," 448.

52 On another occasion, Shibusawa clearly stated: "I was engaged in commerce between 1873 and 1900 ... I have never done any wrong to other people, and I honestly have never told a lie. I can say clearly that commerce is possible without lying" (lecture at meeting of principals of nationwide commercial schools, 1900, in Ryūmonsha, *Shibusawa Eiichi denki shiryō*, vol. 26, 834).

53 Shibusawa, "Seien sensei kungen," 450.

3 Public-Private Connections and Boundaries: From Shibusawa Eiichi's Experience to a Global Historical Perspective

PATRICK FRIDENSON

The distinction in any economy between what belongs to the private (business) sphere and what belongs to the public is very ancient. The existence of enterprise itself dates back to antiquity worldwide.[1] Such a distinction, however, might change over time: it has a history. Moreover, it does not mean that the public and private spheres are decisively separate.[2] The connections and boundaries between them are constantly shifting.

This topic is directly related to Shibusawa Eiichi's own career as he experienced and played a direct role in the introduction of capitalism into Japan. Capitalism everywhere has regularly reshaped the respective place of the private and public spheres and the connections between them. Japan is no exception. Shibusawa commented on this issue under both his own name and the pseudonym "Master Seien." Having seen the superiority of the public sphere in the precapitalist Japan of his youth, he clearly opposed it, repeatedly expressing himself in favour of the private. For him, "the prosperity of merchants and industrialists becomes the prosperity of the nation," a fundamental position that he applied in his own life. After spending eight years in public administration, he went into banking, industry, and a variety of services.[3] Yet he remained deeply interested in the support that private business could get from the state. He also understood the policies of Meiji-era governments that created state-owned enterprises in some sectors to develop the national economy and that later decided on their privatization. Indeed, as is well known, in early capitalist Japan, for quite a while the boundaries between the private and public spheres were not the same as they were in the West during the same period – the result of differences not only in their resources and constraints, but also in their national experiences and cultures. Shibusawa, though favouring the private sphere, learned from his travels abroad the importance of both private philanthropy and public services.

To carry further this broad theme of a shifting divide and circulations between the public and private spheres, my purpose in this chapter is fourfold. First, I consider the part actually played by the ideas of a businessman who becamea utopian socialist, Henri de Saint-Simon (1760–1825), and his followers in Shibusawa's views on the dynamics of the private sphere and on the possible connections between the public and private spheres. Second, moving from Shibusawa's personal contacts with the West to a short history of capitalist economies since the nineteenth century, I sketch the porosities between the public and private spheres during this long period. Third, I review the overlaps between the two spheres: some businesses are public, some governments are in business, and many cases exist of an enterprise or agency operating on both sides of this porous line. Fourth, I offer comments on exchanges and appropriations between the public and private spheres in the same period.

Analogies between or Contacts with Saint-Simonism

How can one account for the fact that Shibusawa, while extolling private business, did not advocate a totally privatized economy and society? Indeed, in his early views on *gapponshugi*, he called for a market economy suitable for Japan and imbued with a deep concern for the morality of the actors. Even much later, until the very end of his long and remarkable life, his advice was "an agreement between economy and morality."[4] His French biographer has explained this stance by an approach rooted in the history of ideas. He stresses Shibusawa's original deep Confucian beliefs and the later impact of foreign doctrines such as evolutionism and organicism on his thought, and speaks of a "combination of ideological traditionalism and associative modernism."[5] It is worth noting here that this is a feature often observed by academics who have studied major entrepreneurs worldwide since the nineteenth century. In addition, like earlier scholars, the biographer also suggests that, having spent twenty-two months in France on a study mission initially linked with the Universal Exhibition of 1867, Shibusawa was sensitive to the influence of Saint-Simonism, at least "in its renewed version of the French Second Empire."[6] Given that Saint-Simonism was influential worldwide and clearly dealt with public-private issues, this is not a minor topic. It raises two distinct questions: Was there a direct relation between Shibusawa and Saint-Simonism or an indirect one? What would the contribution of Saint-Simonism have been to Shibusawa's framework at this stage?

Referring to Shibusawa's will to build modern enterprises with the abacus and the Analects of Confucius, the late Japanese business historian Hara Terushi cautiously remarked that Shibusawa's thought "is not without analogies to Saint-Simon's."[7] Two recent studies by Japanese and French scholars have suggested that Shibusawa benefited from the influence of Saint-Simonism during his first visit to France, in 1867–68.[8] According to them, it was Paul Fleury-Hérard (1836–1913) who introduced Shibusawa to Saint-Simonism. A banker and merchant, Fleury-Hérard lived in Japan until the end of the shogunate. As the French consul in Edo (Tokyo) and the "banker and attorney in France" of Léon Roches, France's ambassador to Japan, he became the first honorary consul of Japan in Paris on Roches's recommendation. He "assisted" Shibusawa and the other Japanese delegates during their entire stay.[9] As a banker, Fleury-Hérard had close links with both the French Ministry of Foreign Affairs and a leading bank, the Société Générale, one of whose main founders was Paulin Talabot, a Saint-Simonian. Thanks to his conversations, Shibusawa is said to have become interested in Saint-Simonism, a social industrialism relying on the dynamics of railways and the ability of banks to facilitate investment. Colonel Léopold Villette, the army officer whom the French emperor appointed as Shibusawa's tutor in France, was likewise a Saint-Simonian.[10] However, the Japanese business historian Yago Kazuhiko, Hara's successor at Waseda University, has observed that Shibusawa never clearly referred to Saint-Simonism, and cautions scholars against the idea of a "direct encounter" between Shibusawa and Saint-Simonism. Indeed, Saint-Simon's name never appears in Shibusawa's complete works.[11] It seems safer, therefore, to infer that Shibusawa was indirectly exposed to Saint-Simonian ideas, that he met some Saint-Simonians, and that his economic thought combined reflections derived from Confucius and from the eighteenth-century Japanese small merchant and ethicist Ishida Baigan with French ideas, including elements of Saint-Simonism. New research shows, however, that there is not one version of Saint-Simonism, but two.

Indeed, Saint-Simonism recently has attracted a renewed interest from scholars internationally. One French historian has published a book on Saint-Simon's immediate followers, showing them as prophets of a new world where progress would indissociably be spiritual and material.[12] Another French historian has written the history of the influence of Saint-Simon's ideas in France up to 2000.[13] Following ten years of research, the first edition of Saint-Simon's complete works, in four volumes, appeared at the end of 2012.[14] And in 2014 a British historian examined how, among this group of engineers and doctors, some "spearheaded bank reform, railway building and urban transformation in the 1850s."[15] Beyond Saint-Simonism, of course, these four publications consider Saint-Simon himself as the founder of sociology, of socialism, of anarchism, and of the theories of management. In the nineteenth century, he inspired such diverse thinkers as the liberal historian Augustin Thierry, the positivist philosopher Auguste Comte, the socialist Pierre Leroux, and the technocratic economist Michel Chevalier. His thought was very open. Its very openness was one of the sources of its success: it could answer different agendas and various demands and perspectives.

What came from Saint-Simon himself? He belonged to an aristocratic family, whose male members traditionally served in the army. Initially a French officer in the American Revolution, in 1790 he became a businessman, specializing in real estate and in textiles. In 1802 he changed his life and became an intellectual, attracting many followers, most of them engineers. He also lost his fortune. An admirer of American society and the British economy, in his numerous publications he argued in favour not only of industry's priority in economy and society, applying science and supported by banking and credit, but also of a meritocracy: competence and talent would be privileged, and experts would rule thanks to the centralization of credit and their sense of the general interest. His direct followers therefore argued that inheritance should be abolished, because it was not a sanction of personal achievements; some even proposed to abolish personal property. Their idea was that, beyond economic success, the role of engineers – some of them eloquent supporters of the doctrine – and of the new managers more generally was to let everybody benefit from the fruits of technological progress. Many of Saint-Simon's direct followers had visited industrial regions, and were aware of the difficulties different types of workers faced. It led them to assign managers a social priority: "The goal of every social institution should be the gradual improvement of the moral, physical, and intellectual condition of the largest and poorest class." They relied on Saint-Simon's last published book, entitled in English translations *The New Christianity* (1825), which called for moral reform by the development of Christian brotherly love, to sketch out an indissolubly social and moral utopia that equated a conversion of the economy with a redistribution of wealth and with a new morality that was centred no longer on the observance of tradition and hierarchy, but on work and skill.

What Shibusawa might have discovered in France in 1867–68, however, was not this first version of Saint-Simonism, which was a doctrine for debate among intellectuals and, more broadly, in the public sphere. Rather, it was a second version, crafted by one group of his followers who turned doctrine into action. Their accomplishments reached a climax under the Second Empire (1852–70). They created most of France's earliest large-scale enterprises, including banking based on joint-stock companies and the introduction of retail banking to serve a larger number of customers. They were also key players in modern transportation, in both steam shipping and railways, where they supported infrastructure building and the operations of companies' networks on concessions from the state, thus transforming the system of public concessions to private firms inherited from the Roman Empire into new public-private relationships, which brought about the beginning of analytical accountancy and large-scale human resource management in France. The building of the Suez Canal in Egypt, which would also operate on a public concession, was part of the same strategy. Finally, they were major actors in the growth of public water and gas utilities, serving the growth of large cities. This program also included hotels, tourism, a department store, and real estate. In addition, they were sensitive to communicating with the public, and developed internal communications in large companies, financial communications, newspapers, magazines, and advertising. They tried to be "apostles of modernity" in France, in its new colonies, and abroad; they were a demanding stimulus to governments, yet still claimed they were serving the general progress. But 1867, when Shibusawa came to France, was also the year the major Saint-Simonian banking corporation, Crédit Mobilier, went into bankruptcy for having invested too much short-term capital in real estate operations at the request of the Bank of France, which, although a fully private bank, still regulated credit in the entire French economy in the name of the French government. Carrying a consistent and wide vision of public-private relations had been one of the origins of the prosperity of leading Saint-Simonians. Nevertheless, such relations were finally the direct source of the death of the largest and most creative business group they had fostered.[16]

It is worth adding that Saint-Simon's writings were directly at the origins of the thought of French engineer and manager Henri Fayol (1841–1925), who developed a general theory of management, and stressed the distinction between managers and owners.[17] Fayol's main book of 1916 was translated three times into Japanese. Japanese translations of Saint-Simon's works, however, were belated: *The New Christianity* (1825) was translated and published in Japan in 1928; *Le catéchisme des industriels* (1823–24) *and Lettres d'un habitant de Genève* (1802) only in 1948. The first comprehensive translation of Saint-Simon's writings was accomplished by Mori Hiroshi and published in 1987–88 in five volumes.[18]

The complex encounter by Shibusawa in his early life with some ideas derived from Saint-Simon's doctrine, the managerial practices of the latter's most business-oriented followers, the transformation of French cities that Shibusawa saw with his own eyes, and the conclusions he soon drew on the roles of the private and public spheres immediately invite historical qualifications and comparisons: How did public-private boundaries shift over the next one hundred and fifty years in industrial capitalist societies? Were there channels or bridges between these two domains?[19]

Porosities

Since the nineteenth century, the boundary between public and private in Asian and Western economies has been full of holes. A striking example of the porous boundary is the recruitment of high-ranking civil servants by private companies in France and Japan.

In France, beginning in the mid-eighteenth century, the state has developed a separate higher education system that trains thousands of engineers and administrators for state jobs. These students receive a salary while learning. A growing proportion of them is hired away by private sector firms. This happens at two different stages of their careers. During the ten years following the completion of their studies, French corporations compensate the government for the salaries paid, but thereby acquire managers or engineers with an elite label and their accompanying network.[20] This system has survived despite the growth of universities and schools of commerce because it ensures the reproduction of elites and because of the salary gap between the public and private sectors. Then, at mid-career, there is a second flow of civil servants with considerable experience and developed networks to senior management positions. Since the 1990s, public opinion has induced regulations against the re-employment of leading bureaucrats in sectors that were under their responsibility.[21]

In Japan this circulation of elite civil servants dates from the Meiji era, more than a century later than in France – Shibusawa himself is a clear example of this process – and might be attributed to the acute needs of a quickly growing private sector for expertise in top management. Later, however, it turned into an institutionalized system. The Second World War played a role in two ways. Within the Ministry of International Trade and Industry (MITI), "the practice of all classmates or seniors resigning when a new vice-minister takes over appears to have originated in October 1941 ... In the postwar world 'respect for seniority' developed concomitantly with the tremendous expansion of the bureaucracy."[22] Since the end of the war, vice-ministers and chiefs of the secretariat have contacted companies to find good positions for talented civil servants in their fifties. This process creates second careers, and is termed *amakudari* (descent from heaven) – because "heaven" is the upper echelons of the civil service, and state agency leaders are the functional equivalent of the former nobility or aristocracy.[23] The system has been criticized for creating "hand-in-glove relationships" and "preferential access to the government." But, on the whole, it has not diminished the independence of the private sector.

In the United States and the United Kingdom, by contrast, except at the very top, the divide between managers, engineers, and scientists in public agencies and private corporations is much firmer. Governments pay such employees far less than do leading corporations, but the attraction of public service, and perhaps of influence on policy, is substantial. Meanwhile, prominent politicians and military officers retire from administrative positions to take senior jobs in lobbying and management, notably in the defence supply sectors. In the United States the revolving door also moves senior federal administrators whose party has lost an election into law firms, a holding zone where they bide their time until later electoral success, when they return to lead agencies and commissions. In the United Kingdom the circulation of elites between the public and private sectors traditionally has been weak, but in the past twenty years, governments and parliaments have introduced men and women from the private sector to the top of the civil service – symbolically, the national school of government was closed in 2012.

A second example of the porous boundary is the issue of regulatory capture, which existed long before its theory was developed by, among others, the American economist George Stigler in 1971.[24] According to this theory, regulatory agencies might become inclined either to defend the interests of the industry they are charged with regulating or to deny the importance of the negative externalities that the public, academics, or – more recently – whistleblowers expose. Examples abound in sectors such as agribusiness, energy, telecommunications, pharmaceuticals, and finance. The games interest groups and lobbyists play, however, meet opposition from rival interest groups, citizens' movements, and the media. Some of the better means to combat such regulatory capture include greater transparency, exemplary judicial decisions, and research and teaching in public ethics.

A third example of the porous boundary between public and private is the system of public concessions to license business monopolies at particular places. Created in ancient Rome to recover taxes, in the early modern era concessions were extended to infrastructure,[25] and are present today, most notably in airport management (from Osaka's Kansai to Toronto's Pearson) and in sports arena retailing. They have also been extended and refined into public-private partnerships, which originated in Britain in 1992 and have multiplied globally. Such partnerships might lead to privatization, as in Greece recently or as was applied to many water authorities globally in the late twentieth century. These relationships often commence without first establishing rules for behaviour or performance, which can lead to corruption or abuse of trust and conflicts of interest.

Overlaps

Overlaps occur when private and public institutions compete or share similar responsibilities. Two different cases have drawn much attention: hospitals and banks.

Let me deal first with hospitals in continental Europe. In western Switzerland from the 1920s onward, private clinics have competed with public hospitals. The latter have had to adapt by welcoming poorer patients, reorganizing their management, reinforcing their links with specialized private hospitals, and introducing technological innovations.[26] In France in the late twentieth century, the phenomenon was illustrated by competition between public and private hospitals. Although politicians see health care as a public good and, thus, hospitals as important, the critical issue is cost. Public hospitals provide slow service and are not individualized or responsive to patients, whereas private hospitals focus on areas that are profitable and on more affluent patients. In the 1990s the government planned a rationalization process designed to replace competition with division of labour – for example, public hospitals would provide high-tech devices that private clinics could not afford. Local health care advocates resisted, however, arguing that this approach would lead to a lack of proximity and accessibility for citizens, creating private clinics for the rich and public hospitals for the rest. That was indeed the outcome. As private clinics multiplied, moreover, hospitals for workers and the poor began closing due to insufficient revenues. Income from sophisticated, high-tech devices could not cover deficits for primary care, while state funding shrank.

In the United States public health became a state priority during the immigration decades, generating the establishment of large public hospitals and health clinics in major cities and community hospitals in small towns and rural areas. Religious groups and medical schools also created hospitals, many of which were operated privately, if by nonprofits. Eventually, public hospitals collapsed (except those for military veterans) in the 1970s as governments no longer provided the subsidies necessary for more expensive technologies and for serving the poor. Thus, medical care in the United States has become almost entirely private, though funded through a maze of public agencies and profit-oriented insurance companies. In consequence, tens of millions of the uninsured have no regular care, and crowd emergency wards when illness arrives, even as profit-seeking high-tech medical corporations nationwide are consolidating chains of hospitals for the privileged. Pricing medical services, in consequence, has become chaotic, with item-by-item negotiations between providers and insurers. Such problems led to the Affordable Care Act of 2010.

In banking, though private institutions have high visibility, public banks are not trivial: consider the Bank of England, the US Federal Reserve, the Bank of France, and the Bank of Japan, or such international banks as the Bank for International Settlements, created in 1930, or the European Central Bank. Look at the reorientation of public postal systems. In 2007 the French postal system transformed its savings and chequing account unit, started in 1918, into a full-service but public bank that competes with high-street banks throughout the nation. It is not yet clear that it can simultaneously serve the poor and seek custom from the rich, who provide sizable deposits that can be placed as loans. Small account holders now face high fees for overdrafts and services, an unexpected consequence of public-private competition. Also, in a world of privatization and globalization, many states have started sovereign investment funds, using government funds to purchase ownership shares in national and international enterprises.

Critics argue that state-business competition stimulates inefficiencies and crowds out private initiatives, given the differential resources and power of the two parties. Yet an alternative look at the US health care system might suggest that such crowding out could provide ample public benefits and yield efficiencies instead. After all, no public policy benefits every stakeholder. In a third domain, large-scale military contracting has generated more mixed reviews, for although it deflects enterprises from their own interests and plans, it does commit the state to paying the bill for potentially transformative innovations.

Exchanges and Appropriations

Historical research has highlighted at least three types of exchanges between the public and private spheres in modern economies. The first is management models and methods. In Germany and France between 1870 and 1914, models of management of human resources in large firms sometimes came from the army; in a number of railways, coal mines, and department stores, discipline or internal promotion systems were inspired by military practices. Some theoreticians of business in Germany proposed the army as a general model of organization: complex but efficient. Another reference for big business in Germany during the same period was the civil service. For some historians, it was used as a catalyst to design forms of administration of large-scale companies in industry and commerce; for others, it was the state bureaucracy that benefited from the efficiency of the private sector. In France, despite an old bureaucratic tradition, large companies either copied the civil service (banks, railways, gas) or tried to innovate with delay and difficulty.[27]

A second channel is the development of dual technologies, serving both military and civilian uses (in aviation, space, optronics, bionics, and so on). A third type consists of what US historian Philip Scranton proposes to call dual enterprises, which operate across the boundary. Military-industrial corporations are obvious members of this club, but so too were the Rothschild bankers who vetted and marketed bonds for governments and companies alike. The modern military itself constantly disrespects its border with the private world.

Finally, the boundary is crossed by devoting public facilities to private interests or appropriating private capabilities for public purposes.

Historically in the United States, private developers have licensed public lands to extract timber, develop oil reserves, and recently to exploit shale gas. Along the Atlantic shore, owners of oceanside homes have routinely blocked public access to beaches. In France it became necessary for the government to draft a special law, passed in 1986, to regulate such appropriations of seashore, confirming citizens' access and the state's right to establish littoral parks as a preservation step. However, the costs of maintaining such territories became so substantial that the managing authority has moved to establish public-private partnerships to secure funding, including concessions for commercial retail operations.

Symmetrically, governments have found ways to appropriate private property, if only for a limited period. At the local level, governments can intervene in property use through planning und restriction. From the seventeenth century until the Revolution, privately held salt marshes and wetland in western France were subjected to royal control to assure supply for the state monopoly in salt extraction.[28] On the national level, the issue is state nationalization, confiscation, and reorientation of private property and its uses, but these actions do not put an end to history: there are cycles. At the end of the twentieth century, a number of large enterprises in Europe and Asia had completed the cycle from private to public to private again, and recently, threatened by the global financial crisis, a few private enterprises have gone back to substantial public involvement.

Since the 1950s a number of national governments have created sovereign wealth funds to invest financial assets in private companies, mostly abroad. Originating in the Persian Gulf, Norway, and Canada, all rely on the growth of oil exploitation, and have been followed by funds created by Singapore, then by China and Russia. They play two games, behaving as private powers and as arms of national interests.

Concluding Remarks

Shibusawa Eiichi argued for the primacy of the private sector. In most countries, however, historical evidence shows that the logic he outlined was not initially followed. The public sector kept growing, if irregularly, a motion partly motivated by considerations of external defence and internal unification.[29] Since the late 1970s the trend has reversed, as ideological change, the level of public debt, the growing reluctance of the middle classes to pay high taxes, the power of financial markets, and the action of international organizations all have led more and more national or local political majorities to reduce the weight of the public sector. This evolution, however, has met several limits.

First, the issue of morality in the private and public sectors and in public-private relations has remained on the agenda. Neither the period of growth of the public sector nor the period of its decline were able fully to meet the kind of targets of morality that Shibusawa set for business in general and in the Japanese context. Very early this was recognized by various pioneers both outside and inside business – in the Western world by Catholic movements and Protestant ministers, business associations, and business schools. It is worth mentioning here that a dean of the Harvard Business School, Wallace Donham, a former banker, introduced the teaching of business ethics at the school in 1928. In Europe in the same period, one should also mention the French Confederation of Christian Business Leaders, formed in 1926. Together with the Dutch and Belgian confederations and in the presence of observers from Italy, Germany, and Czechoslovakia, it constituted the International Christian Union of Business Executives in 1931, renamed UNIAPAC in 1949 when it enlarged to include business-people in other countries.[30] In a recent book, US sociologist Gabriel Abend distinguishes three levels of morality for business: "moral and immoral behavior, or the behavioral level; moral understandings and norms, or the normative level; and the moral background, which includes what moral concepts exist in a society, what moral methods can be used, what reasons can be given, and what objects can be morally evaluated at all. This background underlies the behavioral and normative levels; it supports, facilitates, and enables them." This leads him to identify two types of moral background in the modern history of Western business: "'Standards of Practice' characterized by its scientific world view, moral relativism, and emphasis on individuals' actions and decisions," and "the 'Christian Merchant' characterized by its Christian world view, moral objectivism, and conception of a person's life as a unity."[31] It would be useful to conduct parallel research into Japanese business and to assess the outcome of the reinterpretation of Confucian values combined with some ideas and concerns of Western origin that Shibusawa started. It would also be worthwhile to rank, according to the three levels of morality distinguished above, the numerous initiatives that, in nations as well as in international organizations, have emerged since the 1950s to inspire higher business morality and to regulate the behaviour of business in both the public and private sectors. In doing so, it would be necessary to study their effectiveness or their avoidance.

Second, following recent international research in business history, we have seen that both the growth and then the reduction of the public sector have been accompanied by renewed porosities, overlaps, and exchanges or appropriations between the public and private spheres. This does not blur the two trends. It tells us that the shifts in the distinction between public and private do not tell the entire story, and that they are surrounded by unceasing circulations between the two.

Third, many worldwide crises have emerged, born of the effect of the heightened level of private and public business on the ecosystem. Such crises have fueled theories of public goods since the 1950s and of sustainability since the 1970s. Both types of theories have contributed to a rejuvenation of pre-industrial practices for managing the commons and to new citizens' movements to control or solve the social costs of agriculture, industry, commerce, and finance. In a way, they could be connected to Shibusawa's recognition, as a major businessman, of the importance of the public interest. Even if there is often a gap between discourse and reality and between self-regulation or government regulation and actual practice, the idea that preserving and extending public goods could be a common goal for the private and public economic spheres seems to be gaining ground.

NOTES

1 David S. Landes, Joel Mokyr, and William J. Baumol, eds., *The Invention of Enterprise: Entrepreneurship from Ancient Mesopotamia to Modern Times* (Princeton, NJ: Princeton University Press, 2010).

2 Morton J. Horwitz, "The History of the Public/Private Distinction," *University of Pennsylvania Law Review* 130 (1982): 1423–28; and Jeff Weintraub, "The Theory and Politics of the Public/Private Distinction," in *Public and Private in Thought and Practice*, ed. Jeff Weintraub and Krishan Kumar, 1–42 (Chicago: University of Chicago Press, 1997).

3 Claude Hamon, *Shibusawa Eiichi (1840–1931), bâtisseur du capitalisme* (Paris: Maisonneuve et Larose, 2007).

4 Claude Hamon, "Ethique et diplomatie chez Shibusawa Eiichi," *Ebisu* 34, no. 1 (2005). Shibusawa's full speech of 13 June 1923 is in Japanese *kanji* on 151–2, and in French translation on 154–8.

5 Ibid., 150.

6 Ibid.

7 Hara Terushi, "Les facteurs psychologiques et culturels de la modernisation japonaise: le cas de Eiichi Shibusawa," in *Autour de Alain Peyrefitte*, ed. Raymond Boudon and Pierre Chaunu (Paris: Éditions Odile Jacob, 1996), 120.

8 Kashima Shigeru, "Saint-Simon shugisha – Shibusawa Eiichi," *Shokun* 31, no. 8 (1999) through 36, no. 1 (2004); Hamon, *Shibusawa Eiichi*, 54–7.

9 Shibusawa Eiichi, *The Autobiography of Shibusawa Eiichi: From Peasant to Entrepreneur*, ed. Craig Teruko (Tokyo: University of Tokyo Press, 1994), 106, 123, 157, 159, 163, 182–3; Meron Medzini, *French Policy in Japan during the Closing Years of the Tokugawa Regime* (Cambridge, MA: Harvard University, East Asian Research Center, 1971); and Elisabeth de Touchet, *Quand les Français armaient le Japon: l'arsenal de Yokosuka 1865–1882* (Rennes, France: Presses Universitaires de Rennes, 2003).

10 France, Service historique de la Défense, Archives, Catalogue général des manuscrits, 1672, lieutenant-colonel Léopold Villette, Rapports et lettres sur une mission au Japon (Vincennes, France); Hara, "Facteurs politiques et culturels," 125; and Teramoto Noriko, *Lettres de Léopold Villette à Akitake Tokugawa: de l'Exposition universelle de Paris en 1867 à la Guerre russo-japonaise* (Tokyo: Hitotsubashi University, Center for Historical Social Science Literature, 2009).

11 Yago Kazuhiko, "Introduction of French Managerial Thought and Practices in Japan," in *Managerial Thought and Practice in France, 19th–21st Centuries: Assessment and Future Prospects*, ed. Gilles Garel et al., available online at http://mtpf.mlab-innovation.net/en/, accessed 30 May 2013; see also the comment by Kimura Masato, in discussion with the author, 5 April 2013.

12 Antoine Picon, *Les saint-simoniens: raison, imaginaire et utopie* (Paris: Belin, 2002).

13 Christophe Prochasson, *Saint-Simon ou l'anti-Marx* (Paris: Perrin, 2005).

14 Henri de Saint-Simon, *Œuvres complètes*, 4 vols. (Paris: PUF, 2012).

15 Pamela M. Pilbeam, *Saint-Simonians in Nineteenth-Century France: From Free Love to Algeria* (Basingstoke, UK: Palgrave Macmillan, 2014), 5–24, 69–103.

16 For an overview, both online and in English, see Hervé Le Bret, "The *Saint-Simonisme*: Doctrine and Practice of Management," in Garel et al., *Managerial Thought and Practice in France*.

17 Jean-Louis Peaucelle, "Saint-Simon, aux origines de la pensée de Henri Fayol," *Entreprises et Histoire* 12, no. 34 (2003): 68–83; Jean-Louis Peaucelle and Cameron Guthrie, *Henri Fayol, the Manager* (London: Pickering and Chatto, 2015); and Blanche Segrestin, "Le tournant fayolien: des révolutions industrielles à la naissance de l'entreprise moderne," Entreprises et Histoire 25, no. 83 (2016): 5–12.

18 My thanks to Professor Kimura Masato for these details.

19 The following pages are based on my research seminar on the public and private spheres at the École des hautes études en sciences sociales in the 2005–06 and 2007–08 academic years, but they have been transformed through close collaboration with the US historian Philip Scranton; they also incorporate his ideas and writing. Thus, these pages draw on Philip Scranton and Patrick Fridenson, *Reimagining Business History* (Baltimore: Johns Hopkins University Press, 2013): 92–6, and the relevant bibliography, 96–8.

20 Christophe Charle, "Le pantouflage en France (vers 1880–vers 1980)," *Annales: Économies, Sociétés, Civilisations* 42, no. 5 (1987): 1115–37; Dominique Chagnollaud, "Du pantouflage ou 'la descente du ciel,'" *Pouvoirs* 80 (January 1997): 77–88; Hervé Joly, *Diriger une grande entreprise au XXe siècle: l'élite industrielle française* (Tours, France: Presses de l'Université François-Rabelais, 2013), 340–4.

21 Hervé Joly, "Grands corps et pantouflage: le vivier de l'Etat," in *Dictionnaire historique des patrons français*, ed. Jean-Claude Daumas, 796–803 (Paris: Flammarion, 2010).

22 Chalmers Johnson, *MITI and the Japanese Miracle: The Growth of Industrial Policy, 1925–1975* (Stanford, CA: Stanford University Press, 1982), 66.

23 Chalmers Johnson, "The Reemployment of Retired Government Bureaucrats in Japanese Big Business," *Asian Survey* 14, no. 11 (1974): 963–75; and idem, *MITI and the Japanese Miracle*, 11, 21, 63–73, 254, 266–71, 299, 312. See also Tuvia Blumental, "The Practice of Amakudari within the Japanese Employment System," *Asian Survey* 25, no. 3 (1985): 310–21; Kent E. Calder, "Elites in an Equalizing Role: Ex-bureaucrats as Coordinators and Intermediaries in the Japanese Government-Business Relationship," *Comparative Politics* 21, no. 4 (1989): 379–403; idem, *Strategic Capitalism: Private Business and Public Purpose in Japanese Industrial Finance* (Princeton, NJ: Princeton University Press, 1993); Richard A. Colignon and Chikako Usui, *Amakudari: The Hidden Fabric of Japan's Economy* (Ithaca, NY: Cornell University Press, 2003); and Eva-Maria Zopf, *Amakudari: Descent from Heaven and Its Implications on Doing Business in Japan* (Saarbrücken, Germany: Verlag Dr Müller, 2009).

24 George Stigler, "The Theory of Economic Regulation," *Bell Journal of Economics and Management Science* 2, no. 1 (1971): 3–21.

25 Xavier Bezançon, "Histoire du droit concessionnaire en France," *Entreprises et Histoire* 14, no. 38 (2005): 24–54.

26 Pierre-Yves Donzé, *L'ombre de César: les chirurgiens et la construction du système hospitalier vaudois (1840–1960)* (Lausanne, Switzerland: Éditions BHMS, 2007), 118–48.

27 Jürgen Kocka, "Industrielles Management: Konzeptionen und Modelle in Deutschland vor 1914," *Vierteljahrschrift für Sozial- und Wirtschaftsgeschichte* 56, no. 3 (1969): 332–72; idem, "Family and Bureaucracy in German Industrial Management, 1850–1914: Siemens in Comparative Perspective," *Business History Review* 45, no. 2 (1971): 133–56; Robert R. Locke, *The End of the Practical Man* (Greenwich, CT: JAI Press, 1984), 249–50; Patrick Fridenson, "Authority Relations in German and French Enterprises, 1880–1914," in *Bourgeois Society in Nineteenth-Century Europe*, ed. Jürgen Kocka and Allan Mitchell, 223–44 (Oxford: Berg, 1993); and Heinrich Hartmann, *Organisation und Geschäft: Unternehmensorganisation in Frankreich und Deutschland, 1890–1914* (Göttingen, Germany: Vandenhoeck und Ruprecht, 2010).

28 Yannis Suire, *Le Marais poitevin: une écohistoire du XVIᵉ à l'aube du XXᵉ siècle* (La Roche sur Yon, France: Centre vendéen de recherches historiques, 2006).

29 Robert Millward, *The State and Business in the Major Powers: An Economic History, 1815–1939* (London: Routledge, 2013).

30 Joseph B. Gremillon, *The Catholic Movement of Employers and Managers: A Study of UNIAPAC* (Rome: Gregorian University Press, 1961); Jeffrey L. Cruikshank, *A Delicate Experiment: The Harvard Business School, 1908–1945* (Boston: Harvard Business School Press, 1987), 164; André Grelon, "Le patronat chrétien," in Daumas, *Dictionnaire historique du patronat français*, 1055–60; and Gabriel Abend, *The Moral Background: An Inquiry into the History of Business Ethics* (Princeton, NJ: Princeton University Press, 2014), 210–24.

31 Abend, *Moral Background*, 260–356.

4 Capitalism by the "Visible Hand": The Joint-Stock Company System, Business Leaders (*Zaikaijin*), and Shibusawa Eiichi

MIYAMOTO MATAO

The rapid development of the joint-stock company system is among the most conspicuous features of Japan's modern economic history, and one almost predicted by Shibusawa Eiichi's concept of *gapponshugi*. How was the emergence of the system possible in such a short span of time, given Japan's lack of experience in joint ventures during the Edo period (1603–1867)?

As is well known, it was a noteworthy feature of Shibusawa's entrepreneurial activities that he not only served as a top manager of many companies; he was also the most powerful among the *zaikaijin* (business leaders). Why did Japan need *zaikaijin* such as Shibusawa at that time, and how was Shibusawa able to maintain his powerful influence over the business world for so long? This chapter attempts to answer those questions.

Development of the Joint-Stock Company in Japan

There still might be some room for debate as to whether the meaning of *gapponshugi* as coined by Shibusawa Eiichi means anything more than "starting a company via a joint-stock organization." There is no doubt, however, that Shibusawa believed the joint-stock system prevalent in western Europe to be an effective device for the economic modernization of Meiji Japan (1868–1912), and that this belief was shared by the Meiji government and intellectuals of the time – as evidenced by the way in which they were actively involved in establishing companies, improving understanding of how companies work by issuing texts relating to company establishment such as *Rikkai ryakusoku* (Outline of setting up companies), by Shibusawa Eiichi; *Kaisha ben* (On companies), translated by Fukuchi Gen'ichirō; and *Taisei shōkai hōsoku* (Outline of companies in western countries), translated by Kanda Kōhei. Indeed, the first two of these texts were distributed to the prefectures, where they had a legal role as the basis of promulgations relating to company establishment.[1]

The government, Shibusawa, and the others were not disappointed, and the joint-stock system soon spread rapidly throughout Japan. It took some time to establish company law, but, starting with the 153 national banks established in accordance with the National Bank Act of 1872, several fully fledged joint-stock companies had emerged by the second decade of the Meiji period, followed by a sudden boom in the formation of new enterprises around 1888, so that the *kaisha* (company) became one of the symbols of westernization during the Meiji period.[2]

Table 4.1 shows the development process of joint-stock companies following the implementation of the Old Commercial Code in 1893 and the establishment of the New Commercial Code in 1899. As early as 1896, joint-stock companies already accounted for 56.2 per cent of the total number of companies, and 89.9 per cent of the total paid-up capital for all companies. Thereafter, due to the influence of the tax system, relatively large enterprises selected the joint-stock company form, while family and individual enterprises selected general or limited partnerships. Still, in terms of total paid-up capital, joint-stock companies continued to account for more than 85 per cent of firms over the entire period.[3]

Even in Europe, which has a long history of joint ventures, it took several centuries for joint-stock companies to become commonplace. Why, then, did they spread so rapidly in Japan? What kind of impact did the rapid development of this kind of joint-stock company system have on management and corporate governance? I believe that these questions are closely related to Shibusawa's concept of *gapponshugi*. Accordingly, in this chapter I discuss the role of *zaikaijin* such as Shibusawa in terms of the process of starting up a joint-stock company during the Meiji period, as well as in corporate governance thereafter, with a focus mainly on the Osaka Cotton Spinning Company Limited, the founding of which was led by Shibusawa.

The Effectiveness and Feasibility of the Joint-Stock Company System

As economic historian Alexander Gerschenkron explained, Meiji Japan had the "advantage of relative backwardness."[4] The huge gap between

Table 4.1 Companies, Capital Assets, and Capital per Company, Japan, 1896–1939

Year	Companies Total	Per cent Partnership	Limited Partnership	Joint-Stock Company	Paid-up Capital Total (millions of yen)	Per cent Partnership	Limited Partnership	Joint-Stock Company	Paid-up Capital per Company Average (thousands of yen) Total	Partnership	Limited Partnership	Joint-Stock Company
1896	4,596	7.5	36.3	56.2	397	3.1	6.9	89.9	87 (100)	43 (100)	19 (100)	139 (100)
1900	8,588	9.1	41.4	49.5	779	4.9	5.8	89.3	91 (105)	49 (114)	13 (68)	164 (118)
1905	9,006	14.2	39.0	46.8	975	6.2	5.8	88.0	108 (124)	47 (109)	16 (84)	203 (146)
1910	12,308	20.3	38.9	40.8	1,481	9.5	6.5	84.0	120 (138)	56 (130)	20 (105)	248 (178)
1915	17,149	17.8	40.2	41.8	2,167	8.4	5.9	85.7	126 (145)	60 (140)	20 (105)	258 (186)
1920	29,917	15.7	30.0	54.2	8,238	7.0	4.6	88.4	275 (316)	123 (286)	42 (221)	456 (328)
1925	34,345	15.1	33.6	51.1	11,160	8.0	6.6	85.3	324 (372)	171 (398)	63 (331)	543 (391)
1930	51,910	16.4	46.2	37.4	19,663	8.5	6.5	85.0	378 (434)	139 (323)	38 (200)	612 (440)
1935	84,146	19.5	52.8	27.7	22,352	7.8	6.9	85.3	266 (305)	79 (184)	26 (137)	610 (439)
1939	85,122	17.9	43.0	39.0	34,025	5.5	4.0	90.5	400 (460)	92 (214)	32 (168)	693 (499)

Note: Figures in parentheses are indices: 1896 = 100.

Sources: Before 1915, Nōshōmushō, Nōshōmu tōkei hyō [Statistical report of the Department of Agriculture and Commerce] (Tokyo: Department of Agriculture and Commerce); after 1920, Shōkōshō, Kaisha tōkei hyō [Statistical report of companies] (Tokyo: Department of Industry and Commerce).

Japan and the advanced countries of western Europe in terms of their relative levels of technology and economic development meant that were great entrepreneurial opportunities in Japan even for people without original technologies or specialist knowledge of certain kinds of business.

In contrast to the enormity of these entrepreneurial opportunities, however, there seems to have been a scarcity of suitable management resources (such as capital and entrepreneurial skills) or an eligible labour force for modern industries. With excess demand for entrepreneurial and managerial resources, businessmen had to cooperate with one another to use scarce resources effectively, and the situation inevitably required "organized entrepreneurship," the particular importance of which Nakagawa Keiichirō has emphasized in the course of Japan's industrialization.[5]

Setting up a joint-stock company became a typical case of organized entrepreneurship. Starting up an industry transplanted from the West – such as railways, textiles, banking, insurance, sugar manufacturing, paper manufacturing, and electricity – required both an enormous amount of capital and a willingness to take huge risks given that these were unknown industries. However, the kind of personal capital that could allow individuals to cover the cost on their own was slow to grow. If one wished to invest large amounts of capital in the modern industry sector all at once, then, apart from the *zaibatsu*, which could finance projects with capital from within a single family, there was no option other than to rely on joint-venture mechanisms.

In terms of human resources, although there were people with eligible entrepreneurial skills for modern industry and the desire to start a business, in most cases they lacked the financial means to do so. On the other hand, those with the financial means – former merchants from the Edo period, affluent members of the former samurai class, and the aristocracy – were poorly informed about the new era, and lacked the courage to undertake a new business such as a transplanted industry. In this respect, the mechanism of a joint-stock company, one of the attributes of which is the separation between owners and management, was certainly an effective way of matching these two groups of people.

The feasibility of the joint-stock company system and the role of zaikaijin

In this way, the joint-stock company system was an extremely effective device for starting modern transplanted industries in the Meiji period, but there was also the problem of feasibility.

The basic elements of the joint-stock company system include: (1) legal personhood (a joint-stock company exists as a permanent business entity, distinct from any individual "natural person"); (2) a system for joint-stock enterprise and its maintenance; (3) separation of ownership and management; and (4) a system of limited liability for all investors. I will refrain from a detailed discussion about joint ventures during the Edo period, except to note that, in terms of legal personhood (the first element above), there were corporate names and shop names as distinct from the names of investors, and that in light of the strong restrictions imposed on ownership by the heads of families, large merchants had effectively established corporate status, but corporate status had not been stipulated by public law.[6]

In relation to the system for joint ventures (the second element above), it has been clearly shown that, even during the Edo period, there were joint ventures among members of the same family, as well as joint ventures based on regional bonds (such as Ōmi merchants); the management of cargo vessel businesses via joint ventures had also been developed.[7] As Takamura Naosuke points out,[8] the fact that the joint-venture mindset – that is, the concept that, when someone else is attempting to start up a business, it is acceptable to provide funds on the condition that one will receive a share of the profits – had already begun to sprout was extremely important in the history of the emergence of the joint-stock corporation, and it is worth noting that this idea was already in place in the Edo period to a certain extent. Nevertheless, joint ventures of this period were mostly kinship-based or regional relationship-based unions. These joint ventures were not realized via an open capital market, and investments were not objectified as stock certificates, which meant that these rights were not traded in the market.[9]

Turning to the third element above – the separation of ownership and management – it is clear that it was quite common for large merchants to delegate the management of their business to a manager or clerk. In almost every case, however, a manager employed to run the business had received training at the merchant house since he was very young, and was able to assume such a position only once he had demonstrated his loyalty to his master's family and had been recognized as almost a member of the family. This meant that it was not easy for an employee manager to deviate from the traditional management policies of the merchant family, in terms of either carrying out his tasks or in his basic mindset.[10]

As for the fourth element, a system of limited liability, unions similar to limited partnerships – whereby some investors have limited liability – had been established during the Edo period, but joint-stock companies, where all investors have limited liability, had not.[11]

Thus, there was already some experience of joint ventures in the Edo period, and this experience can be regarded as a precondition to the establishment of a modern joint-stock company system, but a huge gulf still had to be crossed first. Of the four elements discussed above, (1) and (4) would present various organizational problems for corporate enterprises during the second decade of the Meiji period, with ceaseless imbroglios surrounding the system of limited liability in particular, but these problems were resolved for the time being with the establishment of the Commercial Code. The problems that remained were elements (2) and (3).

Achieving joint ventures

Ideally, the way a joint-stock company system is supposed to work is that information about a certain enterprise – such as the details of its business and its profitability – is made known to investors via a market, and investors then decide whether or not to invest based on this information. Meiji Japan, however, had an urgent need to introduce a joint-stock company system rapidly at a stage when capital markets had not yet been established, making it impossible to adopt the kind of ideal method just described. Instead, stock capital had to be raised using "non-market methods" that relied fully on the personal connections and reputation of the founder. Funds had to be raised using a *hōgachō* (donation register) system in much the same way as donations were gathered for a shrine or a temple.

Moreover, modern transplant industries requiring large amounts of capital could not permit potential sources of funds to be limited to just a kinship-based or close community-based unit as had been the case during the Edo period. Instead it was necessary to target different levels of society as potential sources of funds. At the time, the only people with the kind of capital able to respond to a large-scale stock offering were land owners, large merchants, and members of former *daimyō* (feudal lords of the Edo period) families. On the whole, these people were reluctant to invest in new businesses. They were still important, however, in the sense that, if they could be convinced to participate in a float, this would induce other small capitalists to participate. In order to invite them to join the project, the person at the top of the list in the *hōgachō* needed to be a powerful business leader with a high degree of credibility – that is, a *zaikaijin*.

During the Meiji period, it was quite common for capitalists with sufficient capital to respond to large-scale stock floats to form informal investment associations. For example, one such group of former *daimyō* included the Maeda, Uesugi, Hachisuka, and Mori families.[12] This group bought large amounts of stock in the Osaka Cotton Spinning Company, a company in which Shibusawa Eiichi played a leading role in establishing, but they also invested in other companies. There were several investment associations in Osaka – including the Tanaka Ichibei group, the Fujita Denzaburō group, the Matsumoto Jyūtarō group, the Jisuke group, and so on – and the capitalists in these associations tended to act together. The leaders of these associations were the "bosses" of each region, and were at the top of the list in the *hōgachō* when companies were established, but Shibusawa was at the top of the list at the national level, over and above these regional bosses. For large-scale floats, where the funding requirements exceeded the capabilities of individual regional investment associations, it was necessary to ask multiple investment associations to participate. In such cases, the person at the top of the list had to be someone with the capacity to rally multiple investment associations, as well as the ability to strike a balance between the funding contributions of the different associations. This is where business leaders such as Shibusawa made their appearance.

Looking at the reality of the time,[13] in 1898 there were sixty-three textile companies, of which thirty-three had more than three hundred shareholders. In very few cases did the largest shareholder own more than 20 per cent of the stock, indicating the progress that had been made with the diffusion of share ownership. For most textile enterprises, however, the ten largest shareholders owned between 20 per cent and 50 per cent of the total. In other words, although a relatively small number of major shareholders formed the core of the joint venture, a substantial part of the capital was raised from a broad cross-section of society. Furthermore, major shareholders often had large holdings of multiple textile companies – indeed, these kinds of multilateral holdings were a feature of the investment of the time.

The situation with railway companies was quite similar,[14] with an average of 735 shareholders for each railway company in 1898 (compared with 456 shareholders for textile companies). Here too, according to data from 1902, a trend towards diffusion of ownership is apparent, with very few cases of the largest shareholder's owning more than 20 per cent of the total stock, but once again the portion of the total held by the ten largest shareholders is too big to ignore. Furthermore, railway companies initially had a large number of individual shareholders, but this gradually changed to institutional and other powerful investors distributing their investments across multiple enterprises.

In Europe and North America, the general pattern was for an enterprise to start as a partnership formed by a small number of businessmen and eventually to grow into a joint-stock company as the number of investors increased as the business expanded. In this pattern, the original partners continued to be involved in managing the business as capitalists with a central function even after the partnership became a joint-stock company. In contrast, as described above, founders of companies in Meiji Japan had to start their businesses as relatively large joint-stock companies right from the outset. If the enterprise was a large one, they had to ask multiple investment associations to contribute funds, but at this point each investor was asked to contribute an equal level of funding in order to preserve the balance between different investment associations.

Kataoka Naoharu, who became vice-president of the Nippon Life Insurance Company[15] after its establishment in 1889, in later years had the following to say about its founding:

> At the time when the company was established, the investors in Osaka were divided into multiple factions, such as the Matsumoto faction, the Okahashi faction, the Tanaka faction, and so on, and these factions were all mutually antagonistic toward one another. But the character of a business such as the life insurance business, which deals with the public at large with the objective of delivering wide-ranging social benefits, is such that it should not be monopolized by a single party or faction, and at any rate given that there is no promise that the enterprise is ultimately likely to succeed, all of these factions were added as founders. Moreover, the intention was to seek shareholders from a broad cross-section of the general public, and so even the founders were not allowed to hold more than fifty shares.[16]

Thus, the joint-stock companies of the Meiji period were forced to have the character of a motley assortment of uniform rentier-like capitalists, lacking a strong interest in the management of a particular business.

On the other hand, looking at it from the perspective of the investors, they were no more than rentier-like capitalists hoping for a stable return on their investment, without any intention of actively participating in the management of a particular company. Some of them aimed for capital gains from appreciating stock prices, rather than high dividends from good corporate performance. Accordingly, investors avoided putting all of their assets into one particular enterprise, often preferring to diversify their investments over several companies. Such major shareholders would become company directors after the company was founded, but as they typically held directorships in multiple companies, these part-time responsibilities meant that they lacked specialist knowledge of or interest in the particular business activities of any single company. Inevitably, day-to-day management activities and the drafting of management strategies were left up to managerial employees, who effectively fulfilled the role of top management.

These two peculiarities of large joint-stock companies during the Meiji period – namely, the hodgepodge composition of major shareholders making uniform contributions and the delegation of company administration to managerial employees – eventually caused problems of corporate governance. One such problem was ceaseless complications among shareholders who represented a patchwork of different investment associations. Another problem was that the managerial employees who effectively assumed the top management positions were not infrequently subject to criticism from shareholders who were more interested in short-term investment returns than in the details of the company's business or its future prospects. In both cases, somebody was needed to step in to resolve disagreements and imbroglios among shareholders, or between part-time directors and employee managers. In most cases, the person who fulfilled this role was the founder at the top of the list of subscribers. Shibusawa was a typical example of such a person.

Achieving separation of ownership and management

As discussed earlier, the separation of ownership and management had already taken place in large merchant houses during the Edo period. In most cases, however, the person to whom management was delegated was a servant who had been trained since childhood within the merchant house in question.

In contrast, the enterprises of the modern transplant industries of Meiji Japan had not yet developed these kinds of skilled people within their own enterprises. The founders of the companies had either to look externally to find people with management skills or new knowledge and technologies, or to develop such people from scratch. It was the role of the founder at the top of the list of subscribers to appoint such talented people, to develop and supervise them after the company was established, and, depending on the situation, to support them when they came under fire from shareholders.

Summary

The joint-stock company system was an extremely effective form of organization for starting a business in a modern transplanted industry in Meiji Japan. The experience of joint ventures in the Edo period contributed to the rapid development of the joint-stock company system during the Meiji period and beyond, but there was still a huge gulf between the joint ventures of the Edo period and the joint-stock companies of later periods. This is because the mechanisms for raising stock capital from a broad cross-section of society – in other words, capital markets – were not yet mature, and because there was a need to find and develop managers and technicians who were suitable for modern transplant industries. The people who filled in the gaps for the functions that were not provided adequately by the market and enterprises were the *zaikaijin*. Such business leaders, among whom Shibusawa Eiichi was pre-eminent, were deeply involved in the development of the joint-stock company system. Shibusawa advocated the importance of *gapponshugi*, but it might rather be said that *gapponshugi* itself needed the existence of Shibusawa. To establish this hypothesis, I present the case of the Osaka Cotton Spinning Company.

The Osaka Cotton Spinning Company

The Osaka Cotton Spinning Company Limited – now known as Toyobo Co., Ltd. – established in 1882, was Japan's first successful cotton spinning enterprise.[17] The central figure in the founding of the company was Shibusawa Eiichi. To begin, the company raised ¥280,000 in capital from ninety-five shareholders, including former *daimyō* and powerful merchants of major cities. A breakdown of the contributions reveals that seventeen former *daimyō* contributed 38 per cent, fifty-six merchants from Osaka contributed 31 per cent, and seventeen merchants from Tokyo contributed 29 per cent, with the remaining 2 per cent coming from five other shareholders. At its establishment, the company's share ownership was highly concentrated, with the top ten shareholders owning 49.7 per cent of the total number of shares issued. Fujita Denzaburō and Matsumoto Jyūtarō used their emerging positions as the most powerful business leaders in Osaka to cooperate with Shibusawa, making a huge contribution to extracting seed funding from Osaka merchants in various areas, who tended to be reluctant to invest in new businesses.

As major shareholders, Fujita (the shareholder with the largest holding at the end of 1883) and Matsumoto (the shareholder with the eighth-largest holding at the end of 1883) were selected as the first president and director, respectively, while Kumagai Tatsutarō (manager of the Osaka branch of the First National Bank, which Shibusawa controlled) was also named director. As the greatest shareholder, Shibusawa joined the board as an adviser, together with two major shareholders from Tokyo, Fujimoto Bunsaku and Yajima Sakurō. In this way, major shareholders occupied seats on the board, but none of the directors, including Shibusawa, devoted himself to the duties of senior management. Shibusawa held similar positions at numerous other companies, and because most of these companies were in Tokyo, it was quite unusual for him to come to Osaka. Fujita and Matsumoto ran diverse businesses in various fields. Not one of these directors had any specialist knowledge in relation to the machinery or manufacturing technologies used in the modern cotton spinning industry, which had been transplanted from the West.

Under the circumstances, the delegation of management rights to managerial employees was unavoidable. Shibusawa believed that the major reason modern spinning companies had all failed in Japan up to that point was the lack of talented people to manage the business and provide technical supervision. Accordingly, before the business started, he sent money to Yamanobe Takeo – known as a genius from the Nishi Amane school[18] and who was studying in England at the time – to cover his training costs so that he could master spinning technologies in Lancashire. When Yamanobe returned to Japan, Shibusawa installed him as the Osaka Cotton Spinning Company's engineering manager. Yamanobe played a critical role, together with Kamata Seizō (who was appointed commercial manager after being head clerk at a Kyoto crepe wholesaler) and Kawamura Rihei (who became the second commercial manager after originally working for the cotton wholesaler Akiba Shōten).

The engineering and commercial managers received a monthly salary of ¥50; in contrast, the company president was paid only ¥30 and directors ¥20 yen, indicating that these managerial employees effectively functioned as the top management. They were not necessarily able to act freely, however, but were subject to all kinds of restrictions imposed by major shareholders and directors. At the time, the attendance rate at general meetings of shareholders was relatively high, at more than 30 per cent, and shareholders often would make special requests of the management team. Yamanobe recorded the following on the tendencies of stockholders of joint-stock companies in those days, and the duties of managers in light of this:

> Being dazzled by the huge profits of other existing companies, a number of investors are hastily planning to set up new companies expecting similar high profits as those gained in other companies without deliberation over the uncertainty of profitability in a new company. Being captivated by a temporary boom in the stock market, some investors become the stockholders of companies purely for speculative purposes without any interest in the long-term prospects of the company, and thereby easily change their mind depending on dividends and stock prices. It is very natural and inevitable for investors to behave in this way. Therefore, persons in charge of management, and responsible for the future prosperity of the company, have a duty to please stockholders by keeping dividends as high as possible, understand the situation under which the company was set up, as well as make efforts to strengthen the foundation of the company from the perspective of long-run development.[19]

The fact that the Osaka Cotton Spinning Company sacrificed internal reserves and depreciation for the first few years after its foundation in order to increase both the dividend rate and the payout ratio is likely a consequence of Yamanobe's attentiveness to the needs of shareholders.

As a result of this strategy, the company's share price rose steeply, making it easy to raise additional funds. Between 1884 and 1889, its paid-up capital increased from ¥280,000 to ¥1,200,000, while the number of shareholders increased from 95 to 384. Yamanobe had succeeded in gaining the favour of shareholders. From the second half of the 1890s, however, the company faced stiff competition from competitors entering the market. When it found itself taking second billing to other companies in terms of profitability, growth, market share, and so on, Yamanobe came under attack from major shareholders, particularly those close to the company president of the time, Matsumoto Jyūtarō. Shibusawa left the following testimony:

> There were also troubled times for the [company]. Perhaps finding it difficult to overcome these, Yamanobe dropped in to Tokyo one day, and things had reached the point that even the indefatigable Yamanobe was unexpectedly thinking of quitting the company. Although I was not unaware that the spinning industry was in dire straits as a result of the current economic situation, such action would burst the bubble which our efforts had created so far and so I said that I was irrevocably opposed to this, and gave him words of encouragement.[20]

Okamura Katsumasa, who worked underneath Yamanobe as a spinning technician for the company, had the following to say:

> After the boom following the Sino-Japanese war in 1897 there was a turnaround … and the Osaka Cotton Spinning Company made a significant loss. The Osaka directors, including Matsumoto Jyūtarō, who was the company president at the time and who was already hostile to the influence that Yamanobe actually had within the company, came out and said that the company had made a loss under Yamanobe's management, so he should resign. At shareholder meetings Yamanobe was the target of various attacks and defamations, so that he became quite despondent, and discussed various matters with us. It was around that time that he went to the Shibusawa residence in Asukayama to say that he wanted to resign. However, from the following year [1898] the views of President Matsumoto suddenly fell out of favor, and his attitude came under attack. In 1898 Yamanobe replaced Matsumoto as company president, and in 1899 business conditions recovered and a considerable profit was recorded, so that Yamanobe was triumphant.[21]

Yamanobe overcame such ordeals and became company president in 1898. This was a groundbreaking moment insofar as it was the first time that a Meiji-period joint-stock company controlled by major shareholders doubling as directors had appointed an employee manager to the board. Nonetheless, a great many major shareholders continued to attend shareholder meetings and to make statements about dividend policies, funding policies, share price trends, and the financial burden on shareholders, so Yamanobe and the other employee managers found themselves caught between the interests of shareholders and those of the company.

Nevertheless, from the beginning of the twentieth century, the power of the employee managers grew relatively stronger as the attendance rate at shareholders' meetings fell steadily as the number of shareholders and silent owners increased, major shareholders were replaced, and fault-finding shareholders withdrew. Initially the company had achieved a high dividend rate and payout ratio by sacrificing depreciation and internal reserves. After the turn of the century, it switched to a financial strategy of withholding dividends, increasing internal reserves, and actively recruiting capital from new investors in order to invest in the latest machinery and equipment such as automated looms. If the company's managerial team had continued to be restricted by the views of shareholders focused on short-term profits, it is unlikely that such aggressive policies would have been adopted. In this way, the hegemony of employee managers such as Yamanobe gradually became established.

One also needs to pay attention, however, to the presence of Shibusawa, who, as a core shareholder, continued to support these employee managers in the background. From the time the company was founded until at least 1905, Shibusawa remained its top-listed shareholder, although he initially held only 12.3 per cent and in 1909 just 2.6 per cent, so possession alone was not the source of his power. Perhaps the real source of Shibusawa's power was the organizational abilities he demonstrated when the company was founded, as well as his subsequent coordinating skills and his presence as a famous business leader.

Conclusion: The Significance of Business Leaders

Why did Meiji Japan need business leaders such as Shibusawa Eiichi? In most cases, new businesses in the Meiji period required the introduction of systems and technologies from the West, but the rich reservoir of such systems and technologies meant that a talent for invention or specialist business knowledge was not required on the part of Japanese capitalists. At the same time, the reservoir of capital in Japan was generally shallow – those with wealth did not necessarily have the desire to start businesses, while those with the desire to start businesses lacked capital.

Because of such circumstances, the ability to receive accurate economic information was of primary importance. Even if a business had already matured overseas, there were still risks associated with introducing it to relatively backward Japan. Also needed was the ability to build organizations to take advantage of new technologies and new knowledge. This meant the creation of joint-stock companies to muster capital from numerous people, as well as the gathering of talented people with managerial skills and knowledge. In other words, collecting information and building organizations entailed huge costs.

Accordingly, above all else people attempting to start new businesses were expected to be well-informed and to be good at building consensus. Personal connections to politicians or foreigners with useful information, a respected reputation among the business community, and the ability to coordinate different groups with different interests were needed. This kind of entrepreneurial talent was scarce, however, and concentrated in a limited number of persons in each era and region. In Kyoto this role was played by Tanaka Gentarō, in Nagoya it was Okuda Masaka, and in Osaka it was first Godai Tomoatsu and then, after his passing, Fujita Denzaburō, Tanaka Ichibei, Doi Michio, and others. But in Tokyo this role was played by Shibusawa for a long period that extended through the Meiji, Taisho, and Showa periods. The role these people were expected to play lay in gathering information and building organizations during the early stages of the creation of an enterprise; once the enterprise was on track, their mission was over. For this reason, they became involved with many companies, one after another, before moving on to new fields. This meant that they extended their reach into fields that were not necessarily interrelated, and that they never amassed wealth based on a single industry, or formed *zaibatsu* (combines) of the likes of Mitsui or Mitsubishi.

A famous Meiji politician, Ōkuma Shigenobu, made the following historical assessment of Shibusawa, and I think it can be described as a fair assessment:

> [Shibusawa] acts as a special advisor or director for dozens of companies, like the so-called "Jack of all trades." He does not turn down any request so long as it is ethically sound … Commerce and industry in Japan today is in an era of transition. And in an era such as this, men such as Shibusawa are needed. However, if the people of the future were to imitate such behavior the result would be disastrous. In the next era, men with specialist knowledge will take up specialized businesses. Such people exist in Germany and America, but in England there are very few. This is because in England the orderliness of business has already been established, and the foundations are already fixed in place. In a country such as Japan where the business world is not yet fully developed, men like Shibusawa are needed.[22]

These "leader type" entrepreneurs also needed a particular philosophy. Meiji Japan needed to modernize rapidly under political and economic pressure from the West; as such, leaders did not have the luxury of time to make gradual, cumulative progress with technological advances or improvements to management structures based on their own experience or trial and error.

To plug the gap between Japan and the industrialized nations, these business leaders adopted a sense of public duty – expressed as "for the country" or "for society" – rather than the kind of individualistic Western-style entrepreneurial philosophy based on calculated rationalism and self-help. It was along this line of thinking that Gustav Ranis, an American scholar of entrepreneurial history, focused on the strong nationalism and orientation to the national interest apparent in the entrepreneurs of Meiji Japan, and that he took to be a form of "community-centered entrepreneur," different in type to the "auto-centered entrepreneur" of the West.[23] Although it is beyond the scope of this chapter, I believe that Shibusawa's thesis that "morality is compatible with economy" can also be interpreted as another instance of this type of ideology. Viewed in this way, it must be said that these entrepreneurs of the business-leader type had a terribly irrational side as private capitalists. Nevertheless, a society in a phase of great upheaval requires both leaders coloured by this kind of irrational belief and the divergent actions of their followers. In Meiji Japan the organizational, entrepreneurial activities of Shibusawa and other financial leaders were rational when viewed from the perspective of the entire society.

I would like to conclude with two messages with respect to Shibusawa's *gapponshugi*. First, for Shibusawa, *gapponshugi* meant not only the combination of capital among anonymous persons, but also the personal ties among people acquainted with one another, although the ties were beyond kinship- or community-based ones. Second, trade associations, including general business associations, are interpreted as being between a market and individual firms. The function of trade associations or their leaders is to supplement managerial resources insufficiently supplied by either the market or firms.

In the days when the capital market was immature, stock capital could not be raised through a capital market, but rather was recruited by a "non-market" method that depended fully on personal connections and the trust of promoters such as Shibusawa. In other words, Shibusawa's companies were formed not by the "invisible hand," but by the "visible hand" of Shibusawa. In this sense, Shibusawa functioned as a substitute for the market. Given a mature market economy and individual firms that were able to provide the necessary managerial resources for themselves, the space for the activities of *zaikaijin* such as Shibusawa would have been much smaller. As a result of their activities, however, the market economy began to develop, leading to economic development through the open-market system, as Professor Shimada points out in Chapter 1 of this volume. I think this was of utmost importance in the entrepreneurship of Shibusawa.

NOTES

1 Miyamoto Matao, "Sangyōka to kaisha seido no hatten" [Japan's industrialization and the development of the company system], in *Nihon Keizaishi 4: The Age of Industrialization*, ed. Nishikawa Shunsaku and Abe Takeshi (Tokyo: Iwanami Shoten, 1990).
2 Ibid.
3 Ibid.
4 Alexander Gerschenkron, *Economic Backwardness in Historical Perspective* (Cambridge, MA: Belknap Press of Harvard University Press, 1962), 6–8.
5 Nakagawa Keiichirō, "Nihon no kōgyōka katei ni okeru soshikika sareta kigyōka katsudō" [Organized entrepreneurship in the process of Japan's industrialization], *Keieishigaku* [Japan Business History Review] 2, no. 3 (1967): 8–37.
6 Miyamoto Matao, "The Management Systems of Edo Period Merchant Houses," *Japanese Yearbook on Business History* 13 (1997): 121.
7 Ibid.
8 Takamura Naosuke, *Kaisha no tanjō* [The birth of the corporation] (Tokyo: Yoshikawa Kobunkan, 1996).
9 Miyamoto, "Management Systems," 108.
10 Ibid.
11 Ibid.
12 Miyamoto, "Sangyōka to kaisha seido no hatten."
13 On this point, see Sugiyama Kazuo, "Kabushikikaishaseido no hatten" [The development of the joint-stock company system], in *The Studies of Japanese Business History*, vol. 1, ed. Kobayashi Masaaki et al. (Tokyo: Yuhikaku, 1976).
14 Ibid.
15 For the history of Nippon Life Insurance Company, see Nippon Life Insurance Company, ed., *The 100-year History of Nippon Life* (Osaka: Nippon Life

Insurance Company, 1992); and Miyamoto Matao and Abe Takeshi, "The Corporate Governance of Japanese Firms at the Early Stage of Industrialization: Osaka Cotton Spinning and Nippon Life Assurance" in *The Development of Corporate Governance in Japan and Britain*, ed. Robert Fitzgerald and Abe Etsuo (Burlington, VT: Ashgate, 2004).

16 Interview with Kataoka Naoharu (Nippon Life Insurance Archives), 1894.

17 For the history of the Osaka Cotton Spinning Company, see Tōyō Bōseki Kabushikikaisha, *Hyakunenshi Toyobo* [100 years' history of Toyobo] (Osaka: Tōyō Bōseki, 1986); Miyamoto Matao, "The Products and Market Strategies of the Osaka Cotton Spinning Company, 1883–1914," *Japanese Yearbook on Business History* 5 (1989): 117–59; and Miyamoto and Abe, "Corporate Governance of Japanese Firms."

18 Nishi Amane was a distinguished Confucian scholar; the Nishi Amane school, Ikueikai, cultivated many young diligent students through teaching English.

19 Yamanobe Takeo, "Bōseki-gyō kōchaku shihon shōkyaku oyobi son'eki keisan ni kansuru shisetsu" [My opinion on the depreciation of fixed capital in the spinning industry and the profit and loss account], *Bōseki rengō geppō* 2 (1889).

20 Uno Yonekichi, ed., *Yamanobe Takeo-kun shōden* [Short biography of Mr Yamanobe Takeo] (Osaka: Bōsekizasshisha, 1918).

21 Interview with Okamura Katsumasa, in Ryūmonsha, ed., *Shibusawa Eiichi denki shiryō* [Shibusawa Eiichi biographical materials], vol. 10 (Tokyo: Shibusawa Eiichi denki shiryō kankōkai, 1956).

22 Kimura Tsuyoshi and Waseda University Historical Archive, eds., *Ōkuma Shigenobu sōsho*, vol. 1, *Ōkuma Shigenobu wa kataru – Kokon tozai jinbutsu hyōron* [Ōkuma Shigenobu series, vol. 1, Shigenobu Ōkuma speaks – Commentary on significant figures of the East and West, past and present] (Tokyo: Waseda University Press, 1969).

23 Gustav Ranis, "The Community-Centered Entrepreneur in Japanese Development," *Explorations in Entrepreneurial History* 8, no. 2 (1955): 80–98.

5 "Obtaining wealth through fair means": Putting Shibusawa Eiichi's Views on Business Morality in Context

JANET HUNTER

Shibusawa Eiichi's views on business morality should be placed in the context of broader debates on commercial morality in the late nineteenth and early twentieth centuries. It is also useful to examine the actual forms of behaviour that gave rise to charges against Japan of commercial immorality, and the practical problems business leaders faced as they worked to introduce new techniques and forms of business and to secure social respect within Japan for business and commercial activities. In this chapter, I show how Japanese business and political leaders, as well as the press, became part of a broader discourse on norms of commercial behaviour, and I argue that Shibusawa's ideas, although in many respects distinct, were also very much the product of their time. Shibusawa was engaging with issues of morality and economy that were of profound concern to his contemporaries inside and outside Japan, and that were highlighted as Japan increased its engagement with the global economy and the transnational spread of ideas.

Shibusawa's ideas of *gapponshugi* can be regarded as having two main strands: the relationship between morality and economic activity, and the organization of business activities by bringing together financial and human resources (both of which are discussed in other chapters in this volume). These two strands came together in Shibusawa's belief that the inseparability of morality and economic activity was integral to the management of any *gappon*-capitalist enterprise, and that economic activity needed to contribute to the broader interest of the community. In this context Shibusawa argued clearly that business should not be conducted through *fuseitō no shudan* (unjust means), and he emphasized the importance of morality and honesty in the conduct of business. Immoral business behaviour, he suggested, led to a loss of trust. Without trust business would falter, and the very future of the nation would be threatened. In articulating these views, Shibusawa was engaging with the issue of what many of his contemporaries, in both Japan and the West, referred to as "commercial morality." Shibusawa himself did not like the term,[1] and rarely offered explicit examples of what he considered to be manifestations of immoral business practice. He did, however, argue in his lectures at the Tokyo Higher Commercial School that commercial morality consisted of two core principles: not telling lies, and not prioritizing private individual profit.[2] One should not lie to benefit oneself, and one should not conduct business by deceiving others.[3]

Although Shibusawa's reference point was Confucianism, his concerns nevertheless have a striking resonance with the Christian-influenced discourse on commercial morality that had evolved in the West during the nineteenth century and that had been taken up in Japan beginning in the 1890s. Moreover, Shibusawa's growing concern with the relationship between morality and business coincided with the growth of complaints in Europe and the United States about the "immoral" conduct of Japanese merchants in international transactions. He would have been well aware that Japan was widely viewed in the West as demonstrating a "want of commercial morality."[4] Like many of his contemporaries, he acknowledged the legitimacy of these concerns, and believed strongly in the need to raise standards of business ethics in the Japanese business community. There seems little doubt, therefore, that Shibusawa's views on the immorality of accumulating wealth through unjust means were informed not just by the Confucian Analects, but also by the realities of existing circumstances and institutional frameworks. The international discourse on commercial morality was an important part of that environment.

Following naturally on Shibusawa's concerns about the low standing of merchants in Japanese society, the issue of morality in the actual conduct of business allows one to explore in greater depth the extent to which Shibusawa's ideas might have been a response to the practical problems that he and his contemporaries experienced. Although Shibusawa's *gapponshugi* ideas were in many ways distinct, in respect to business morality at least, they were also very much a product of their time and of the environment in which Japanese business was operating during the decades after the Meiji Restoration. These discourses on commercial morality can be explored through contemporary publications, including journals and newspapers. Although the views articulated in these publications were often partial or distorted, such means of communication had significant consequences for the process of industrialization, helping to transmit economic ideas from one country to another and promoting the formulation of a national economic discourse.[5] In England, indeed, the press was regarded as "the jealous guardian of commercial ethics."[6]

In the first section of this chapter, I offer an outline of the Western, Christian-influenced discourse on commercial morality that emerged from the late eighteenth century, focusing in particular on Britain. In the second section, I analyse Western attitudes to commercial morality in Japan that were informed by this discourse, identifying the specific business practices that gave rise to accusations of business immorality. In the final section, I consider the Japanese discourse on commercial morality, analysing the views of Shibusawa Eiichi alongside those of his contemporaries.

Western Discourses on Commercial Morality

Discussions of commercial morality in western Europe were strongly rooted in the doctrines of Christianity. Medieval and early modern theological discussions of the compatibility between Christian belief and the making of profit continued for centuries to be reflected in debates about how to conduct business so as to uphold appropriate religious and ethical values. The clergyman Thomas Gisborne, for example, argued in the 1790s that honesty and probity were the fundamental moral virtues needed by anyone engaged in business, and that business should be conducted "according to the rules of fairness and plain dealing."[7] Works such as Gisborne's were informed by examples of undesirable business behaviour and practices, but it was only somewhat later, in the context of the rapid growth of Britain's trade, industry, and finance, that there emerged pronounced public debates making use of the terms "commercial morality" or "mercantile morality." Although the developing discourse retained the older emphasis on morally undesirable behaviour, it was strengthened by the association of such behaviour with undesirable economic outcomes. Unethical business practices on occasion might be individually profitable, but it was increasingly argued, even in treatises whose prime purposes were religious, that over the longer term such practices were damaging both to the individual concerned and to the community. One publication in the 1860s identified a recent spate of business scandals caused by deception and fraud not only as evidence of immorality, but also as potentially damaging to the stability of British commerce.[8]

This concrete link between "immoral" business practices and negative economic outcomes spread concerns beyond the religious and educational communities, drawing business and economic groups into discussions of the business conduct of individuals and organizations. In January 1868, just at the time of Japan's Meiji Restoration, the issue of commercial credit and commercial morality seized the attention of the British press. These well-publicized debates, fueled by a wave of company collapses and bankruptcies many attributed to fraudulent practices or speculation, set the tone for the discourse on commercial morality that persisted in Britain through the late nineteenth and early twentieth centuries. It is not always easy to know exactly what forms of behaviour were regarded as constituting a departure from mercantile morality, but rash speculation was invariably regarded in itself as an evil, in line with traditional maxims about only borrowing what can be repaid. The honouring of contracts was said to be paramount. More specific lapses included the adulteration of goods, the failure to deliver goods on time, the issuing of false bills of exchange and of lading, the use of unregistered mortgages as a false basis of credit, and the false labelling of products.[9]

The role of legislation in encouraging bad behaviour was widely debated. Members of the Liverpool Chamber of Commerce, which established a special committee to report on the issue, were particularly concerned about the inducements offered by the bankruptcy laws and by post-nuptial settlements. In the case of bankruptcy, criminal proceedings could not be taken against the individual even where fraudulent behaviour was suspected, leaving the dishonest bankrupt free to engage in further fraudulent transactions.[10] A post-nuptial settlement concluded by someone engaged in risky or dishonest ventures allowed the individual to transfer a main part of his assets to his wife's name, enabling him to avoid all liability in case of failure.[11] It was recognized, however, that legislation by itself was not enough to ensure that individuals and groups engaged in business acted within the bounds of what was deemed appropriate behaviour: individuals chose to behave well or badly. Many argued that legislation would never have the desired effect unless it was backed up by appropriate social constraints. A consensus appears to have emerged that the business community itself needed to take the lead in ensuring proper modes of behaviour among its members, and that it was ultimately the moral responsibility of the individual to refrain from engaging in behaviour that brought disrepute on the community more broadly. Although some commentators stated that the extent of "departures from rectitude" should not be exaggerated, it was acknowledged that the credit standing of business as a whole suffered from the moral lapses of the few, and there was a real danger that fraudulence would become accepted as normal mercantile practice, disadvantaging those who engaged in legitimate competition and dealings. The declining reputation of "Manchester goods" because of adulteration, for example, was a real danger both to the competitiveness of British products and to the reputation of British merchant activity more broadly.[12]

Business conditions were recognized as a major stimulus to fraud. In times of commercial prosperity or where the prospect of profits was particularly high, as in the wake of the American Civil War, the temptation to engage in "overtrading and extravagance" was undoubtedly increased.[13] At the same time, acute competition in difficult markets could be an encouragement to cheat, and some members of the Lancashire cotton industry in the 1870s claimed that remaining honest threatened their very survival.[14] The substantial growth of credit on which much of Britain's industrial and trading expansion was built, however, was charged with much of the responsibility for the growth of fraud and speculation, as it made dishonesty more difficult to detect and meant that lapses in individual conduct had far-reaching consequences for others.

This discourse on commercial morality persisted through following decades. One campaigner around the turn of the century, Sir Edward Fry, an eminent retired judge, argued that, as long as fraud remained profitable, people would continue to engage in it. He condemned a number of practices that, although not necessarily illegal, threatened the reputation of the British as fair dealers, and the moral and credit standing of the whole mercantile community. These included adulteration of goods, fraudulent trademarks, secret commission payments that effectively amounted to bribery, false advertising, and overinsurance.[15] Well after the First World War, there continued to be concern in Britain that a minority of traders and producers were failing to act not only according to the law, but even in accordance with the spirit of the law and accepted moral values. Although the terms "commercial morality" and "mercantile morality" became less conspicuous, the sentiments were unchanged.

Concerns about business behaviour were not limited to Britain. Mercantile handbooks published in the United States emphasized the moral way of going about discrete areas of business, such as buying or selling, and success manuals stressed the equation between individual morality and material progress, and virtues such as honesty, industry, and frugality. Wrong business methods, such as misrepresentation by the seller, speculation with borrowed capital, and taking advantage of bankruptcy laws to evade debt payment had to be avoided.[16] The financial machinations undertaken by individuals such as Jay Gould came in for heavy censure, and contributed to ongoing debates about commercial morality. The *New York Times* denounced Wall Street, accusing some of its denizens of victimization and deception in the pursuit of profit.[17] Concerns persisted into the 1920s, and fed into the inclination of the country's top business schools to offer training in business ethics. The author of one book on business ethics published in 1926 believed that, although the situation had improved considerably compared to a generation earlier, there continued to be "a fringe of unscrupulous men" who were "constantly engaging in questionable practices, for the sake of immediate gain, and bringing the industry into disrepute."[18] For this author, though, the bottom line was the damaging effect that business immorality had on trust, without which business itself could not function properly: "Modern business is built on credit. It is carried on by borrowing, by the exchange of promises to pay in the future. The term itself implies mutual trust. The extent to which credit is used is a witness to the standard of honesty that has grown up in the business world. Merchants have discovered that it pays to have a reputation for integrity and fidelity, for on this depends their credit rating, the terms they can secure, the cost of doing business, and in many cases the difference between success and failure."[19]

Worry about the morality of certain business practices in the pursuit of profit was not limited exclusively to the Anglo-American world. Wherever self-interest was regarded as the driving force behind economic activity, its relationship to broader issues of morality was likely to come under discussion.[20] It was Britain and the United States, however, that became Japan's major trading partners in the years after the Meiji Restoration, and that played the major role in shaping the contours and institutions of Japan's trade relations in the late nineteenth century. Perceptions of Japan in these countries, therefore, were of particular importance.

Western Attitudes towards Japanese Commercial Morality

Shibusawa Eiichi and his contemporaries were exposed to these concerns through their interactions with Westerners. Particularly worrying for them was the reputation that the Japanese themselves acquired as being unusually deficient in commercial morality. Despite their dubious domestic reputation, the international reputation of Britain's merchant traders remained high relative to that of traders from other countries. In effect, there appears to have been an international consensus that a global hierarchy of standards of commercial morality existed, with Britain at its apex and developing economies, including Japan, towards the bottom. As the first and most advanced industrial nation, Britain was the first to have to cope with the real challenges to commercial honesty posed by the development of a sophisticated credit system, and the majority of its businesses, it was suggested, had come through this challenge with flying colours. It was when British trade and investment came up against very different commercial practices in a host of developing, mainly non-European, countries, and under a balance of power that sought to impose western European and American "rules of the game," that traders and producers from these very disparate countries came to be charged with lack of business integrity. It is hard to refute the claim that there was a strong element of double standards associated with the accusations. There is also evidence that some Western businessmen believed it was legitimate to adopt lower standards of business behaviour in dealings with foreign countries than they were expected to adhere to at home.[21] Moreover, although many Europeans rejected the idea that foreigners could be "cheated with impunity," there is substantial evidence of distinctly unethical practices by Western merchants in Japan and the existence of a widespread belief that, in treaty port trade, honesty and integrity did not necessarily pay.

In some respects the charges against Japan differed little from those levelled at countries such as Greece or Brazil, but Japan was conspicuous by its position at the bottom of the hierarchy. At the time of treaty revision in 1899, Japanese commercial morality was said to be far lower than "that of Hindoos and Turks,"[22] and Japan was frequently compared unfavourably with China, identified by a number of commentators as possessing the highest standards of commercial morality in Asia. Even those who questioned the high standards of Chinese commercial probity agreed that they were far superior to those of the Japanese.[23] The reputation of the Japanese for integrity in commerce, therefore, was far below the level that might have been suggested by the country's growing status in international trade. A major factor in this, I would suggest, was the threat that effective Japanese competition posed to the status quo. The charges of commercial immorality levied at Japan can only be understood in this context.

In England, concerns over Japanese trading methods became conspicuous in the 1880s, fuelled by statements from those involved in the trade. Although it was up to the consular courts in Yokohama and Kobe to deal with specific instances in which Japanese merchants were supposed to have acted inappropriately,[24] many of the reports in late nineteenth century British newspapers focused more on general issues of character – charges not out of line with the similar emphasis in British debates of the period. Through the 1890s the criticisms became increasingly vocal, as the prospect of treaty revision provoked anxieties about the extent to which Japanese courts would be able or willing to uphold the rights of Western merchants. Claims about Japanese deficiency in commercial morality remained frequent through the first decade of the twentieth century, and re-emerged strongly after the end of the First World War. Over time the charges became much more specific, with critics identifying particular business practices that were deemed to be against (Western) law and/or to demonstrate inadequate levels of morality.

The "deficiency" was normally explained with reference to two specific factors. The first was the traditional low standing of merchants in pre-modern Japanese society, which had pushed them into self-serving and immoral behaviour. The second was the specific circumstances of treaty port trade, where a lack of adequate controls, combined with the attraction the ports offered to unscrupulous traders in search of a quick profit, offered an environment in which many Westerners hardly offered a model of business probity. This in turn attracted to the ports Japanese traders with little experience of Western business practices and even less compunction about fleecing foreigners, by fair means or foul. In Western eyes the Japanese rapidly established themselves as "rapacious" traders who "violated all rules of business."[25]

Consular reports played an important role in abstracting the morality issue from the emotive language and sentiments of those who were directly involved, thereby establishing the inferior standard of commercial morality in Japan as a widely accepted truth in Europe. Although consular reports offered explanation and analysis, rather than simple indictment, their appraisals served as a foundation for comment in the press that often lacked the same degree of objectivity. The Austrian consul in Yokohama was reported as having compared the level of honesty of Japanese merchants unfavourably with that of their Chinese counterparts, and having commented that the "universal contempt" associated with the traditional low social status of merchants in Japan meant that there was "no possibility of the development of moral quali-ties."[26] Another consular report from Kobe was cited in support of the argument that the unwholesome commercial habits and want of com-mercial morality in Japan were exacerbated by the existence of trade "in too many instances devoid of those principles of honesty which in the West are considered, acknowledged, and accepted as the true and genuine indications of civilization."[27] One former British consul, Joseph Longford, took a particular interest in commercial morality, and com-pared the Japanese unfavourably with the Chinese. He emphasized that, although standards in the new modern firms were high, the aver-age Japanese merchant was not to be trusted: "The Japanese traders as a class have, according to the universal verdict of those who deal with them, to this day the unsavoury reputation of absolute unreliability in the fulfilment of any obligation, or having failed to acquire in their com-mercial transactions even the most elementary principles of common honesty."[28] Longford, like many others, noted that the environment of the open ports had failed to offer adequate inducements to Japanese merchants to modify what he saw as their inability to embrace com-mercial integrity, and he expressed his hope that raising the merchants' status and ending the treaty port system would improve the situation.

The views expressed in these reports were taken up in travel records and serious publications on Japan beginning in the 1890s, in which authors invariably expressed admiration for Japan's "progress," but rarely dissented from the view that Japanese commercial behaviour left much to be desired. Joseph Llewellyn Thomas, describing a highly pleasurable trip to Japan during the 1890s, noted that both English and American merchants were inclined to speak of their Japanese counter-parts as "dishonest, tricky, and altogether unscrupulous."[29] Even the strongly pro-Japanese Arthur Diosy, founder of the Japan Society of London, felt obliged to address the issue of the "dishonest Japanese trader" in his best seller *The New Far East*.[30] The German economist Karl Rathgen noted that Japanese methods of competition were not always pretty or praiseworthy, while emphasizing that those who engaged in trade with Westerners were invariably "the most unscrupulous ele-ments."[31] Both Diosy and Rathgen apportioned some of the blame to the behaviour of Western treaty port merchants. These stereotypical views of the Japanese persisted. Erich Pauer suggests that, even after the First World War, German engineers and their families regarded Jap-anese as members of a lower-class race, adhering to the stereotype of being imitators, rather than innovators.[32]

What exactly was it, though, that led Westerners to these sweeping assumptions? The earliest charges against the Japanese appear to relate to general deceit and deception. Townsend Harris was reported to have called the Japanese "the greatest liars upon the face of the earth,"[33] a charge later echoed by Algernon Mitford.[34] The haggling over prices common not only in Japan, but in many countries, including some in Europe, was regarded as symptomatic of a general lack of honesty and of civilization. One visitor to Japan in the 1890s commented that the custom that sales prices were based not on the value of the article, but in line with what the purchaser could be made to pay, was among the indicators of the low standard of Japanese commercial morality.[35] More specific charges of dishonest business practices increasingly were used to back up these general complaints about dishonesty and lack of integrity. Most conspicuous were charges of failing to honour contractual obligations, supplying defective or substandard goods, and branding and trademark fraud, which became a particularly poisonous issue.

Japan's reputation for failing to honour contracts was established early on. The American traders studied by Murphy complained of Japanese merchants ordering foreign goods and then refusing to accept them or trying to renegotiate the price, often leaving importers with surplus goods that they then had to offload at an uneconomic rate.[36] A Japanese inclination to flout contractual obligations was reiterated in newspaper articles and more popular publications. Even Diosy noted persistent accusations that small traders in Japan neglected obligations, did not fulfil contracts, and failed to honour debts.[37] Ex-consul Joseph Longford stated that "the most formal contracts are unblushingly repudiated, or at best their execution postponed when their prompt fulfilment involves a loss of even contemptible significance," and emphasized that, following treaty revision, most Westerners had little confidence in the ability of Japanese courts to uphold their contractual rights, and even less in the willingness of the Japanese merchant community to take action against one of their own.[38] Charges of failing to honour contractual obligations persisted through the early decades of the twentieth century, gaining particular prominence in the economic downturn after the First World War.

Knowingly supplying inferior goods, either through adulteration or through the provision of goods inferior to the sample ones that had led to the contract, was the second major "crime" identified by Japan's critics. Like contract violation, such acts were also likely to be contrary to the law, but it was the lack of morality that was highlighted in public statements. Complaints that Japanese merchants tried to sell goods inferior to the contracted quality were frequent during the treaty port era,[39] but with the growth of trade and direct purchasing after the repeal of the unequal treaties, Western commentators became increasingly vocal about such practices. A purchaser presented with high-quality samples by the seller or at an industrial exhibition would place a large order, only to find on delivery that the goods did not match up to the sample. In other cases large parts of a consignment might be unfit for purpose. Among the products said to be affected were *habutae*, a sheer lightweight silk fabric that was a significant contributor to Japan's export earnings. The French author Pierre Leroy-Beaulieu highlighted recurrent problems with the inferior quality of Japanese goods, including matches and *habutae* silk, though he attributed this more to the rush to compete than to intentional negligence.[40] As late as 1920 the Manchester Chamber of Commerce was being told that, "when Indian buyers had bought goods from Japan they had found them correct half-way down the case and entirely different in the other half."[41] In most cases obtaining redress from the Japanese seller proved extremely difficult.

It was the issue of trademarks, branding, and product protection, however, that provoked the most fury among Japan's critics, particularly from the 1890s onward. Deceiving the public by misrepresenting products had long been legally actionable in Britain, but only beginning in the mid-nineteenth century did western European countries and the United States move towards a national registration system for trademarks. By the end of the century, legislation offered some protection for trademarks and branding within these countries, but protection was problematic in overseas markets with different cultural traditions and lacking equivalent legal protection.[42] Examples of infringements can be found early in the period of treaty port trade: "Routine violations included Bass and Guinness ale, brandy, wine, condensed milk, preserved beef and, at one restaurant, any drink a customer preferred, where it was only necessary to wait for the barman to affix the appropriate label."[43] Trademark registration under Japanese as well as Western law, a move recommended by the British Embassy in Tokyo,[44] offered only limited protection. One *cause célèbre* was the suit brought by the whisky producer Buchanan's of Glasgow against an Osaka merchant who marketed a local product with an almost identical label. The defendant admitted that he had explicitly copied the label to make it look like an imported product, but Buchanan's lost the case when the court ruled that the domestic product was so obviously inferior to the original that customers were unlikely to be taken in by the deception. Buchanan's eventually succeeded in obtaining the cancellation of the Japanese trademark, but the incident was regarded as typical of the lack of protection offered by the Japanese courts.[45]

Product protection was particularly problematic where Japanese and British producers competed in third markets, especially in Asia, where legal safeguards were minimal. One Japanese imitator of a trademark asserted that he considered himself at liberty to use this particular trademark for the whole of China,[46] while hundreds and thousands of shops in China and Korea were said to be selling grossly inferior cigarettes made in Japan but bearing the names of foreign tobacco companies. "Huntley and Palmer's biscuits, Bryant and May's matches, and other first-class foreign productions are also successfully imitated in appearance though not in quality, and find an increasing sale in place of the more expensive genuine article."[47] Such reports make it apparent that at least some of the imitations were designed with fraud in mind, but the issue also highlighted the ability of Japanese producers to market lower-quality goods in low-income countries at lower prices than their Western competitors, thereby threatening traditional Western dominance. At least one commentator acknowledged this, noting that the British passion to protect their interests in this regard was fuelled by the fact that "we happen to be the owners of most of the valuable property for which we claim respect."[48] British complaints about fraudulent trademarks re-emerged with renewed vigour as the Lancashire cotton industry tried to reassert its dominant global position after the First World War. Japanese sellers were said to be gaining an inappropriate advantage in the Chinese market by using marks very similar to those of British producers, while detailed imitations of British packaging and products such as fountain pens were passed off on consumers for a fraction of the price in Britain. Widespread complaints of trademark infringements in cotton goods, and in products such as cutlery and pottery, continued through the 1920s and into the following decade.[49]

The Discourse in Japan on Commercial Morality

Japan's business and political leaders could not remain unaware of the criticisms regarding the country's low level of commercial morality. Members of the Japanese elite travelling in North America and Europe, as did Shibusawa himself in 1903 and 1909, were often directly confronted with vociferous complaints. Nemoto Tadashi, sent in 1898 on an observation tour of the United States by the minister of agriculture and commerce, reported back on the untrustworthy reputation of Japanese traders stemming from poor value, the breaking of contracts, and other fraud.[50] Speaking to prefectural governors in the spring of 1908, the agriculture and commerce minister, Matsuoka Yasutake, stressed the need for collective action to ensure that goods were of high and uniform quality, and to respect trademarks and other commercial property rights, in order to avoid a damaging loss of trust in Japan's international dealings.[51] The following year the same ministry communicated to chambers of commerce its concern that "merchants and manufacturers are liable to sacrifice the interests of others for the sake of their own temporary gain ... It is to be profoundly regretted for the future of our industries that not a few have imitated or stolen inventions, trade marks, and other industrial rights. Foreign trade marks and trade names have also been abused ... Any act resembling dishonesty or fraud is highly detrimental to our commercial credit."[52] Ōkuma Shigenobu took to the pages of the *Encyclopædia Britannica* to emphasize the Japanese government's commitment to deal with the abuses and to educate the commercial classes in the ethical standards expected by Westerners.[53] One minister who took a particular interest in the problem was Ōura Kanetake. On a visit to Lyon in 1910, he was confronted by purchasers of Japanese *habutae* silk who complained about the product's quality and uniformity, and condemned disparities between samples and the products that eventually arrived. In a series of speeches to businessmen after his return, Ōura called for an investigation into how best to strengthen Japanese commercial morality.[54] A few years later, a new minister, Nakakōji Ren, issued an injunction on "Respect for Commercial Morality," urging businessmen to refrain from actions that destroyed commercial morality in the interests of immediate profit.[55] Among the business leaders who addressed the issue in public statements was Masuda Takashi, head of the Mitsui *zaibatsu*. Masuda faced accusations of lack of morality first-hand on a visit to England, and although reluctant to concede the extent of malpractice, took to the pages of the *Economist* to share his perspective, later elaborating his views in a book published in English.[56]

Western criticisms were thus a part of the international environment in which Shibusawa Eiichi and other leading entrepreneurs of the Meiji period worked to introduce new techniques and forms of business, and to secure within Japan social respect for business and commercial activities. Recognition of the need to play by the Western-imposed rules of the game extended to acceptance of the need to adhere to Western norms for the moral conduct of business, but diffusing knowledge of those norms to the mass of Japanese businesses, let alone getting them accepted, was far from easy. Without such acceptance, however, Japan's business leaders understood that the country's future as an international trader could be put at risk. Shibusawa's views on business ethics, as well as on the overall relationship between economy and morality, therefore evolved in the context of widespread discussion of, and concern about, moral standards in Japanese business. They were the product not only of the need to introduce new business institutions and to turn commerce and business into respectable occupations, but also of the national imperative to dispel these highly damaging views of the integrity (or lack thereof) of the Japanese, particularly of the commercial classes.

Whereas in the early 1880s Shibusawa appears to have been relatively positive about Japanese commercial morality, by around the turn of the century, following the upsurge of complaints beginning in the mid-1890s, his view appears to have been far less optimistic. Analysis of Shibusawa's lectures to the (Tokyo) Higher Commercial School[57] also suggests that, after his journey to the West in 1902, he harboured increasing concerns about the morality of those engaged in commerce in Japan, and feared for graduates entering a business world identified with moral shortcomings.[58] Addressing principals of higher commercial schools in 1903, Shibusawa spoke approvingly of the levels of commercial morality in Europe and the United States, and suggested that the future of Japanese commerce could be imperilled by the fact that Japan was far from reaching the same standards.[59] The importance of foreign models is also evident in Shibusawa's references to Western countries that, in the modern period, had moved away from traditional contempt for merchant activity and successfully raised the status of merchants.[60]

As we know, Shibusawa's ideas regarding business principles drew on concepts from Confucianism to argue that wealth accumulation was fully compatible with morality, but he also indicated that the obtaining of wealth should be undertaken in an appropriate way – that is, through *tadashii dōri* (correct means).[61] Shibusawa took issue with the actual term *shōgyō dōtoku* (commercial morality), arguing that its widespread use in the absence of equal discussion of other moralities, such as political morality or academic morality, was largely meaningless. Far better, he suggested, to think in terms of general moral principles that should be adhered to by all groups in the population. He nevertheless acknowledged that the intense discussions about commercial morality resulted from conspicuously bad behaviour on the part of the merchant class, which he attributed to an overemphasis on personal gain, the traditional lack of education of merchants, and popular prejudices about them as a group. Although the warrior class had had the ideals of *bushidō* to establish basic moral principles, the merchant class had had only the principle of profit. Because of this heritage, much remained to be done to ensure that all merchants spoke and acted with integrity, and adhered to the moral principles of fairness, uprightness, and chivalry.[62]

Most of Shibusawa's comments on the importance of correct behaviour on the part of merchants and other businesspeople were at the more general level, but he did make some references to more specific issues. Putting profits first, he suggested, should not necessarily lead to the breaking of contracts or the telling of lies, and adhering to signed contracts, even where doing so might entail a short-term loss, was the essence of fairness and integrity.[63] As we have seen, this reference to the breaking of contractual obligations reflected one of the core failings of Japanese traders that foreigners identified. Shibusawa's emphasis on the importance of not prioritizing individual profit was also very much in line with contemporary concerns about the damage the poor image of Japanese traders could do to the national interest. One lecture Shibusawa gave in 1897, for example – at a time when foreign criticisms were on the rise in the lead-up to treaty revision – emphasized strongly the need to prioritize the public benefit over individual profit.[64]

Shibusawa's analysis also offered a relatively nuanced view of the cultural difference between Japan and the West. Foreign customs, he suggested, could not be applied lock, stock, and barrel to Japan. Different countries had different perceptions of what was moral, and moral precepts needed to be tailored to Japanese circumstances and Japanese society. Japan had no traditional custom of respect for the individual or for contracts between individuals in the way that characterized countries such as Britain and the United States, and it was this disparity and lack of experience that gave rise to so much of the condemnation of Japan.[65] For Shibusawa, therefore, the commercial morality controversy raised the much broader issue of the transnational spread of norms and ideas, even while he recognized that, in the Western-dominated world of the early twentieth century, it was highly damaging for the country's industry and commerce for any Japanese to continue to act in a way that jeopardized Japan's international trust and credit standing.

Shibusawa was far from alone in the first decade of the twentieth century in giving serious thought to the moral qualities deemed desirable in the West, to the specific circumstances that might have contributed to Japan's poor reputation in commerce, and to the need to better educate those anticipating a career in business. Moves to strengthen commercial education had already brought with them instruction in business ethics. Nakajima Rikizō, professor of Western philosophy at the Imperial University, published a textbook in 1901 on commercial morality containing lectures he had given at the Higher Commercial School.[66] In his preface Nakajima argued that it was a matter of urgency to correct the evil customs that characterized contemporary Japanese commerce and to improve the progress of commercial morality. The publisher's preface emphasized similar concerns, drawing attention to the confusion between old and new customs in a period of rapid change, and highlighting the importance of shared religious values in shaping morality in Europe and North America over a sustained period. The lectures focused on the virtues required to secure trust and to manage a business and on the importance of civic responsibility on the part of the commercial classes. Nakajima, like Shibusawa, argued that a distinction between general morality and commercial morality was meaningless, but he stressed the need to cultivate in merchants the moral qualities essential to the engendering of trust as the foundation of the credit system, without which commerce and civilization would not continue to progress. Nakajima, too, cited Confucius in arguing that the virtues of honesty and truth were fundamental to the securing of trust.[67] The lectures in other respects made points very similar to those found in the Western literature on commercial morality and in some of Shibusawa's statements. First, Nakajima's identification of the importance of credit led directly to the claim that a high level of morality in commerce was in the long-term interest of the individual and of Japan as a whole. Second, the virtues that were called for included the same ones stressed by English writers in the eighteenth and nineteenth centuries and by Shibusawa – namely, honesty and integrity, and also perseverance, diligence, frugality, scrupulousness, promptness, and contribution to *kōkyōshin* (the public good).

Nakajima had extensive contact with the American Congregationalist minister and Yale professor of moral philosophy, George Trumbull Ladd, who spent a number of years as adviser to the Japanese government in the 1890s and also lectured at the Imperial University. On his third visit to Japan in 1907, Ladd was invited by the Higher Commercial

School to lecture on commercial morality; his lectures were also shortly afterwards published in book form.[68] Despite the book's title, and despite Ladd's brief involvement in business in his youth, the focus of the lectures was essentially on the abstract virtues required of all people – in particular, courage, moderation, constancy, fairness, truth, compassion, and being a *zen'i no hito* (person of goodwill). Students at the Higher Commercial School, therefore, were receiving a consistent message regarding the need for ethical business conduct from different sources, not just from Shibusawa.

Business ethics lectures continued to have a core place in commercial education throughout the remaining years of Shibusawa's life. In 1913, for example, it was reported that the vocational school at Koishikawa had introduced monthly lectures for the public with a view to improving commercial morality as well as providing information on economic problems and commerce.[69] Ishikawa Bungo, author of a textbook on retail business published in the 1920s, reiterated Shibusawa's earlier view that commercial morality could not be separated from morality in general: those in commerce should adhere to standard principles of honesty and integrity. Ishikawa acknowledged that lapses in commercial behaviour such as contract violation, the delivery of inferior goods, or deceptive advertising caused enormous damage, but he argued that such behaviour was evidence of moral failings on the part of individual merchants, rather than of a low standard of commercial morality in Japan as a whole. The responsible trader who adhered to the requirements of commercial morality was also careful about his choice of business partners and worked hard to preserve commercial stability.[70] The history of Japanese commercial activity continued to have an important explanatory role in textbooks on commerce. Emphasis on the importance of public benefit from commercial activity, as opposed to just private profit, was also notable in the 1930s.[71]

Concerns about morality in commerce are also found in more scholarly works on Japanese trade and commerce, notably those by Japanese scholars working abroad who would have been exposed to Western criticisms on a regular basis. Hattori Yukimasa, for example, who took his doctorate at the Johns Hopkins University around the turn of the century, emphasized in his analysis the importance of the circumstances of Japan's trade with the West as a source of problems – in particular, the indirect nature of much of Japan's trade through the open ports, its general lack of commercial experience, and its ignorance of foreign commerce. The political and cultural transition, Hattori suggested, was compounded by economic factors in Japan such as the traditional lack of credit and of a credit system, and high interest rates. Hattori did not deny, however, that Japanese merchants were guilty on occasion of dishonest business practices. He wrote of the want of uniformity in the quality of Japanese manufactures, and used the specific phrase "the low tone of commercial morality among the Japanese merchants."[72]

The broader context of concerns about morality in Japanese business expressed by Shibusawa is nowhere better demonstrated than in the attention paid to the issue both by business journals and daily newspapers. The journal *Jitsugyō no Nihon*, for which Shibusawa wrote quite frequently,[73] campaigned vigorously to improve business morality in a succession of editorials and articles by leading businessmen. *Jitsugyō no Nihon* had good contacts with Japanese consuls and businessmen engaged in foreign trade, who could supply first-hand information on criticisms from overseas. These criticisms were prominent in its editorials: typical were statements such as, "every time an American opens his mouth it is to complain about the lack of morality of Japanese producers or traders,"[74] or "to openly request that English merchants, renowned throughout the world for their integrity, go along with [Japanese merchants'] dishonest practice is not only a declaration of their own lack of morality, but affects a host of other honest merchants, and sullies the reputation of our country as a whole."[75] In one of the journal's earliest issues, Japan's consul in London identified how the immorality of merchants was hindering the development of Japanese trade.[76] Over the next few years, Takahashi Korekiyo, Katō Takaaki, Sonoda Kōkichi, Morimura Ichizaemon, Hatano Shōgorō, and Asano Sōichirō all took to its pages to comment on the issue, as did Koyama Kenzō, principal of the Higher Commercial School.[77] The main concern of these members of Japan's elite was the damage that the poor reputation of Japanese traders overseas was doing to the prospects for Japanese trade and foreign investment. The litany of complaints from Westerners regarding the breaking of contracts, the supply of inferior goods, and deception over commercial rights was repeated, and apparently accepted. Although the bad behaviour might be on the part of only a small minority, this was all it took to sully the national reputation and national interest.

Jitsugyō no sekai – which started life as *Mita shōgyō kai*, and to which Shibusawa contributed an article in 1911 concerning the relationship between Confucian ideas and business activity[78] – was another business journal that addressed the issue of morality in Japanese business practice. In 1908 Kamata Eikichi, who would become education minister in the 1920s, highlighted the low standard of morality of Japanese merchants, whose failure to keep promises and comply with deadlines was a major problem for Japanese business. Kamata cited England as a model of how to conduct commerce, and contrasted Japanese merchants unfavourably with their Chinese counterparts, who recognized that bad behaviour was likely to lead to commercial loss.[79] A couple of years later, one of the journal's Chinese reporters also contrasted the Chinese emphasis on trust with the rude and unwelcoming attitude of Japanese traders towards their customers.[80] The entrepreneur Morimura Ichizaemon also wrote in the journal's pages about how honesty was the best commercial strategy, a theme later taken up by the writer Toyosaki Zennosuke,[81] while the author Kōda Rohan wrote about the identity of public and private benefit.[82]

Discussion of the commercial morality issue had already reached the wider public. As early as 1885, the newspaper *Yomiuri Shimbun* stressed the importance of treating customers fairly, although the argument was less one of abstract moral principles and more one that good conduct was more likely to result in business prosperity.[83] During the 1890s, comment on commercial morality, often making use of the term *shōgyō dōtoku*, became increasingly frequent in the Japanese press. A leading article in *Kokumin Shimbun* called for better commercial education to improve the quality of merchants, pointing to the fact that "men engaged in commerce were for the most part lacking in mercantile education, and in the case of those who possessed any at all it was of an imperfect character."[84] *Asahi Shimbun* reported that the statesman Yamagata Aritomo was deeply concerned about evidence of increasing fraud and corruption in Japan, the lack of trust in dealings with foreign merchants, and a general decline in morality in commerce and industry.[85] *Yomiuri Shimbun* took up the issue with renewed vigour early in 1901, launching a front-page editorial on what it called *shōgyō dōtoku no taihai* (the corruption of commercial morality). The picture painted in the article was as unfavourable as anything to be found in the Western press, suggesting that domestic and foreign trade and business were riddled with corruption and fraud, that manufacturers regularly supplied substandard products, and that senior officials of banks and companies frequently engaged in fraudulent practices for their own enrichment. The important tea and *habutae* industries were being put at risk because of the "deficiency in commercial morality" of those who cheated on both quality and quantity in supplying the goods to make an inappropriate short-term profit. It had become almost normal, the newspaper stated, for there to be a disparity in quality between sample goods and the final product. The leader argued strongly that a commercial world characterized by moral principles, trust, and the honouring of contracts was one that would prosper, and that urgent measures needed to be taken to reform business institutions and organizations and to develop a broader concept of the public interest.[86] Other articles followed, sometimes citing more specific examples of malpractice. Contracts were reneged on, and "the inclination of our merchants to honour contracts is inferior even to that of the Chinese." Porcelain supplied was of low quality, there was widespread disparity between samples and the quality of the consignment, new products were sold initially at low prices, undercutting the market, and the price then gradually raised. Deceptive labelling of products was widespread, with packets of paper said to contain one hundred sheets actually containing considerably fewer.[87] The sentiments expressed by *Yomiuri Shimbun* could have been lifted straight from a British newspaper. "Unless we can reverse the degradation of our commercial morality, respecting morality, paying attention to credit standing and to contracts, along the lines of economic society in Europe and North America, then however much we may support and encourage business we must be concerned that the results will not be as we would wish.[88]

The issue was taken up by other papers, particularly after the victory against Russia opened new prospects for trade on the Asian mainland. *Asahi Shimbun* noted that free entry into the Korean market was characterized by "lack of regard for commercial morality," and reported that warnings had been issued to Japanese peddlers and shopkeepers that defrauding purchasers in Korea through the sale of inferior goods would jeopardize future trade. For the first time there was mention of fraud in relation to trademarks.[89] *Asahi Shimbun*, too, published leaders on business ethics,[90] arguing that Japanese traders were excessively focused on short-term profit and engaged in practices profoundly damaging to Japan's international trading position. The major forms of behaviour Westerners condemned – contract violation, fraudulent trademarks, supply of inferior goods, disparity between sample and consignment, mixing in crude-quality goods in repeat transactions – were accepted as fact. The paper put the responsibility squarely on the commercial community. It argued, for example, that an Osaka firm whose Chinese agent had copied German trademarks was itself to blame, as "acceptance of the counterfeit [by the Japanese firm] is in itself already a deficiency of commercial morality."[91]

Although some journalists did attempt to defend Japan against foreign accusations, articles continued to highlight dubious practices in both domestic and foreign dealings, often of a sensational nature. Gunboat suppliers had used bricks instead of steel plate, and shoe suppliers horse leather instead of cattle hide.[92] Half a consignment of silk *habutae* for the United States had been burned as unfit for use, thus posing a real threat to Japan's exports to North America.[93] The boom and bust of the First World War in some ways intensified the discussion. In August 1914, just after the start of the conflict, *Asahi Shimbun* called for a special kind of commercial morality suited to wartime imperatives amid concerns that rising prices would be fuelled by hoarding and speculation.[94] Another article in 1915 described a litany of adulterated and substandard products and a lack of uniformity in consignments. In one large lacquerware order from the United States, the wood had been insufficiently dried, causing the lacquer to crack. However easy it might be to explain the reasons for the problems, the bottom line was that the poor reputation of Japanese export goods was the result of "a deficiency of commercial morality."[95] With the end of the war, transactions hitherto viewed as profitable ceased to be so. US manufacturers, in particular, were affected by Japanese purchasers' reneging on contracts, a practice condemned by some Japanese commentators as reinforcing the overall perception of declining standards of commercial morality in Japan and thus damaging to business. The reputation of Japanese merchants was said to be worse than that of Jewish merchants.[96] As the wartime boom collapsed, the behaviour of many involved in proposed new businesses provoked criticism of actions that, "even though they did not breach the law were not permissible in terms of commercial morality."[97] The lax approach to business ethics of those who argued that they could not be expected to adhere to strict principles of commercial morality at a time of acute economic instability was sharply condemned.[98] Japanese consuls overseas continued to report that goods were not delivered as promised, were adulterated, were of substandard quality or uneven in quality, and not up to the quality of sample products. The lack of commercial morality denoted by such practices was seen as a real impediment to the continued growth of Japanese trade.[99] A fifty-strong delegation to Britain led by Dan Takuma of Mitsui faced complaints about infringement of cutlery trademarks when it visited Sheffield in January 1922, and on a number of occasions during the visit Japanese delegates felt obliged to assure their hosts that they in no way condoned this, or any other practice commensurate with dishonesty and a lack of commercial morality.[100]

Although discussion of commercial morality in the Japanese press appears to have declined markedly after the early 1920s, accusations of dishonesty and fraud never went away. A meeting of business groups in Osaka in 1938 was told that a major area of German complaints against Japan was Japan's shameless copying of German designs and products and the lack of any spirit of commercial morality on the part of the Japanese.[101] Efforts continued to defend Japan's integrity and to argue that it was unjust to make generalized charges of deficient moral character of the Japanese as a whole because of the bad behaviour of the few, but the issue remained of profound concern to leading business-men, to the authorities, and to educators. Shibusawa Eiichi's views on morality and economy and on the importance of morality in the actual conduct of business, therefore, were formulated in the context of shared concerns about these very concrete issues.

Unresolved Issues on Business Ethics

Individual ideas are formulated in a context of practical dilemmas and shared debates, and the *gapponshugi* beliefs of Shibusawa Eiichi were no exception. Shibusawa's ideas on morality in business conduct must be located in the broader context of Japan's changing position in the global economy in the late nineteenth and early twentieth centuries, and in the evolving discourse on commercial morality that accompanied it. Although Shibusawa's ideas were in many ways distinct, they were also the product of their time. Shibusawa engaged with issues that were of profound concern to his contemporaries inside and outside Japan, and that were put into ever sharper perspective as Japan increasingly engaged with the global economy and the transnational flow of ideas. This is not to say, however, that their relevance is in any way limited to that time. Early in the twenty-first century, we are still grappling with the complex relationships among weaknesses in the structures of rules and systems, intentional violations of accepted norms by individuals or groups, and their practical consequences for business outcomes. The border between illegal and immoral conduct remains indistinct, and the historical example of Japan reminds us of the difficulties that cultural complexity and the existence of multiple ethical standards can pose in economic decision-making and the practice of business.

NOTES

1 Shibusawa Eiichi, *Seien hyakuwa* [Seien's 100 stories] (Tokyo: Kokumin Kyōiku Kai, [1913] 1926), 60–6.
2 Tanaka Kazuhiro, "Dōtoku keizai gōitsu setsu no Shin'i" [Real mean-ing of the idea of the unity of morality and economy], in *Shibusawa Eiichi*

to hitozukuri [Shibusawa Eiichi and development of human resources], ed. Kikkawa Takeo, Shimada Masakazu, and Tanaka Kazuhiro (Tokyo: Yuhikaku, 2013), 61.

3 See Tanaka, Chapter 2, in this volume.

4 "Japanese Commercial Morality," *Economist Monthly Trade Supplement* 10 (October 1891), 9.

5 Rachid L'Aoufir, *La Prusse de 1815 à 1848: l'industrialisation comme processus de communication* (Paris: L'Harmattan, 2004), 121–54, 373–6.

6 "Commercial Morality," *South Australian Register*, 27 February 1862.

7 Thomas Gisborne, *An Enquiry into the Duties of Men in the Higher and Middle Classes of Society in Britain* (London: B. & J. White, 1795), 200–18.

8 Anon., *Mercantile Morals: A Book for Young Men Entering upon the Duties of Active Life* (London: James Blackwood, 1861), 128.

9 Leader, *Times* (London), 6 November 1873, and Letter to the Editor, 8 November 1873; *Manchester Guardian*, 7 April 1868; "The alleged degeneration of England in commercial morality," *Economist*, 14 January 1868, 22 November 1884.

10 *Manchester Guardian*, 30 January 1868; "Commercial credit and morality," *Times* (London), 30 January 1868.

11 "Liverpool on commercial morality," *Economist*, 1 February 1868.

12 Ibid.; Leader, *Times* (London), 6 November 1873.

13 *Manchester Guardian*, 30 January 1868.

14 Leader, *Times* (London), 6 November 1873.

15 "Sir Edward Fry on commercial morality," *Times* (London), 6 September 1899, "Sir Edward Fry on commercial morality," 5 December 1904, 25 January 1905; "Sir Edward Fry on commercial morality," *Spectator*, 19 November 1896.

16 Judy Hilkey, *Character Is Capital: Success Manuals and Manhood in Gilded Age America* (Chapel Hill: University of North Carolina Press, 1997), 4, 127, 133–4.

17 Reported in "New York commercial morality," *Manchester Guardian*, 2 October 1872.

18 Edgar L. Heermance, *The Ethics of Business: A Study of Current Standards* (New York; London: Harper & Brothers, 1926), 21.

19 Ibid., 107.

20 See, for example, Richard Ehrenburg, *Der Handel: Seine wirtschaftliche Bedeutung, seine nationalen Pflichten und sein Verhältnis zum Staate* [Trade: Its economic significance, its national obligations and its relationship with the state] (Jena, Germany: Verlag von Gustav Fischer, 1897), 44–9.

21 See, for example, Leader, *Times* (London), 6 November 1873, and Letter to the Editor, 8 November 1873.

22 "Japan," *Economist*, 22 July 1899.

23 See, for example, Edward Bartrum, *Wanderings, West and East* (London: S.W. Partridge, 1899), 104; Letter to the Editor on "Trading with the Chinese," *Economist*, 24 August 1929; Henry C. Emery, "Chinese Commercial Morality," *Harper's Monthly Magazine* (July 1923), 227; Joseph H. Longford, "The Commercial Morality of the Japanese," *Contemporary Review* 87 (January/June 1905), 705.

24 See, for example, J.E. Hoare, *Japan's Treaty Ports and Foreign Settlements: The Uninvited Guests, 1858–1899* (London: RoutledgeCurzon, 1995); and Yuki Allyson Honjo, *Japan's Early Experience of Contract Management in the Treaty Ports* (London: Routledge, 2003).

25 Kevin Murphy, *The American Merchant Experience in Nineteenth-Century Japan* (London: RoutledgeCurzon, 2002), 30–2, 68, 109, 117ff.

26 "Japanese commercial morality," *Times* (London), 26 September 1888.

27 *Economist*, 10 October 1891.

28 Longford, "Commercial Morality of the Japanese," 706.

29 Joseph Llewellyn Thomas, *Journeys among the Gentle Japs in the Summer of 1895* (London: Sampson Low, 1897), 179.

30 Arthur Diosy, *The New Far East*, 5th ed. (London: Cassell, 1904), 283–93.

31 Karl Rathgen, *Die Japaner in der Weltwirtschaft* [The Japanese in the world economy] (Leipzig: B.G. Teubner, 1911), 122, 138.

32 Erich Pauer, "Deutsche Ingenieure in Japan, japanische Ingenieure in Deutschland in der Zwischenkriegszeit [German engineers in Japan, Japanese engineers in Germany in the inter-war period]," in *Deutschland-Japan in der Zwischenkriegszeit* [Germany-Japan in the inter-war period], ed. J. Kreiner and R. Mathias (Bonn: Bouvier Verlag, 1990), 309–11.

33 R.B. Peery, *Gist of Japan* (Edinburgh; London: Oliphant, 1897), 67.

34 Murphy, *American Merchant Experience*, 138.

35 Peery, *Gist of Japan*, 119.

36 Murphy, *American Merchant Experience*, 159.

37 Diosy, *New Far East*, 283.

38 Longford, "Commercial Morality of the Japanese," 710.

39 Murphy, *American Merchant Experience*, 159.

40 Cited in Jean-Pierre Lehmann, *The Image of Japan: From Feudal Isolation to World Power, 1850–1905* (London: Routledge, [1978] 2011), 77.

41 "Japan's cotton trade – Use of fraudulent trade marks – A movement to stop it," *Manchester Guardian*, 27 November 1920.

42 P. Duguid, Teresa da Silva Lopes, and J. Mercer, "Reading Registrations: An Overview of 100 Years of Trademark Registrations in France, the United Kingdom, and the United States," in *Trademarks, Brands and Competitiveness*, ed. Teresa da Silva Lopes and Paul Duguid, 9–30 (New York:

Routledge, 2010); and David Higgins, "Trademarks and Infringement in Britain, c.1875–c.1900," in da Silva Lopes and Duguid, *Trademarks, Brands and Competitiveness*, 102–18.

43 Murphy, *American Merchant Experience*, 51.

44 "British trade marks in Japan," *Manchester Guardian*, 26 December 1907.

45 "Justice in Japan – The violation of foreign trade marks," *Manchester Guardian*, 17 October 1907; "Trade marks in Japan – Buchanan Whisky case," *Manchester Guardian*, 20 March 1908.

46 "Trade with Japan – Some Lancashire difficulties," *Manchester Guardian*, 1 June 1907.

47 *Manchester Guardian*, 17 October 1907.

48 "Trade marks in the Far East," *Manchester Guardian*, 10 February 1909.

49 "Japan's cotton trade – Use of fraudulent trade marks – A movement to stop it," *Manchester Guardian*, 27 November 1920; "Japanese mission at Sheffield – Visitors and the relations of capital and labour," *Manchester Guardian*, 27 November 1920; "Japan's copying of trade-marks – Minister's promise," *Manchester Guardian*, 7 January 1922; *Manchester Guardian*, 7 December 1933.

50 Nemoto Tadashi, "Honpō Shōnin no Heifū" [Evil practices of Japanese merchants], *Jitsugyō no Nihon* 2, no. 15 (1898): 13–15.

51 *Tokyo Asahi Shimbun*, 14 April 1908.

52 Cited in "Commercial morality in Japan – An official appeal," *Manchester Guardian*, 26 January 1909.

53 "Japan," *Encyclopædia Britannica*, 11th ed. (1910/11).

54 *Yomiuri Shimbun*, 5 September 1910, 20 September 1910, 15 December 1910, 22 April 1911; "Japan – Commercial morality – Formosan sugar and tea industries," *Economist*, 24 December 1910.

55 *Tokyo Asahi Shimbun*, 8 January 1913.

56 *Economist*, 14 January 1908; Masuda Takashi, *Japan: Its Commercial Development and Prospects* (London: Sisley's, 1908).

57 The Tokyo Commercial School became the Higher Commercial School in 1885, and was renamed Tokyo Higher Commercial School in 1902. It retained this designation until becoming the Tokyo University of Commerce in 1920, and eventually Hitotsubashi University in 1949.

58 Tanaka, "Dōtoku keizai gōitsu setsu no Shin'i," 65–89.

59 Yamafuji Ryūtarō, "Chūtō shōgyō kyōiku no fukyū to kōritsu shōgyō gakkō" [Spread of commercial education at middle schools and public commercial schools], in *Shibusawa Eiichi to hitozukuri* [Shibusawa Eiichi and building human capital], ed. Kikkawa Takeo, Shimada Masakazu, and Tanaka Kazuhiro (Tokyo: Yuhikaku, 2013), 178.

60 Kenjō Teiji, *Shibusawa Eiichi – "Dōtoku" to keizai no aida* [Shibusawa Eiichi – Between "morality" and economy] (Tokyo: Nihon Keizai Hyoronsha, 2008), 186.
61 Shibusawa, *Seien hyakuwa*, 52.
62 Ibid., 60–6.
63 Ibid., 65–6.
64 Kenjō, *Shibusawa Eiichi*, 186.
65 Shibusawa, *Seien hyakuwa*, 65–6.
66 Nakajima Rikizō, *Shōgyō dōtoku kyōkasho* [Commercial morality textbook] (Tokyo: Dōbunkan, 1901).
67 For a brief summary of the main points in the lectures, see ibid., 1–13.
68 G.T. Ladd, *Shōgyō dōtoku – Lectures of G.T. Ladd*, trans. Moriya Tsunetaro (Tokyo: Tokyo Kōtō Shōgyō Gakkō/Hakubunkan, 1907).
69 *Tokyo Asahi Shimbun*, 7 May 1913.
70 Ishikawa Bungo, *Shōgyō jūnikō* [Twelve lectures on commerce] (Tokyo: Shimizu Shoten, 1926), 415–18.
71 See, for example, "Nihon shihonkatachi no aikokushin naki o tsūfun su" [Indignation at the lack of patriotism of Japanese capitalists], *Jitsugyō no sekai* 28 (October 1931); Arima Hiromasa, "Shōgyō dōtoku" [Commercial morality], in *Nihon shōnin shi* [History of merchants in Japan], ed. Nihon Rekishi Chiri Gakkai (Tokyo: Nihon Gakujutsu Fukyūkai, 1935).
72 Hattori Yukimasa, *The Foreign Commerce of Japan since the Restoration, 1869–1900*, Johns Hopkins Studies in Historical and Political Science (Baltimore: Johns Hopkins Press, 1904), 30. Other works of this kind by Japanese scholars in Western languages include Kinoshita Eitarō (Yetarō), *The Past and Present of Japanese Commerce* (New York: Columbia University Press, 1902), xvi, 1; and Tateishi Sajiro, *Japan's Internationale Handelsbeziehungen, mit besonderer Rücksichtigung der Gegenwart* [Japan's international trading relations, with special regard to the present] (Halle: Hofbuch Druckerei von C.A. Kaemmerer, 1902).
73 Shibusawa Eiichi Kinen Zaidan, ed., *Shibusawa Eiichi o shiru jiten* [A dictionary of Shibusawa Eiichi] (Tokyo: Tokyodo, 2012), 135.
74 Editorial, *Jitsugyō no Nihon* 3, no. 9 (1899).
75 Editorial, *Jitsugyō no Nihon* 6, no. 10 (1902).
76 Arakawa Minoji, "Kaigai bōeki fushin no gen'in oyobi shinsaku no hōhō" [Causes of inactivity in foreign trade and means of promoting it], *Jitsugyō no Nihon* 1, no. 5 (1897).
77 Koyama Kenzō, "Shōgyō dōtoku kōryo" [Consideration of commercial morality], *Jitsugyō no Nihon* 1, no. 13 (1898); Morimura Ichizaemon, "Jitsugyō rikkoku no hōshin" [How to build up our national business], *Jitsugyō no Nihon* 3, no. 20 (1899); Sonoda Kōkichi, "Shōgyō dōtoku yōsei no

hitsuyō" [Need to cultivate commercial morality], *Jitsugyō no Nihon* 4, no. 1 (1900); Katō Takaaki, "Gaikoku bōeki jō no shōgai" [Obstacles to foreign trade], *Jitsugyō no Nihon* 4, no. 15 (1900); Asano Sōichirō, "Kaigai bōeki kakuchō saku" [Strategy for expanding overseas trade], *Jitsugyō no Nihon* 4, no. 22 (1900); Hatano Shōgorō, "Waga shōnin wa hatashite fushin'yō naru ya" [How our merchants end up untrustworthy], *Jitsugyō no Nihon* 5, no. 2 (1901).

78 Shibusawa Eiichi Kinen Zaidan, *Shibusawa Eiichi o shiru jiten*, 161.

79 Kamata Eikichi, "Wagakuni no shōgyō dōtoku o takamuru saizen sairyō saku" [Best strategies for improving the standard of commercial morality in our country], *Jitsugyō no sekai* 5, no. 1 (1908).

80 Hō Risei, "Zannen nagara Nihonjin wa Shinjin yori shōbai ga kaku no gotoku heta de katsu sai nai" [Unfortunately Japanese are inferior to the Chinese when it comes to trade], *Jitsugyō no sekai* 7, no. 7 (1910).

81 Morimura Ichizaemon, "Gyōdōtoku no kaizen wa daiyoku o kosui suru ni kagiru" [Improvement in business morality constrained by advocacy of greed], *Jitsugyō no sekai* 5, no. 3 (1908); Toyosaki Zennosuke, "Shōtorihikijō ni okeru shinyō no kachi" [Value of trust in commercial dealings], *Jitsugyō no sekai* 10, no. 21 (1913).

82 Kōda Rohan, "Kōtoku kōeki to shitoku shieki to" [Public morality, public benefit and personal morality, personal benefit], *Jitsugyō no sekai* 10, no. 15 (1913).

83 *Yomiuri Shimbun*, 1 October 1885, 11 December 1885.

84 Cited in A.H. Lay, "Report on Commercial Education in Japan," United Kingdom, British Parliamentary Papers, *Commercial and Consular Reports, Japan*, vol. 10 (Shannon: Irish University Press, [1899] 1971), 15/477.

85 *Tokyo Asahi Shimbun*, 18 August 1901.

86 *Yomiuri Shimbun*, 6 January 1901.

87 *Yomiuri Shimbun*, 21 January 1901.

88 *Yomiuri Shimbun*, 6 January 1901.

89 *Tokyo Asahi Shimbun*, 5 August 1904.

90 See, for example, *Asahi Shimbun*, 18 October 1906, 30 November 1907.

91 *Osaka Asahi Shimbun*, 30 November 1907.

92 *Yomiuri Shimbun*, 5 January 1910.

93 *Yomiuri Shimbun*, 5 May 1911.

94 *Osaka Asahi Shimbun*, 25 August 1914.

95 *Tokyo Asahi Shimbun*, 9 February 1915.

96 *Yomiuri Shimbun*, 19 December 1918; *Tokyo Asahi Shimbun*, 19 December 1918.

97 *Tokyo Asahi Shimbun*, 12 September 1920.

98 *Tokyo Asahi Shimbun*, 28 April 1919, 7 March 1920.

99 *Tokyo Asahi Shimbun*, 25 March 1921.
100 "Japanese trade mission – A visit to Manchester arranged – Dr. Dan on Washington and China," *Manchester Guardian*, 21 December 1921; "Japanese mission at Sheffield – Visitors and the relations of capital and labour," *Manchester Guardian*, 7 January 1922.
101 *Yomiuri Shimbun*, 17 July 1938.

6 Shibusawa Eiichi's View of Business Morality in Global Society

KIMURA MASATO

Throughout his life Shibusawa Eiichi based his principles and actions on *gapponshugi* and the ideal union of morality and economics. This chapter clarifies the characteristics of his views on business morality by also considering trends in the global society of his time and Japan's involvement in it.

The period between the late nineteenth century and the beginning of the First World War was characterized by the social Darwinism–based principle of the survival of the fittest, when liberal thinking and the market economy transcended borders and rapidly spread throughout the world. Having opened itself to the world in 1853, Japan increasingly felt a sense of crisis as its neighbour, China, became semi-colonized after the First Opium War through invasions by Western powers such as Britain and France. Japan, however, managed to save itself from intervention by Western powers in the transition from the Tokugawa shogunate to the Meiji government, which set goals of wealth, military strength, and the encouragement of new industry in an effort to catch up with developed countries amid intense competition with foreign traders. Although the treaties concluded at the end of the Edo period were unequal, the new Japanese government tenaciously tackled revisions of those treaties throughout the Meiji period. By the early twentieth century, Japan had become capable of making international deals with Western countries nearly as an equal partner. Consequently, Japanese international trade and economic growth far outpaced expectations.

This period exactly coincides with the ninety-one-year life of Shibusawa Eiichi. Born in 1840 at the outbreak of the First Opium War, Shibusawa died in 1931, when Britain left the gold standard system and Japan triggered the Manchurian Incident amid the global depression that stemmed from the 1929 stock market collapse on Wall Street. During his lifetime, Shibusawa experienced the tectonic shift of global society and Japan's turning points. Aware of the critical importance of cultivating a sense of morality when developing business activities in international relations, Shibusawa proactively engaged both global society and Japanese domestic society through private economic diplomacy.

In discussing Shibusawa's priorities of raising awareness about business and improving the status of businesspeople, the thorough practice of business morality in international trade, and proactive business morality, the analysis makes it clear that Shibusawa's view of business morality exhibited two major trends. One was consistency based on the Analects of Confucius; the other was change in response to trends in international economics characterized by rapid globalization, and to harsh criticism of Japanese economic activities from overseas, as discussed by Janet Hunter in Chapter 5.

Raising Awareness about Business and Improving the Status of Businesspeople

Shibusawa stressed the need for a bold shift in thinking about business from two perspectives: raising awareness about business, and improving the social status of businesspeople.

As Tanaka Kazuhiro details in Chapter 2, Shibusawa maintained that business activities did not contradict the teachings of Confucius, especially the Analects, which were the philosophical foundation of the education of the samurai, who were the ruling class in the Edo period. Rather, Shibusawa argued that making profits and accumulating wealth could accompany morality. He successfully persuaded others that creating a rich society would stabilize people's lives and help them practice morality, and that businesspeople were on an equal level in society with politicians, the military, and bureaucrats because of their economic contribution to international society.

Shibusawa was exposed to these ideas while staying in France in 1867–68 as a member of a group of delegates to the Paris Exposition. In Paris he placed great trust in a French banker named Paul Flüry-Hérard (1836–1913),[1] the honorary consul general for Japan. Indeed, Shibusawa learned a wide range of economic knowledge from the French. The biggest concern for Shibusawa, who was assigned to take care of general affairs and manage the Tokugawa delegation's stay in Paris, was to make enough money to support his master Tokugawa Akitake in studying abroad. However, the outbreak of the Boshin War between

the Tokugawa shogunate and forces wishing to return Japan to imperial rule discouraged Shibusawa from counting on the shogunate for
remittances. He thus tried to save money in ways such as relocating to
a less expensive hotel and cutting unnecessary expenses to make ends
meet. This is when he met Flüry-Hérard, who taught him the French
ways of meticulous accounting and asset management.

Observing the mechanisms of the French economy, Shibusawa grew
particularly interested in aspects such as convertible paper currency,
public securities, bank management, and the joint-stock system. In the
days of Napoléon III, France enjoyed an economic boom, and Paris was
brimming with vigour. Shibusawa was advised to buy railroad securities, and did so with his spare money. The price of the securities soared
by the time he returned to Japan, allowing him to sell them off at a great
profit and the Japanese delegates to return to their country with money
to spare. Before long, the economic knowledge Shibusawa acquired
in Paris became of value in the Meiji Restoration. In obedience to the
emperor, Tokugawa Yoshinobu had vacated Edo Castle and confined
himself to the feudal domain of Shizuoka, where Shibusawa met him
and established Shizuoka Shōhō Kaisho, Japan's first *gappon-kaisha*, or
joint-stock corporation,[2] whose purpose was to support the Shizuoka
Domain financially.

In Meiji Japan's effort to catch up with Western powers, Shibusawa
cited three significant obstacles to industrialization that had to be overcome above all else:[3] high interest rates (in western Europe the annual
lending rate was between 3 and 6 per cent, while in Japan it reached
between 7 and 13 per cent); a shortage of capital, which meant it was
hard to obtain funds for long-term investments; and a shortage of
trained personnel needed to start machine-related industries. Nevertheless, Shibusawa believed these obstacles could be overcome. He argued
that, if a business aligned with society's needs, it would definitely
become profitable in the long term, notwithstanding high interest rates;
cutting unnecessary expenses and increasing the number of stockholders would help overcome capital shortages; and the human resources
needed for industrialization could be trained by setting up commercial
law institutes and other educational institutions and by consistently
providing students with specialized and practical education.

Gapponshugi

The approach Shibusawa employed to overcome these obstacles was
the principle of *gapponshugi*, or capitalism infused with moral values.

Gapponshugi has already been discussed in preceding chapters from different perspectives. Here I wish to summarize its meaning briefly, since a full understanding of the concept is imperative when considering the morality of a banker.

Based on Shibusawa's thinking and the lectures he gave, *gapponshugi* is defined as the principle of developing a business by assembling the best possible people and funding to achieve the mission and with the aim of pursuing the public good. Usually, the Japanese terms *gappon-kaisha* and *kabushiki kaisha* are regarded as almost the same – namely, a joint-stock company. According to the sixth edition of the *Kōjien* dictionary, *kabushiki kaisha* is defined as a limited liability company whose capital is divided by an equity-based form of stock and organized by investors (shareholders). Shibusawa's definition of *gappon-kaisha*, however, was considerably different from the behaviour of stock companies and stockholders in today's capitalistic world. As Shimada Masakazu mentions in Chapter 1, the five hundred or so companies that involved Shibusawa in their establishment included unidentified companies and limited partnerships as well as stock companies. This is because Shibusawa's *gapponshugi* consisted of three factors: the mission, human resources and their networks, and capital.

THE MISSION

For Shibusawa the mission of businesses should be that of *gappon-soshiki* – an organization that pursues the public good. This required stockholders and business managers to understand and be motivated to achieving that goal before making investments and running a company. The company did not always have to take the form of a stock company; it needed only be an organization suitable for fulfilling the aim of a company.

HUMAN RESOURCES AND NETWORKS

Shibusawa placed importance on the human resources needed to engage in corporate management and business activities. While business managers had to understand the mission of their company, the need pursue the public good, and the importance of acquiring profits through business operations, Shibusawa stressed that it was even more important that profits were evenly distributed to all investors. He stubbornly objected to monopolizing businesses and profits and pursuing the development of a homegrown conglomerate, as is obvious in his famous debate with Iwasaki Yatarō on competition: Iwasaki preferred monopolized companies in order to compete with foreign companies, but Shibusawa insisted that monopolies were not good because they often gave rise to corruption.

In that regard Shibusawa looked for managers who were not only able to develop a business properly, but also who had a broad vision, were cooperative enough to seek partners and work with them, and had a network to support both the company's vision and the spirit of cooperation. To that end, he deepened his involvement in the establishment and management of educational institutions such as the Tokyo Commercial School (the forerunner of Hitotsubashi University) and other commercial schools around the country.[4]

CAPITAL

Starting and developing a business requires abundant capital. During his time in Paris, Shibusawa learned that banks were the driving force for setting up a joint-stock company. After returning to Japan, he took the initiative in putting that lesson into practice, introducing, through the Meiji government, a banking system, supporting the establishment of banks such as Dai-Ichi Kokuritsu Ginko (First National Bank), and extending the banking system nationwide.

In introducing a banking system for modern Japan, the Meiji government chose the American form, which, because it allowed banks to issue paper currency, appeared more suitable for the collecting of clan notes, oval gold and silver coins, and bronze coins that had circulated during the Edo period. In 1872 the Meiji government enacted the National Bank Act, based on US legislation, to which some elements of the British bank system were added. In 1873 Dai-Ichi Kokuritsu Ginko was set up in compliance with the Act. In the process, people such as Ito Hirobumi, Yoshida Kiyonari, Ōkuma Shigenobu, Matsukata Masayoshi, Inoue Kaoru, and Shibusawa Eiichi engaged in heated discussions inside the government about such questions as the concepts of banks and banking, their translation into Japanese, and the ideals of a banking system.[5]

Shibusawa strongly believed it was necessary to impart the concept and mechanism of a Western-style bank throughout Japanese society, irrespective of outdated differences in social classes, in order to improve Japan's ability to raise capital. He expressed this aim eloquently in a contribution to a bank advertisement:

First of all, a bank is like a large river. It serves limitless purposes. Even if a substantial amount of money is collected, it will, however, be worth nothing more than water in a ditch or drops of water unless it is kept in the bank. It may be hidden in the storehouse of a wealthy merchant or farmer, or may be kept in the pocket of a day worker or an elderly woman. This will not make the money work for benefiting people or enriching the country. Even if water is capable of flowing, it will be useless if an embankment or a hill blocks it. Collecting money from storehouses and pockets amounts to a great deal of capital, which makes trade prosper, increases products, develops industries, facilitates learning, improves roads, and makes everything in the country evolve into a brand new state.[6]

Shibusawa also cited publications such as his *Ryūkai ryakusoku* (The rules of establishing a company) and Fukuchi Gen'ichirō's *Kaishaben* (How to establish a company) to explain practical operations of a bank as a *gappon-soshiki*.

The morality of a banker

Shibusawa firmly believed that the role of a bank was to invest in what would lead to the public good, to create something new – in other words, to change intangible money into tangible wealth – and to support the investment financially so that would function well. Bankers' judgments about financing should be based on whether the investment was expected to generate a healthy return relative to the capital invested. Bankers should also gain insight into whether the investment was truly necessary for the nation and society.

From the perspective of business morality, Shibusawa emphasized two points in setting up Dai-Ichi Bank. First, he tried to collect capital from as many people as possible. Since all banks that would be established under the National Bank Act would be private enterprises, Shibusawa tried to avoid allowing a single major capitalist to monopolize the bank, and so he declined Mitsui's offer to handle all aspects of the bank. In the end, he persuaded seventy-one stockholders – individuals as well as companies – to invest in the bank.

Second, he decided to disclose publicly the names of the investors and the amounts invested. During the Edo period, major money-changers such as Mitsui and Kōnoike had also undertaken financial activities such as *daimyōgashi* (lending money to *daimyo*, or feudal lords), but they had never dared to disclose the names of investors or the amounts they invested. Mutual aid organizations called *tanomoshikō* and *mujin*, dating back to the Kamakura period, handled small loans to commoners, and they, too, maintained the privacy of such transactions. Given this tradition, many investors were reluctant to have the details of their involvement disclosed. Shibusawa, however, considered banks to be the core of *gapponshugi*. To him, ensuring transparency was imperative for clarifying investors' responsibilities. With repeated efforts, he finally succeeded in persuading major investors, including Mitsui and Onogumi, to agree to this approach. As Shibusawa argued, "bankers are positioned above other people engaged in commerce and industry. Bankers enjoy people's respect and honour. This is why they must always be willing to assume heavy responsibilities."[7] This kind of awareness-raising was also needed to persuade talented individuals to pursue a career in commerce.

Raising awareness among bankers and instilling in them a sense of responsibility also required improving the status of banks in Japanese society. For this purpose, Shibusawa established Takuzen-kai (later, the Tokyo Bankers' Association) in the late 1870s with the aim of offering bankers opportunities to exchange information and develop friendships through friendly competition. As part of the economic circle, Takuzen-kai cooperated with the likes of the Tokyo Chamber of Commerce in submitting recommendations and proposals to the government about such issues as finance and trade policy.[8]

Shibusawa strictly required bankers to have a strong moral compass, yet many bankers and businesspeople failed to live up to his standards. Indeed, during the economic boom that followed the First World War, their behaviour deteriorated, as represented by the Ishii Sadashichi affair.[9] Ishii, an Osaka-based lumber dealer, had achieved success as a war profiteer through transactions involving wood and three staples: stocks, rice, and cotton yarn. Having temporarily recovered from the post-war depression, in 1921 Ishii bought up rice in an attempt to take advantage of a poor rice crop, but this did not go as he had expected. He then he bought up stock in Kanebo, a major textile company. Such speculative economic activity, based solely on expectations of future price increases, was only temporarily successful, however, and his company, Ishii Shoten, ultimately went out of business, leaving a gaping debt that rendered Ishii bankrupt and with a reputation as the "king of debt." More than forty banks – including Sumitomo Bank, a homegrown conglomerate – had financed Ishii Shoten. The affair exposed the extent to which the post-war Japanese economy had been driven by highly unrealistic speculation and a lack restraint in the banks' attitudes towards corporate financing. These immoral acts by economic figures, particularly bankers, were abhorrent to Shibusawa, who regarded banks as the core of *gappon-kaisha*.

As the trump card against kanson-minpi

Another reason Shibusawa focused on banks in applying the principle of *gapponshugi* was his belief that this was essential for Japan to break away from *kanson-minpi*, the tendency to respect bureaucrats and look down on the citizenry. When travelling in Europe in 1867, Shibusawa was amazed by the way local businesses represented precisely what he considered *gappon-soshiki* (in their pursuit of the public good) and by the intimacy of public-private interactions. This led him to believe that, once commerce and industry developed in Japan by *gappon-soshiki* principles, the status of those engaged in them would rise and the relationship between public and private would become more intimate.

In his youth, Shibusawa was repeatedly summoned to the magistrate's office of the Okaya Domain on behalf of his father, and had been disgusted by the officials' overbearing attitudes and thinking. The experience led him to decide that doing away with *kanson-minpi* would be his primary goal in life.[10] Officials who wielded authority despite having no talent were, of course, intolerable. Shibusawa also grew increasingly frustrated with merchants who did nothing more than pursue their own profits, and lacked the courage to defy the government or other higher-ups. Shibusawa, who was strongly influenced by the philosophy of Odaka Jyunchū[11] in studies of *Mitogaku* – a school of thought that believed the emperor, rather than the Tokugawa shogun, was the proper sovereign of Japan[12] – considered that the Japanese people needed to become aware of their possible role in changing Japan into a modern, European-style society with industrialization as its core, and that this required a system in which citizens could fully exercise their skills and knowledge.

As a member of the Meiji government, Shibusawa was involved in collaborative efforts by the *Kaisei Kakari* (reform office) in both the Ministry of Civil Affairs and the Ministry of Finance to draft, design, and implement numerous institutional reforms aimed at nation-building. These efforts included land tax reform; the introduction of monetary, banking, and postal systems; conversion to the metric measurement system; and the use of the solar calendar. Shibusawa then left the government and, as a private businessperson, helped to establish and run numerous companies and organizations under the leadership of ordinary citizens and in cooperation with the government. Dai-Ichi Bank was the start, followed by the Oji Paper Manufacturing Company, the Osaka Spinning Company, the Tokyo Marine Insurance Company, and numerous others, many of which are still active today. Shibusawa indeed put into practice his notion that it was the Japanese people who had to take the initiative in nation-building.

Besides Shibusawa, like-minded figures such as Godai Tomoatsu, Doi Michio, and Masuda Takashi also resigned from their positions in the central and local governments and entered private economic circles, taking the initiative in starting companies and businesses and spear-heading economic growth. Instrumental to the development of the private sector were the spirit of self-reliance and theory of commerce promulgated by the author, educator, and entrepreneur Fukuzawa Yukichi. Such men were confident that the entrepreneurial activities of private economic figures and the wealth that accrued from them would lay the economic foundation for making a democratic society function.

As this all shows, Shibusawa's idea of *gapponshugi* was designed to pursue the public good and involved stronger norms than those of an ordinary stock corporation. In other words, it was based philosophically on the compatibility between morality and economy or, as Shibusawa expressed it, *rongo* (The Analects of Confucius) and *soroban* (abacus).

The Thorough Practice of Business Morality

How did Shibusawa handle issues that concerned business morality in a narrower sense? The *Daijirin* dictionary defines *shōgyōdōtoku* as the internal norm that must be followed in business activities. To follow *shōgyōdōtoku* means to comply with common morals as represented by sincerity and faith, and to avoid excessive competition, insincere contracts, false/exaggerated advertising, overproduction of inferior goods, excessive profit, cornering the market, raids, and other malicious acts. Injustice and unfairness in international trade have existed since ancient times the world over, in some cases resulting in armed conflict.[13]

Shibusawa issued frequent messages about business morality. These can be summarized as: "Do not lie," and "Do not give priority to your own benefit." They contained spiritual arguments, the abstract principle of business morality, his answer to criticism about unfairness or injustice concerning trade imbalances, and concrete suggestions for creating a just and equal environment for trade in which both parties could be fully committed.

Criticism of Japanese products

As Janet Hunter details in Chapter 5, the unethical behaviour of Japanese merchants met with a great deal of criticism from foreign traders and newspapers after the opening of Japanese ports at the end of the Edo period. In particular, criticism concerned breaches of contract, the supply of defective or substandard products, and, more harmfully, false advertising and trademarks. If taken at face value, much of the criticism pointed out inexcusable problems for which the Japanese side was absolutely responsible in light of Shibusawa's view of business morality. This criticism posed a continual headache for Shibusawa, who had consistently emphasized the importance of morality in international trade since the first year of the Meiji period. In 1902, when the Anglo-Japanese alliance was concluded, Shibusawa made a second visit to Europe via the United States. Again he was bombarded with harsh criticism in both the United States and Britain concerning problems of quality and illegal acts involving Japanese products. He had never imagined this. It was a particular shock for him to be reprimanded by Britain, the country he respected for retaining a high level of business morality. As president of Dai-Ichi Bank and chairman of the Tokyo Chamber of Commerce, Shibusawa believed that the Japanese economy to some extent had become modernized. In fact, however, Japan had scarcely acquired a good reputation beyond its military strength. He learned that Japanese entrepreneurial activities still lagged far behind the standards of the international community. On his way home to Japan, he grew so exasperated that he found himself hating the sight of Westerners' faces.

The reputation for corrupt behaviour among Japanese businesspeople was greatly attributable to the fact that, since Japan had maintained a policy of national isolation since the early seventeenth century, the activities of its merchants had been limited to the domestic market and to contacts with the West at certain specified locations, including the islands of Dejima (Nagasaki), Tsushima, the Ryukyus, and Hokkaido. Japanese merchants were not blessed with opportunities to learn practical knowledge from resident foreign merchants like those of the East India Company because, unlike other Asian countries such as India and Indonesia, Japan luckily had escaped being colonized by Britain, the

Netherlands, or other Western powers. With no experience in transactions with Western countries, Japanese merchants had no knowledge of Western business customs. This made Japan unique among Asian countries. To make matters worse, differences in language and business customs seem to have amplified misunderstandings between both sides and to have contributed to the harsh criticism of Japan.[14]

The arrogance of foreign merchants

There were also problems, however, with foreign merchants, who tended to be arrogant and unwilling to understand Japanese business customs. From the end of the Edo period to the early Meiji period, illegal or unfair dealings by so-called *gaishō* (foreign merchants) were easily noticeable.[15] Having been closed from the outside for more than two hundred years, Japan had developed no shipping industry, marine insurance, or foreign exchange dealings to facilitate foreign trade when the country launched full scale into its industrialization and international trade. It also lacked legal preparations for international trade or a merchant organization to negotiate with the *gaishō*. As a result, Japanese merchants were charged exorbitant prices for imports, while the prices of their exports were hammered down.

An example is transactions of raw silk, a representative export of Japan, in Yokohama after its port was opened. The arrogance of foreign merchants became too much to tolerate. Since the foreign mercantile houses handled all aspects of exports, Japanese merchants were limited to selling the silk to the *gaishō* in their settlement. The *gaishō* did not even issue receipts or storage certificates for the products they received, so the Japanese merchants had no influence over how the silk was kept and shipped to overseas markets after it was sold. The products were transported to the warehouse in Yokohama and underwent simple inspection by the *gaishō*. If a quality problem occurred when a product was marketed overseas, the sales contract might be broken without notice and no money paid for the purchase. This happened quite often.

Without considering the problems that might have occurred at different points in the supply chain, *gaishō* and foreign newspapers criticized the poor quality of Japanese raw silk and the inconsistency of samples, which Japanese merchants, and Shibusawa, saw as unfair. Some raw silk merchants, including Arai Ryōichirō, started travelling to New York to conduct trade directly, rather than go through the *gaishō*.[16]

While admitting problems on the Japanese side, Shibusawa believed it was necessary to organize Japanese raw silk merchants to fight back against the injustice and high-handedness of the *gaishō*. He recommended that Dai-Ichi Bank, Dai-Ni Bank, and Mitsui Bank advance ¥5 million or more to help Yokohama-based raw silk merchants set up a *Rengo Niatsukaishō* (associated freight office), which would serve as a mechanism and opportunity for the conduct of normal trade transactions, a move that the foreign merchants in Yokohama opposed. Meanwhile, Japanese raw silk enjoyed steady demand overseas, and direct trade in New York was on the rise thanks to efforts by Arai and other Japanese merchants. In 1911 both the Anglo-Japanese Treaty of Commerce and Navigation and the Treaty of Commerce and Navigation between Japan and the United States were revised, and Japan obtained tariff autonomy. Thereafter, problems with the *gaishō* began to wind down.

Arguments in the Japanese media about business morality rapidly declined after the early 1920s as Japan gained more experience in international trade and more Japanese companies expanded their business to cities such as New York and London. Nevertheless, accusations of injustice and fraud concerning Japanese products never ceased overseas. Defending the Japanese for their sincerity, Shibusawa continued to insist that it was unreasonable to criticize all Japanese businesspeople for a lack of morals on the part of a few, but the issue remained of great concern among Japanese financial circles, authorities, and educators.

Trade imbalances: The search for fairness and justice

Shibusawa was devoted to increasing international economic transactions. At the turn of the twentieth century, he placed great importance on the development of economic relations between Japan and the United States, and in 1909 led a mission – called the Honorary Commercial Commissioners of Japan – of dozens of Japanese businesspeople to that country, which he expected would become Japan's most important partner. Besides knowledge about economics and business management, Shibusawa intended to make members of the mission learn more background information about politics, society, culture, education, and religion. The Japanese mission visited more than sixty US cities in a three-month period from September to the end of November 1909. Its aim was to replace the so-called unequal treaty concluded at the end of the Edo period with a more equitable treaty suitable for international trade in a time of advancing globalization. The mission, likened to a business version of the diplomatic Iwakura Mission of the early 1870s, was the largest-scale such effort Japan ever undertook.[17]

In many places they visited, the Japanese businesspeople heard voices of unexpectedly strong frustration by Americans about the trade imbalance between the two countries. Speeches by American businesspeople at welcome parties were often scathing on this issue, though they did not go so far as to ruin the party atmosphere. One speaker at a banquet organized by the Chicago Chamber of Commerce blamed the Japanese for caring only about selling their own products, in response to which Shibusawa said that the aim of the mission was to increase Japan's purchase of US products, not to expand outlets for Japanese products.[18] He also stressed the need to increase the overall amount of Japanese-US trade. During its subsequent visits to New York and Boston, the Japanese mission was bombarded with complaints about the poor quality of Japanese products, which were considerably inferior to samples. In this regard, the Americans' allegations were indisputable, and a great irritant for Shibusawa.

According to the memoir of Machida Tokunosuke, a member of the mission, some of the Japanese visitors were exasperated by the Americans' allegations.[19] One, Iwahara Kenzō, a board member of Mitsui, rebuked Shibusawa upon their return to Japan: "You said you heard the Americans say Japanese merchants are selfish, only care about selling Japanese products and couldn't care less about buying US products. I have heard nothing of the kind, and if I heard such complaints I would immediately refute them." Iwahara said the Americans, not the Japanese, were to blame, and the complaints typically came from a talentless bunch of Americans. If a product were to arrive from France or Britain and an American merchant intended to export it instead, the only thing he should do is to make a good product and sell it to Japan. According to Iwahara's logic, the American merchants needed to learn more about Japan.

In his memoir Machida statistically compared the two countries in terms of buying power, and concluded that the unfavourable US trade imbalance was unavoidable. Machida likened Shibusawa, Iwahara, and himself to the famous analogy in which Oda Nobunaga (Iwahara) would kill a little cuckoo if it did not sing, Toyotomi Hideyoshi (Machida) would employ any means to make the cuckoo sing, while Tokugawa Ieyasu (Shibusawa) would patiently wait until it sang. This episode speaks eloquently to the patience of Shibusawa, who tried to teach these hot-blooded Japanese businesspeople the meaning of the long-term and low-profile task of private economic diplomacy.

Mutual visits by Japanese and US missions identified further bilateral differences in their understanding of trade relations. The US argument was represented by Robert Dollar (1844–1932), president of the Dollar Steamship Company. Dollar argued that, although the United States bought many products from Japan, Japanese imports came largely from Britain and Germany, rather than from the United States. Dollar said Japan and the United States should respect reciprocity in order to maintain close and effective relations.[20] In other words, he sought to address the situation in which bilateral trade was too favourable to Japan and only played the role of a landing place of Japanese export goods for the market in the eastern United States.

For their part, Japanese businesspeople found Japanese-US trade attractive because it was one of the few transactions in which Japan enjoyed a surplus, and so they did not see the trade from the standpoint of "fairness" or "justice." Matsukata Kōjirō studied at Yale University before returning to Japan to become president of the Kawasaki Dockyard. He participated in the 1909 mission to the United States as chairman of the Kobe Chamber of Commerce. With his fluent English, he opposed the Americans' allegations: "US newspapers criticize Japan for buying few US products and buying European products more. So then why does our trade with the US Pacific coastal area, which is geographically much closer to Japan than Europe, remain stagnant? It would be easier for traders in this area to find products that satisfy demand in Japan." Matsukata attributed the biggest cause to ignorance on the part of both Japanese and Americans, concluding that the problem stemmed from the lack of market research by Japanese and American traders. He argued that, if Japanese and American businesspeople would learn more about one another through mutual interaction, bilateral trade would increase, and that the problem had nothing to do with unfairness or injustice.[21]

Shibusawa believed in the need for the United States and Japan to achieve trade balance, but admitted international trade would need a moderate amount of competition:

> Competition often starts with goodwill and ends with ill will. Neither side will be willing to conduct bad deeds at the start. Ultimately, performing a bad deed is because of competition for victory. Having said that, if the competition has dwindled to nil, people will become as cold as water and

will stop learning, causing advances and discoveries in the world to come to a stop. This would be an unwelcome phenomenon.

Competition is like the temperature of the human body. The temperature will either make a person live or kill him. Similarly, competition will either make a merchant live or kill him. Therefore, merchants must keep their *"normal temperature."*[22]

It is interesting to note that trade friction occurred between Japan and the United States from the 1960s to the 1990s over issues of fairness and justice, but the same debate had already occurred early in the twentieth century.

Offering opportunities for entrepreneurial efforts on a global scale

A positive aspect of business morality is creating an environment that supports entrepreneurial activities to facilitate economic transactions on a global scale, including efforts of businesspeople to improve international relations.

Business transactions, long-term investments, and permanent transactions require more than just economic advantage or technological strength; they also require a trust-based relationship among nations and within national organizations in a broader sense that might cover politics, the military, and society. In having this unique perspective, Shibusawa stood out among businesspeople in global society.

One can, of course, find many examples of global entrepreneurs' efforts to improve international relations. US railroad tycoon Edward Harriman concluded the Katsura-Harriman Agreement with the Japanese government in 1905 with the aim of constructing railroads in Manchuria in cooperation with Japan. Shibusawa proactively supported the move, but Komura Jyutarō, the Japanese foreign minister, annulled the agreement upon returning from Portsmouth, New Hampshire, after negotiating the treaty that ended the Russo-Japanese War. Yet Harriman's action was an attempt to improve relations among Japan, the United States, and China by going beyond private interests to build a global transportation network. Likewise Chinese entrepreneur and politician Zhang Jian (1853–1926), visiting Japan in 1903, was shocked by the National Industrial Exhibition in Osaka. After returning to China, he left the Qing government and, based in his hometown of Nantong, devote himself to his country's modernization. In 1915 Zhang went to San Francisco to attend the Panama-Pacific International Exposition commemorating the opening of the Panama Canal the previous year, and then went on to Washington, DC, to meet important people in US political and economic circles – including President Woodrow Wilson – in an effort to improve US-Chinese relations. Also, in the early twentieth century, diplomats such as Komura Jutarō and Kaneko Kentarō were well aware of the influence of public opinion on international relations, as seen in comments such as: "In the past, diplomacy was about relations between emperors or foreign ministers. In the twentieth century, the driving force of diplomacy lies between people. It is no longer something that ambitious politicians can handle alone."[23] These political figures asked the economic community to cooperate in efforts to settle the issue of Japanese immigrants in the United States.

Shibusawa himself long remained committed to the practice of proactive business morality on a much larger scale. He maintained he was a layperson at diplomacy, but he believed that diplomacy could be part of the business morality that private sector leaders should pursue in order to facilitate global entrepreneurial activities. With that role in mind, after turning age sixty, he accepted the Japanese government's requests to travel abroad, visiting the United States four times, Europe once, China once, and Korea several times in active efforts to improve their relations with Japan.[24] Such activities, Shibusawa believed, would help Japanese economic players obtain trust from other countries, thereby helping to enrich the Japanese economy and contributing to international peace.

Formation of a new order after the First World War

Shibusawa was among the first to regard the First World War as a great turning point, believing that, regardless of which side won, the Atlantic-oriented world would come to an end and that the United States, China, Japan, and the Pacific region would begin to play a larger part in international relations. He continued to explore what Japan needed to do to help realize peace and stability in the new world order. His actions, in fact, extended to many different spheres.

In 1914 Shibusawa visited China and met leading figures in Chinese political and financial circles, including President (and future emperor) Yuan Shikai, exchanging opinions on developing infrastructure for the Chinese economy and facilitating cooperation between Japanese and Chinese businesspeople. The Japanese government, however, regarded the war as an opportunity to expand Japan's interests in China and, applying military pressure, imposed on the Chinese government the so-called Twenty-One Demands, which worsened impressions of Japan in both China and the United States.

Shibusawa was sure that the war, which was being waged on an unprecedented scale, would significantly change financial circles as well as commerce and industry around the world. Like Zhang Jian, in 1915 he went to San Francisco to attend the Panama-Pacific International Exposition, and then travelled to the East Coast and met President Wilson and other important people in US political and financial circles. Shortly after the end of the war, the economic boom in Japan was replaced by a post-war depression. The *narikin* (instant rich) who had prospered during the war went bankrupt, and economic circles were pressed with survival issues. At the Paris Peace Conference in 1919, the Japanese delegation was infamously labelled a silent partner uninterested in international order and as speaking only about its own interests. As a consequence, the new international economic order was built mostly around Europe and the United States.

Shibusawa feared that Japan was failing to catch up with trends in global society and that it was also moving in the wrong direction in terms of proactive business morality. Instead of Japan's being one of the Big Five after the war, its politicians, bureaucrats, and military personnel could no longer be counted on to develop an international order to ensure peace, prosperity, and stability. Japan's financial community also faced the need to discover new sources of wealth and to foster the development of the international economy. To this end Shibusawa worked to establish a private organization to explore the future of Japanese society, while involving himself in international trends through the *Kokusai Renmei Kyōkai* (League of Nations Association of Japan), the *Nichi-Bei Kankei Iinkai* (standing committee on Japanese-American relations), the *Kiitsu Kyōkai* (organization for facilitating mutual understanding and cooperation among religious personnel), and the *Kyōchō-kai* (cooperation society), among others.

To solidify the economy's base, Shibusawa focused his efforts on how to handle the post-war depression, which hit Japan after a sharp decline in the Tokyo and Osaka Stock Exchanges in mid-March 1920. In early April, Masuda Bill Broker, a bank that sold bills, went out of business, triggering a great crash in the stock and commodity markets. Turmoil continued, and the wave of depression rapidly spread nationwide. The situation became even more serious in May when Mogi Shoten, a representative raw silk merchant in Yokohama, and its main bank, Shichijushi Bank, went bankrupt. Further corporate bankruptcies and bank runs occurred in succession.

Shibusawa felt that the first thing the government had to do was normalize the economy, whose growth had already reached maturity during the war, and to establish a macroeconomic policy for continued growth. In the short term this meant dispelling financial unrest; in the longer term the enormous military spending had to be reduced since it posed a heavy burden on the Japanese economy. At the same time, Japanese companies had to become more competitive internationally in order to survive the severe competition that was expected to follow the reconstruction of the European economy. Shibusawa therefore welcomed the naval disarmament conference held in Washington in 1921–22, which he attended as an observer. He was convinced that the treaty among the three major naval powers of Japan, the United States, and Britain would contribute to the health of the Japanese economy.

Shibusawa's view of proactive business morality also could often be seen in philanthropy. It is noteworthy that Shibusawa encouraged the moral behaviour of businesspeople in the aftermath of a great disaster. When a magnitude-8.3 earthquake devastated San Francisco in 1906, Shibusawa and other leaders of Japanese financial circles met at the Japan Red Cross office to discuss relief measures. At first many of the attendees opposed or were hesitant about making donations to the affected area, for several reasons: San Francisco was at the centre of the movement to ostracize Japanese immigrants; it was unprecedented for private companies to spend money for a public purpose; and it would be difficult in terms of corporate accounting to handle donations. Shibusawa, however, turned the tide at the meeting by remarking that it should be taken for granted that the business community would spend money generously in times of an urgent and public cause that might concern the fate of the nation. He offered to donate ¥10,000 from Dai-Ichi Bank, which he headed, and further donations were then efficiently collected; ultimately, the sum of ¥170,000 was sent to San Francisco. The United States later reciprocated for Japan's quick action in the form of huge support after the Great Kanto earthquake that struck Japan in 1923. US bankers purchased Tokyo's city bonds, and supplies of food, construction materials, and other necessities to the affected area ensured quick reconstruction.

Shibusawa's Business Morality Lives on in the Twenty-first Century

With the end of the Cold War, capitalism based on a market economy has expanded globally and many emerging economies, notably that of China, are enjoying rapid economic growth. However, Shibusawa Eiichi's views on business morality and its activities still offer important lessons in three areas.

The first concerns the emerging economies. Shibusawa attempted to encourage economic growth in the newly rising nation of Japan by positioning private banks at the centre of *gapponshugi*, improving the monetary system, stabilizing the value of the currency, and facilitating supply. In creating an economic community to change the balance of power in Japanese society, he successfully used Confucianism, the traditional moral base for disciplining leaders of different circles, to change values and morality in business. Under the strict class system in effect during the Edo period, it took a long time for disdain for commercial activities to disappear and for the status of businesspeople to rise. In the early twentieth century, from the end of the Meiji period to the Taisho period, almost all of Shibusawa's efforts were successful. For instance, Kodama Gentarō, the army's vice-chief of staff, visited Shibusawa around 1903 to ask for full-scale cooperation from financial circles for war with Russia, whose outbreak seemed inevitable. This episode was an indication of the recognition economic circles had gained, and of the role Japanese businesspeople were beginning to play in policymaking that would determine Japan's fate. Shibusawa's efforts thus might serve as a useful reference for today's emerging economies in their attempts to counter corruption and narrow the expanding gap between rich and poor. Success in these areas would result from a comfortable relationship between the government and the people, especially between the military and entrepreneurs.

Shibusawa's views also offer lessons for halting today's excessive penchant for finance capitalism, as pointed out by Ronald Dore, a British sociologist well-versed in Japan.[25] Contemporary finance capitalism is overconfident in the market mechanism that is manipulated by the "invisible hand," and leans excessively towards self-interest, resulting in "bubbles" and expanding the gap between rich and poor. Even worse, finance capitalism intrinsically involves the risk of cyclic global depressions as a consequence of bubble collapses. In contrast Shibusawa's *gapponshugi*, where each player is identifiable, can be expected to halt the abuse of finance capitalism by incorporating business morality into the capitalist model.

Lastly, proactive business morality offers a lesson for countries such as China and Japan. In 2010 China took over the world's number-two ranking in gross domestic product from Japan, while Japan has been ridiculed for having "two lost decades." When the Immigration Act of

1924 went through the US Congress, Nitobe Inazō and many other pro-American people in Japanese political, financial, and scholarly circles expressed antipathy towards the United States. Shibusawa remained calm, however, because he placed so much importance on Japanese-US relations, and gave a thought-provoking speech: "No matter what happens, justice always prevails. A good number of Americans sympathize with Japan from the standpoint of fairness, justice, and humanity. These correct public opinions will find themselves embodied in the future. I wish for this to come true as soon as possible." Shibusawa also apprehended the situation within his own country:

> In the face of this domestic and international predicament, Japanese people must be committed to improving national strength. Without national strength, the rest of the world will take us lightly. Domestically, however, politicians are too busy engaging in internal strife to turn their eyes to international issues. Businesspeople are also so preoccupied with trifling disputes that they fail to keep sight of the big picture. The room for business collaboration is vast, whether it is by a steamship line, bank, spinning industry, electric company, or sugar company. If you put aside personal or corporate interests and personal feelings, and are sincerely committed to the lofty cause of national society, business collaboration will be amply possible, though it will entail a degree of difficulty ... Needless to say, today a nation, not a group or a village, should be regarded as a unit. The world should be a single community. In this regard, I want each of the Japanese people to cultivate his or her character as a global citizen and to endeavour to turn the crisis into an advantage.[26]

Shibusawa's views of business morality are imperative for organizing *gappon-soshiki* or *gappon-kaisha*. He stayed true to the ideal in his activities as an international entrepreneur. Businesspeople represent private citizens and act for the benefit of the nation. At the centre of the nation, however, is its people, who need to think of the whole world becoming a community, instead of confining themselves to the narrow perspective of caring only about their own country. Shibusawa, in short, wanted his fellow countrymen to cultivate their character as global citizens. As globalization continues to advance, many countries have adopted the capitalist economic system based on a market economy. Corporate activities and interactions among financial circles are widespread. Today we have a great deal to learn from Shibusawa Eiichi's views on business morality.

NOTES

1 For details about Flüry-Hérard, see Kashima Shigeru, *Shibusawa Eiichi I: Sorobanhen* [Shibusawa Eiichi I: Abacus] (Tokyo: Bungeishunju, 2011).

2 Shōhō Kaisho undertook loans for product mortgages, the management of term deposits in current accounts, and the purchase and sale of rice fertilizer and other materials, among others. *Shōhō Kaisho*'s activities were funded by *kokudaka haishakukin*, a loan payable by the Shizuoka Domain to the new government.

3 Ryūmonsha, ed., *Shibusawa Eiichi denki shiryō* [Shibusawa Eiichi biographical materials], vol. 5, *Koen/Danwa* [Lecture and discourse] (Tokyo: Shibusawa Eiichi denki shiryō kankōkai, 1968), 2–3.

4 Kikkawa Takeo, Shimada Masakazu, and Tanaka Kazuhiro, eds., *Shibusawa Eiichi to hitozukuri* [Shibusawa Eiichi and development of human resources] (Tokyo: Yuhikaku Publishing, 2013).

5 Nihon Ginko hyakunenshi hensan'iinkai, ed., *Nihon Ginko hyakunen shi* [100-year history of the Bank of Japan], vol. 1 (Tokyo: Nihon Ginko, 1982), 3–31.

6 Shibusawa Hideo, *Shibusawa Eiichi* (Tokyo: Shibusawa Seien Kinen Zaidan Ryūmonsha, 1956), 79–80.

7 Ryūmonsha, *Shibusawa Eiichi denki shiryō*, vol. 5, 103.

8 The word *takuzen,* quoted by Shibusawa from the Analects of Confucius, means "lead the way and follow the good." After Shibusawa became chairman of the Tokyo Chamber of Commerce, Takuzen-kai met monthly at the chamber's building.

9 For details about the incident of Ishii Sadashichi, see Arisawa Hiromi, ed., *Showa keizaishi* [Economic history of the Showa period] (Tokyo: Nikkei, 1994); and Miyamoto Mataji, *Osaka shōnin taiheiki Taishōhen jō* [Record of Osaka-based merchants in the Taisho period, part I] (Tokyo: Sogensha, 1964), 190, 204–210.

10 Shibusawa Eiichi, *Amayogatari: Shibusawa Eiichi jiden* [The autobiography of Shibusawa Eiichi], annotated by Chō Yukio (Tokyo: Iwanami Shoten, 1984), 25–8.

11 Odaka Jyunchū (1830–1901) was a cousin of Shibusawa Eiichi and an older brother of Eiichi's wife, Chiyo.

12 *Mitogaku* developed during the nineteenth century in Mito, where the vice-Tokugawa shogun lived during the Edo period.

13 Injustice and unfairness in trade were part of the cause of wars between England (later, Britain) and both Holland and Spain during the seventeenth and eighteenth centuries.

14 Nakagawa Keiichirō, "Nihon no kōgyōka katei ni okeru soshikika sareta kigyōka katsudō" [Organized entrepreneurship in process of Japan's industrialization], *Keieishigaku* [Japan Business History Review] 2, no. 3 (1967): 13–14.

15 For details about incidents involving the injustice of foreign merchants, see Kanno Watarō, *Zoku Osaka keizaishi kenkyū* [Sequel to the study on economic history of Osaka] (Tokyo: Seibundo Shuppan, [1935] 1982), chap. 1.

16 For details about Arai Ryōichirō and other Japanese businesspeople who travelled to New York, see Sakata Yasuo, *Kokusai businessman-no tanjō: Nichibei keizaikankei no kaitakusha* [Emergence of international businesspeople: Pioneers of Japan-US economic relations] (Tokyo: Tokyodo Shuppan, 2009).

17 For details about the Honorary Commercial Commissioners of Japan, see Shibusawa Memorial Museum, ed., *Shibusawa Eiichi America e iku: Hyakunen mae no minkan keizai gaikō* [Shibusawa Eiichi goes to the United States: Private economic diplomacy of 100 years ago] (Tokyo: Shibusawa Memorial Museum, 2009); and Kimura Masato, *Nichibei minkan keizai gaikō 1905–1911* [Japan-US private economic diplomacy: 1905–1911] (Tokyo: Keio Tsushin, 1989).

18 *Chicago Tribune*, 28 September 1909.

19 *Kōden Machida Tokunosuke ō* [Story told by the venerable Machida Tokunosuke], draft in the possession of Machida Jiro, 1924.

20 Robert Dollar, Address to the Japanese Commissioners at the reception in the Merchants Exchange, November 1909 (Online Archive of California, University of California, Berkeley, Bancroft Library, Robert Dollar Papers, carton 5, 70/114). Based on reciprocity, businesspeople on the US Pacific Coast, represented by Dollar, demanded that Japan import more US products.

21 Matsukata Kōjirō, Speech at a luncheon party onboard SS *Saikyō Maru* in honour of the visit of the Honorary Commercial Commissioners representing Chambers of Commerce of the Pacific Coast of the USA, 1 November 1908 (Robert Dollar Papers, carton 6, 69/113).

22 Shibusawa Eiichi, "The Analects and the Abacus," in *Modern Japanese*, trans. Moriya Atsushi (Tokyo: Chikumashobo, 2010), emphasis added.

23 Speech by Kaneko Kentarō in Fuken Rengō Kyōshinkai [local exposition of the western part of Japan] held at Aichi Kenkai Gijidō [conference hall of Aichi Prefectural Assembly], 1909, *Chūō Ginkō tsūshinroku* [Record of communications of the Central Bank], no. 62, 1909, 13.

24 For details about Shibusawa's private economic diplomacy, see Kimura Masato, *Shibusawa Eiichi: Minkan keizai gaikō-no sōshisha* [Shibusawa Eiichi: Pioneer of private economic diplomacy] (Tokyo: Chuokoron-Sha, 1991).

25 For more on Dore and finance capitalism, see Kikkawa Takeo, Chapter 8 in this volume.

26 Shibusawa Eiichi, *Shibusawa Eiichi jijyoden* [Autobiography of Shibusawa Eiichi] (Tokyo: Ijin Resshiden Hensanjo, 1937), 944–5.

7 *Gapponshugi* in Global Perspective: Debating the Responsibility of Capitalism

GEOFFREY JONES

Since the nineteenth century, business leaders such as Shibusawa Eiichi in Japan and his counterparts in the United States, Europe, and elsewhere have talked about the responsibility of business beyond making profits, although until recently such discourse had not received mainstream attention. In the pages that follow, I argue that four factors have driven such debate: spirituality, self-interest, fears of government intervention, and the belief that governments are incapable of addressing major social issues.

The global significance of *gapponshugi* can be found on several dimensions. Shibusawa can be considered one of the pioneer thinkers about the challenges of realizing the public good by accumulating private wealth. He laid out the issues, and suggested the solutions, which are still relevant and being debated today. He made his arguments in a secular fashion, whereas until recently others relied on the overwhelming priority of the interests of their deity to support the case. Finally, his intellectual contribution was undertaken while he was a highly successful business practitioner, creator of the modern Japanese banking system, and founder of nearly five hundred companies.

Shibusawa's evolving insights on the potential for private wealth to contribute to the public good form an important component of a discussion that has featured in many national contexts, both during and after his lifetime. His insistence that morality and economy are consistent with each other and that capitalism could be ethical – and has a responsibility to be ethical – has been echoed in quite different societies than Meiji Japan. However, the issues are complex, and debates on the responsibility of capitalism have continued to the present day.

Shibusawa's concepts were formulated and expressed within his own time and place, even though he was an international traveller who was well aware of, and interacted with, discourses beyond Japan. In this chapter I seek to place his ideas within a broader global historical context extending from the nineteenth century until the present day. I survey both the evolving arguments about the responsibility of business and the changing practices of firms. The chapter is interpretative, rather than comprehensive. I aim to map the terrain, and so to provide a stronger basis for identifying the distinctiveness of Shibusawa's contribution and insights.

The Era of Shibusawa Eiichi, 1840–1931

As capitalism emerged in the Western world, it had an ambiguous relationship with the social values of the dominant religion, Christianity. Famously, the German sociologist Max Weber associated the advent of modern capitalism with the Reformation in the sixteenth century, arguing that the ascetic, rational, and individualist nature of Lutheran and Calvinist beliefs set them apart from Catholic and Orthodox Christianity and shaped behaviour. He identified the "Protestant work ethic" as creating persons who worked hard, were frugal, and strove for success as proof of personal faith. In other words, it shaped entrepreneurs whose values were aligned with "the spirit of capitalism."[1]

Weber set off a famous debate among historians about the cultural basis of entrepreneurial success that has continued until the present day, but this debate has also overshadowed other issues concerning Christianity and the morality of capitalism. In the Gospel of Luke in the New Testament, Jesus is recorded as saying that "it is easier for a camel to go through a needle's eye, than for a rich man to enter the kingdom of God." This hardly provides a compelling incentive to engage in capitalist endeavours. Medieval European societies struggled with the tension between riches and religion, but the tension did not go away as the modern world emerged. In 1776 Adam Smith, in *The Wealth of Nations*, argued that the market was value-neutral, and that its invisible hand promoted the public good out of private self-interest. He considered the science of economics "the great antidote to the poison of enthusiasm and superstition."[2] There was, however, far from a consensus in Western society that business and economic affairs were no concern of God. Indeed Thomas Malthus, a Christian minister, in *An Essay on the Principle of Population*, published in 1798, put God and morality in a central place in political economy.

As the Industrial Revolution took hold during the eighteenth century, the institutionalization of economic activity in the form of firms expanded. The concept of the corporation as a legal person separate from its owners was an invention of Western societies, originating in Roman law during the first two centuries AD, developing during the Middle Ages in both Church and civil law, and further codified by the British and American common law tradition.[3] The role and responsibilities of such corporations was less clear. At first the family ownership of almost all corporations blurred the issue. The personal values of founders and owners were expressed in their firms. The Christian values of founders helped shape a wider societal role for firms in the form of industrial paternalism and welfare capitalism. In Britain a succession of entrepreneurs, from Josiah Wedgwood in the eighteenth-century pottery industry to George Cadbury and William Lever in the late nineteenth-century chocolate and soap industries, provided houses, villages, and health and recreational facilities for their workers. Self-interest coexisted with religious concerns in these endeavours, as entrepreneurs sought to build loyal and stable workforces inculcated with the values of industrial capitalism. Economics also mattered: firms in especially favourable market positions, including Lever and Cadbury, offered extended welfare benefits; most large British firms did not.[4]

Mixed motives are evident in the literature on nineteenth-century paternalism, both in Britain and the United States.[5] Lever built an exemplary model industrial village for his employees at Port Sunlight, outside Liverpool, in 1888. To counter the threat of socialism, however, and in a blatant strategy to keep ideological dissent under control, he also appointed a Wesleyan minister as the company's welfare officer and minister at the church he had built in 1904. In an extraordinary departure from convention, he even confined membership of his church to his employees.[6] The Quaker George Cadbury, who built the new garden village of Bournville around a new chocolate factory four miles outside the crowded industrial city of Birmingham, seemed to go above and beyond concerns to build a stable and docile workforce. In 1900 he even donated the village to a separate trust. Six years later Cadbury articulated his "theory of giving": "Begin at home with your work people, see to their comfort, health ... See that your workshops are light and well-ventilated ... give your people the advantage of living where there is plenty of space. This was our main object in removing from Birmingham into the country. It was morally right and proved financially to be a success, because the business had room to expand."[7] The balance between morality and profits can be debated as much in the Cadbury case as in others, but the evidence of strong religious views driving an agenda concerning responsibility is strong. As Charles Dellheim has observed, "the Quaker business ethic legitimized but also tempered capitalism by defining the proper means and ends of business."[8]

Debates about the motives of the American "corporate paternalists" of the nineteenth and early twentieth centuries in using some of their wealth to support philanthropic ventures and engaging in sophisticated urban and social planning are similar to debates in Britain. The prominent examples of welfare capitalism – including the Houghton family, which built the Corning glass company in upstate New York; the Hershey chocolate company in Pennsylvania; and George Pullman, the railcar manufacturer, who built a large town for his workers outside Chicago in 1880 – are well-known figures in US business history. Company towns became a feature of the American industrial landscape as the century progressed, although, as Hardy Green has suggested, they fell into two types: ostensibly, at least, paternalistic, and downright exploitative of the workers who lived there.[9]

A major difference between the United States and Europe was the growing scale of US business, as well as the enormous wealth of successful business leaders such as Andrew Carnegie and John D. Rockefeller. There was plenty of criticism of the abuse of power by "trusts" such as Rockefeller's Standard Oil, but size also stimulated thoughts about responsibility. "I was taught," Henry J. Heinz, the founder of the Heinz Company, wrote, "that a certain responsibility goes with any large business affecting many people."[10]

Scottish-born Andrew Carnegie, who built a huge steel business in the United States, took the concept of charity to the next level. Believing that "hoarding millions is avarice, not thrift," he went beyond offering his workers good conditions and guaranteed employment to propose what he termed *The Gospel of Wealth*. Carnegie insisted that entrepreneurs had a responsibility to use their wealth to promote social good – not by leaving money to their families, but by funding public institutions such as schools and libraries that would further opportunity for others. Carnegie gave away almost all of his personal fortune of $10 billion (in today's dollars), and established the framework of modern American philanthropy by establishing the Carnegie Foundation in

1911, beginning "the art of spending money for the common good."[11] The foundation was a new form of institution designed to administer large resources and deliver them to multiple recipients. Carnegie had been distressed by sectarian divisions in Scotland, and initially showed little interest in religious matters, but by the time he began his large philanthropic projects, he had become an active Presbyterian. Among his first big projects was giving thousands of organs to churches.[12]

Carnegie initiated a distinctly American view of the responsibility of business leaders: if they made a lot of money, they should give it away to promote the public good. This reflected the idiosyncratic American system, which was at once highly individualistic, yet had a strong sense of community, and which was committed to profit-making, yet believed in social justice. Oliver Zunz has provided an excellent history of American-style philanthropy, which need not be repeated in detail here. The Rockefeller Foundation was created in 1913, six years after Shibusawa publicly criticized John D. Rockefeller for holding on to his wealth and not returning it to society. Between 1915 and 1930 the number of foundations in the United States grew from seventy-seven to two hundred.[13] During the 1920s the Guggenheims almost single-handedly funded the growth of American aviation before later turning their attention to museums and art. In 1936 the Ford Foundation was created. In 1944 the hotelier Conrad Hilton established his foundation to "relieve the suffering, the distressed, and the destitute." There were strong religious beliefs behind many of these figures: the Rockefellers were Baptists, the Guggenheims Jewish, and Hilton a fervent Roman Catholic. Bill Gates, Warren Buffet, George Kaiser, and the Walton family are among the American business leaders who have continued this distinctive tradition until the present day. A key insight of Zunz is that American philanthropy from Carnegie onward evolved from helping the poor to an investment in shaping the future. "Individual Americans return to society some monetary gain," he writes, "with the motivation that it might benefit them in the long run."[14]

Although the view that philanthropy is a responsibility of business has proved immensely important in the United States, by the late nineteenth century there was discussion of other responsibilities. These included responsibility for the natural environment, although this would not become a major concern until much later. By the late nineteenth century, industrial pollution in major US cities such as Chicago and St. Louis was so evident that it encouraged a handful of business leaders to organize to persuade the business community to seek ways to control it voluntarily.[15] A handful of "health reformers" also sought to address concerns about food adulteration, the potential harmful effects of growing sugar consumption, and the use of chemicals to grow crops. Among these entrepreneurs was Dr. John Harvey Kellogg, the inventor of the now famous Kellogg's Cornflakes.[16]

Another responsibility for business appeared during the nineteenth century: patriotism. There was plenty of jingoistic patriotism by business in both Britain and the United States, but it was really in the new nation-states that a powerful rhetoric emerged that business had a responsibility for nation-building. It was the entrepreneurs of Meiji Japan who famously, or infamously, found themselves characterized by Gustav Ranis in 1955 as "community-centered," or willing to pursue nation-building even if it were not a profit-maximizing endeavour. This provoked a famous historiographical debate, with Yamamura Kōzō publishing a debunking of this argument thirteen years later.[17] It is apparent that the key entrepreneurs of the time understood the nature of the threat to Japan posed by the West, and saw themselves playing their part in resisting this threat. It is equally implausible to believe that private entrepreneurs made a practice of pursuing patriotic goals without any regard to their profitability. Wrapping oneself in the national flag was, and is, a rhetorical strategy for entrepreneurs that can only bring benefits and seldom has a downside, unless the flag is besmirched by a wicked government. Shibusawa's own position was somewhat restrained, in support of the country's war effort against Russia during the early 1900s, as well as of the Japanese occupation of Korea and Taiwan, yet later resisting the military's ambitions in China.

The feeling of the patriotic responsibility of entrepreneurs is also evident among important German entrepreneurs in the nineteenth century. For example, Werner Siemens, the famous entrepreneur in the electrical industry, was born in 1816 into a highly fragmented political entity still known as the Holy Roman Empire. He recorded in his memoirs that he inherited from his father a commitment to national unity that led to his early career in the army. "The hope and confidence of a united Germany emerging from Prussia," he wrote, "was one of the decisive factors to enter the Prussian military service in the first place."[18] After the Austro-Prussian War of 1866, Siemens abandoned his earlier liberal views to become an active nationalist supporting Bismarck's mission to unify the country.[19] These sentiments did not mean that Siemens, an astute entrepreneur as well as inventor, pursued business opportunities for primarily patriotic purposes, but such feelings certainly shaped his outlook and motivation.

The Great Depression and Its Aftermath

During the years following the First World War, the emergence of management as a profession took hold. In the United States the creation of business schools attached to prestigious colleges and universities such as Columbia, Harvard, and Dartmouth led to a push to make management a profession on par with law or medicine.[20] This was a particular concern of Wallace Donham, a lawyer who became dean of the Harvard Business School in 1919 and who strove to make the school as prestigious as the longer-established Harvard Law School. He was concerned to develop a code of ethics for managers, and spoke on multiple occasions about the broader responsibilities of business.[21] In 1927 Donham wrote in the *Harvard Business School Alumni Bulletin*: "Unless more of our business leaders learn to exercise their powers and responsibilities with a definitely increased sense of responsibility toward other groups in the community ... our civilization may well head for one of its periods of decline."[22]

The Great Depression, and the consequent public criticism of Wall Street and of unfettered capitalism more generally, prompted extensive discussion about the responsibility of managers. Donham's ideas evolved further. In 1933 he published a widely cited article in the *Harvard Business Review* in which he maintained that business had the responsibility to be ethical, and warned that, if it were not, governments would impose unwise and unnecessary laws on it. He wrote:

> The solution of problems of business ethics, the task of learning how to conduct business so as to add to general security and happiness, must be undertaken primarily by business leaders. Their object must be to do the job so well that the law and the policeman are unnecessary.... All business practices which put too great strains on human nature must be considered unethical, and men must be rated by their fellows less for their ability to appropriate economic power and for the success in accumulating dollars and more for their social imagination and institutional far-sightedness.[23]

During the 1930s, within the context of Franklin D. Roosevelt's New Deal, there was extensive debate on the responsibility of business. In 1932 Adolph Berle, a corporate lawyer who became an adviser to

Roosevelt, co-authored with Gardiner Means *The Modern Corporation and Private Property*.[24] This landmark study laid out the problems of separating ownership and control in large modern corporations. A key (although subsequently overlooked) component of the argument was that the growth of professional managers had broken what Berle considered the historic link between capitalism and social and moral responsibilities to the societies in which firms were based. Berle's view of what had transpired in the past mighty not have been historically accurate, but it is evident that the emergence of limited liability and the joint-stock company proved a considerable challenge for business leaders who sought to combine wealth accumulation with a wider societal role. As their companies went public, managers assumed a fiduciary responsibility to shareholders and the creation of shareholder value.

Berle's solutions were regulatory and legal. He designed a new Securities and Exchange Act to force disclosure of corporate information to make managers more responsive to the social good. During the 1930s Berle debated with the Harvard Law Professor E. Merrick Dodd, who argued that it should be formally recognized that large corporations were social institutions that had responsibilities to numerous stakeholders beyond shareholders. Berle was less confident that managers would ever be fit to exercise such responsibilities, and called for formal government regulation to oblige them to meet broader responsibilities.[25]

There were also important regulatory and institutional developments to facilitate corporate giving in the United States. In 1917 US law was changed to permit individuals to deduct charitable donations from their income tax. The primary motivation was to encourage gifts for charities related to the war effort. It was contested, however, whether corporations could make charitable donations, but the 1935 Revenue Act permitted corporations to deduct charitable donations from tax, and corporate donations rose sharply thereafter. A number of intermediate organizations also emerged that were crucial to corporate philanthropy. In particular the Young Men's Christian Association pioneered methods of fundraising from corporations between 1905 and 1916.[26]

There were echoes of American debates on corporate responsibility in many other Western countries, although they were framed within their distinctive cultures, traditions, and political systems. In Britain churches continued to play a role in making the case for the ethical responsibility of business. A 1918 report by the Church of England noted: "Christianity claims to offer mankind a body of moral teaching which not only is binding upon individuals in their personal and domestic conduct but also supplies a criterion by which to judge their economic activity, their industrial organization, and their social institutions." A book written by a post office executive and published by the Student Christian Movement in 1922 described a new generation of managers who "may provide a priesthood in industry, just as there is a priesthood in worship."[27] As in the United States, there was much discussion of the professionalization of management. Quaker business families such as Rowntree and Cadbury were especially important in the so-called management movement. The former company produced three of the most important writers of those years: Seebohn Rowntree, Oliver Sheldon, and Lyndall Urwick.[28] Chapter 3 of Sheldon's *The Philosophy of Management*, published in 1923, entitled "The Social Responsibility of Management," discussed in detail the responsibilities of business to the well-being of their broader communities and to maintaining high ethical standards.[29]

Meanwhile, beyond debates on societal responsibilities, some American business leaders saw their responsibilities extending to international diplomacy. Among the more famous examples were Henry Ford's Peace Ship during the First World War and the efforts by T.J. Watson, the chief executive of IBM, to head off mounting tensions in Europe in the late 1930s. In 1937 Watson, who was also president of the International Chamber of Commerce, arranged a personal meeting with Adolf Hitler to discourage him from planning another war. Watson was rewarded by Hitler's promise that there would be no war, as well as a special Nazi medal decorated with swastikas. As is well-known, Watson had no more success than Ford – who received a similar medal from the Nazi regime – and after the German invasion of France in 1940 returned his medal.[30]

Beyond the West

There were few parallels in the non-Western world to the precocious modernization seen in Meiji Japan that had stimulated Shibusawa to consider the responsibility of capitalism. The most substantive development in the late nineteenth century was in the southern cone of Latin America – especially Argentina, where substantial industrialization in processing and consumer goods manufacturing occurred. There is no evidence, however, that the large business groups which emerged, such as Tornquist and Bunge, articulated views on the responsibility of capitalism. They were highly cosmopolitan, with strong connections to financial and banking groups in Belgium and Germany in particular, and had limited sense of a national identity that, in Argentina's case, was still being formed. They were also heavily dependent on concessions and favours from the political elites who ran the governments of socially stratified countries such as Argentina. The primary motivation of the business groups of this era was the enrichment of the controlling families and their allies.

In China the new business leaders who began to develop manufacturing and other businesses from the late nineteenth century onward did sometimes pursue wider social and cultural roles, especially in their local cities and regions, although, as in the case of US and British corporate paternalism discussed above, it would be wrong to interpret their motivation as altruistic in a very idealist sense. The case of Zhang Jian (1853–1926), who founded and began building the Dasheng Cotton Mill in Nantong into a diversified business group, has been researched in detail. Zhang Jian invested extensively in educational, welfare, and cultural facilities in Nantong in an extensive program aimed at the modernization of a formerly backward area. It is also evident, however, that Zhang Jian was well aware that these activities would improve his social status and increase his influence. He carefully handled his favourable image in local newspapers, while reducing his actual financial commitments by charging for schools and libraries he founded, often handing over facilities his family founded to the local government.[31]

Within Asia, however, the closest parallel to Japan in terms of both its modern economic development and in discourse on the responsibilities of business was British India. In the middle of the nineteenth century a locally owned modern cotton textile industry had emerged around Bombay (Mumbai). The owners were Parsi families such as Tata, with whom Shibusawa had a close business relationship due to cotton trading. They developed close relationships with the British administration and performed a quasi-intermediary role.[32] The Tata family, moreover, was also an early advocate of the responsibilities of business. "In a free enterprise," the group's founder Jamsetji Tata (1839–1904) noted, "the community is not just another stake holder in the business but in fact the very purpose of its existence."[33] The Tata group developed a distinctive corporate culture characterized by the concept of service to the wider community and high ethical standards that persisted through the twentieth century.

It was also in India that a more radical view of corporate responsibility emerged. During the First World War a new wave of industrial entrepreneurship emerged from the small Marwari community.[34] This group, which has continued to dominate Indian business to this day, is often associated with sharp business practices and little concern for societal matters. Alternative perspectives, however, have also emerged. Jamnalal Bajaj, a Marwari trader and manufacturer, bankrolled Gandhi's independence struggle against British colonial rule, but his contribution to Gandhi's campaign extended well beyond providing financial resources. He and his family, including his wife, took part in demonstrations and passive resistance against the British, and found themselves jailed for long periods as a result. Bajaj articulated the view that business had a patriotic duty to serve India and free it from British domination. The campaign against the British, however, was not the most radical element of Bajaj's views. Following Gandhi, Bajaj affirmed a trustee model of capitalism, emphasizing the responsibilities of firms to all stakeholders as well as the adoption of the highest ethical standards. He gave away most his own personal wealth to charitable causes. Bajaj and his family pursued an ambitious social agenda focused on addressing the needs of the disenfranchised in society, especially the Untouchables and women, as well as rural development and environmental sustainability. In 1928 he opened the doors of his family temple at Wardha to all, including Untouchables, becoming the first temple in India to welcome them. Later in his life, which ended prematurely in 1942 following a long bout of imprisonment, he became an active animal rights campaigner, especially for the rights of the cow. Like many Hindus, he was a strict vegetarian.[35]

Like the Quaker Cadbury and Rowntree families, which strictly avoided businesses related to war out of their pacifist convictions, Bajaj insisted that it mattered how business made profits as well as how funds were used. During the 1930s he refused to follow his peers in diversifying beyond sugar refining into the lucrative business of alcoholic drinks because Gandhi forbade consumption of alcohol. Bajaj's belief that the use of handmade cloth was essential to solving the poverty of the Indian countryside and providing employment opportunities for rural women to facilitate their emancipation also led him to avoid textile manufacturing.[36] The Bajaj companies flourished after Indian Independence in 1947. They are still one of India's largest business groups, and remain noteworthy for their high ethical standards.

The Post-war Decades

The Second World War saw a dramatic improvement in the reputation of big business in the United States, which played an essential role in the Allied victory. The corporations themselves invested heavily in reinforcing this improved public image.[37] Berle (among others) hailed US corporations for accepting that they had a wide range of social and other responsibilities.[38] The new dean of the Harvard Business School, Donald K. David, insisted that business needed to expand its wider role in American society. In 1946 he called for firms to move beyond serving shareholders to acknowledge the "public responsibilities of enterprise."[39] Three years later, in a landmark article in the *Harvard Business Review*, he insisted that American business had a responsibility to show it was a superior system to Russian-style socialism. This meant avoiding a narrow focus on profits and, among other things, treating employees fairly, combatting racial discrimination, and assisting the development of poorer countries.[40]

There remained a significant religious dimension to discourses on business responsibility. In 1953 the National Council of Churches, an interfaith organization, funded a book by Howard Bowen called *Social Responsibilities of the Businessman*. Bowen identified the many stakeholders in a business, and argued that managers needed to serve all of them. Firms made "commercial goods and services," but, Bowen maintained, they also affected the conditions in which such goods were made, including providing employment, the natural environment, and marketing and advertising practices, and managers also had responsibility for these "social products."[41]

During the same era, large US businesses ramped up their corporate philanthropy. These were prosperous and confident years for such corporations, which dominated innovation and led the world in high-tech industries. During the 1950s General Electric invested heavily in social programs in local communities and in education, encouraged by new laws that made corporate giving to charities tax deductible. A new generation of firms established foundations, and firms also invested directly in higher education in particular. Alfred Sloan and other business leaders worked on the Council for Financial Aid to Education to encourage firms to give to universities.[42] During the 1960s some firms ramped up their corporate philanthropy further – for example, Minneapolis-based Dayton Hudson became noteworthy for giving away 5 per cent of its pre-tax profits to philanthropy.[43]

The most radical exponent of the responsibility of corporations was the computer mainframe company Control Data Corporation and its founder William C. Norris. The firm, founded in 1957 in Minneapolis, grew incredibly rapidly, entering the *Fortune 500* in 1965. Norris saw responsibility extending far beyond charitable giving, and made the case for businesses to identify social problems and address them as opportunities. The company proactively sought to employ people with physical handicaps, provided child care for women employees, and built factories in disadvantaged inner-city areas.[44]

The ambitious thoughts of Norris and other business leaders on business responsibility were not without critics, however, even during the 1950s and 1960s. In 1958 the *Harvard Business Review* published an article headed "The Dangers of Social Responsibility," by Theodore Levitt, a marketing consultant who would later join the Harvard Business School faculty and become the *Review*'s editor between 1985 and 1989. Levitt asserted flatly that companies were not designed or equipped to address social issues.[45] In 1970 economist Milton Friedman published his now-classic article in the *New York Times Magazine* stating, "[t]he social responsibility of business is to increase profits."[46] The new liberal era had not yet dawned, but the intellectual case was being made.

It is less easy to track the development of concepts of responsibility in European business during the post-war decades. European firms initially had to reconstruct their business, rather than debate wider responsibilities, and business leaders were more discreet than their American counterparts in discussing their strategies. Many of the foundations established in Germany and elsewhere during the post-war decades were more concerned with retaining family ownership over firms than with philanthropic activity.[47] Europe lacked institutions like the Harvard Business School that could articulate theories of responsibility. In addition, governments in Europe took responsibility for welfare and other issues in ways they did not in the United States, which reduced the perceived need for corporations to be involved in society. In Britain, France, and elsewhere, large segments of the economy had also been nationalized.

Nevertheless, a broadening view of the responsibility of large corporations was underway in Europe during the post-war decades. In the Netherlands, the executives of large corporations, including Philips, Shell, and Unilever, articulated views on the wider responsibilities of companies. Unlike in the United States, there was limited interest in corporate philanthropy, but there was widespread support for concepts of trusteeship and the belief that firms had multiple stakeholders.[48] The consumer products company Unilever was at the forefront of such trends. Paul Rijkens, the company's Dutch chairman during the immediate post-war decade, was a strong advocate of the social responsibility of corporations. He insisted that Unilever had responsibilities not only to shareholders, but also to employees, consumers, and the environment.[49] Rijkens recruited like-minded figures to Unilever, including Pieter Kuin, who became a director in 1961 and published important studies on the responsibilities of business.[50] In 1966 he told an international management conference in Rotterdam that "management should never take up the cause of the rich against the poor, the privileged against the masses, the private against the public good."[51]

It would be mistaken to suggest that Unilever became a consistent exponent of social responsibility: Rijkens's successors were less passionate about the subject. Yet its corporate culture continued to insist that, in the words of an article in the house journal published in 1959, it was a "powerful force for good in the world."[52] During the 1960s the firm's large Indian affiliate, Hindustan Lever, began a program of rural development that over time would emerge as a textbook case of how a large Western multinational can use business to promote development. Seeking more reliable milk supplies, Hindustan Lever provided small farmers guidance about and knowledge of animal husbandry, and intervened with banks to get them loans without corrupt repayments.[53]

Responsibility for sustainability

Also during the post-war decades, a number of entrepreneurs became concerned about the natural environment and interested in the ability of business to improve things. This built on earlier entrepreneurial endeavors which went back to the nineteenth century.[54] There were now growing public concern in Europe and the United States, especially after the publication of Rachel Carson's *Silent Spring* in 1962, which warned of the detrimental environmental impact of widely used and produced pesticides such as DDT. A new generation of small entrepreneurs, frequently located on the margins of society, established startups that sought to promote a more sustainable future.

The desire to roll back the use of chemicals in food production and provide consumers alternative and safer food, grown in a sustainable fashion, was one focus. Frank Ford, prompted into action by the perception that "food is over processed, laced with chemicals, and devoid of nutrition," founded Arrowhead Mills as a farm-to-market company in Texas in 1960. He concluded that the extraction and use of the planet's resources had reached an unsustainable level, and that conventionally produced food "consumes precious energy when we produce it and weakens our health when we eat it."[55] He argued that business had the responsibility to provide an alternative, and set about building a supply and distribution network that would enable consumers to avoid chemically contaminated food if they wished. By the 1970s Arrowhead Mills had grown to become the largest distributor of organic food in the United States.

Ford was a born-again Christian, and a significant number of the new generation of entrepreneurs who built natural foods businesses in the United States were active Christians. This was part of a wider pattern of spirituality driving views about the responsibility of business in this domain, which extended beyond traditional Christianity. The macrobiotic movement in the United States, which created the first health stores in Boston during the 1960s, was driven by ideas borrowed from Japanese spirituality. Nor was this an exclusively American or Western phenomenon. Ibrahim Abouleish, who started and developed a prominent organic farming and retailing business in Egypt in the 1970s called Sekem, was motivated by his Islamic beliefs. In an interview about the role of religion in driving his entrepreneurial endeavours to make the world more sustainable, Abouleish said: "My religion Islam needs more entrepreneurs, entrepreneurs that are able to explain religion in a modern way so they are not considered as greedy people, but as a factor of development, a sustainable development."[56]

The belief that business had a responsibility for sustainability motivated businesses in other industries also. It was particularly evident in clean energy, where the pollution caused by fossil fuels and nuclear energy prompted entrepreneurs to explore more sustainable alternatives, despite the technological and financial obstacles that made profitability a distant dream. This was especially evident in the technologically challenging photovoltaic solar industry. In Japan the solar industry was created and shaped by electronic corporations based in the Kansai region. The pioneer venture was Sharp, founded by Hayakawa Tokuji before the First World War as a metalworking shop with a vision to make people happy. During the 1950s Sharp pioneered solar technologies – and subsequently the use of solar cells in calculators and other electrical products – as well as Japan's space program.[57] None of these activities generated profits, and the continued investment appeared to have been motivated by the personal vision of Hayakawa. "I believe the biggest issue of the future is the accumulation and storage of solar heat and light," he wrote in his 1970 biography, "while all living things enjoy the blessings of the sun, we have to rely on electricity from power stations. With magnificent heat and light streaming down on us, we must think of ways of using those blessings. This is where solar cells come in."[58]

Inamori Kazuo's Kyocera Corporation investments in solar energy during the 1970s were also motivated by wider concerns about sustainability. Inamori's interest in solar power had its origins in his own growing awareness of environmental problems. Japan's rapid industrialization during the 1950s and 1960s resulted in extensive pollution, just as the recent fast growth in China and India has done. Inamori noted that the water from his own factories polluted rivers and killed fish, and by the late 1960s he began investing in water purification technology, even though this forced up the costs of his still medium-sized company. These environmental issues led him into solar power after a fortuitous encounter with a new technology in the United States. As he later described, "Japan had no energy sources and had to import everything including coal, oil, and natural gas, and I thought it was a weak point of the nation." Inamori's views reflected his lifelong belief that "people have no higher calling than to strive for the greater good of humankind and society."[59]

Inamori was ordained into the Buddhist priesthood in 1997, but his views on the responsibility of business to others were primarily shaped by Confucian thought, as were those of Shibusawa Eiichi. In his book *A Compass to Fulfilment*, Inamori stresses the "will of the universe," which he calls a "cosmic force that seeks to cultivate all things, that encourages development and evolution."[60] If a leader is to attain the Confucian supreme virtue of *ren*, he or she needs to attain the will of the universe by encouraging the growth and development of others. Confucian thought also led Inamori to discount narrow concepts of profit maximization. "In the long run," he observed, "actions based on a solid philosophy never result in a loss. Despite the fact that they appear disadvantageous, in the end such genuine actions will profit you."[61]

In the United States also, investment in solar energy was sometimes driven by wider concerns than profitability. The American industry struggled to gain traction until big oil companies entered it during the 1970s. One of the most important of the new investors was Atlantic Richfield Oil Company (ARCO), which formed ARCO Solar in 1977. ARCO's investment in solar energy reflected a long-standing commitment to environmental issues. Robert O. Anderson, who had founded the firm in the 1940s, was an outspoken proponent of the responsibility of business to address the world's environmental problems. He was among the founders of Friends of the Earth in 1969 and a regular speaker at international events on the need to protect the environment. He was actively involved in the preparations for the United Nations

Conference on the Human Environment in Stockholm in 1972. As early as 1969, ARCO appointed a prominent ecologist to work in Alaska as its chief ecologist and environmental adviser, and the firm pioneered techniques to minimize environmental pollution from its operations. ARCO became, for a time, the largest photovoltaic manufacturer in the world, and engaged heavily in research, forming a strategy Anderson described as "growing tomorrow's new industries."[62] Wider sustainability concerns were also important in the early stages of the wind energy industry in the United States, Denmark, and Germany. Pioneering wind entrepreneurs were often environmental activists, and the two activities were intimately interconnected.[63]

The early pioneers of the notion that business had a responsibility for environmental sustainability were far from mainstream, but they built a foundation for the subsequent growth of sustainability concerns in corporate strategies. By 2015 few annual reports of major corporations failed to report and highlight their sustainability activities. Much of this was rhetoric; at its worst, it was "greenwashing." It was striking, however, how firms accepted that they had at least to claim that they were reducing their environmental footprint.

A powerful cluster of profitable business enterprises, whose founders were evangelists for business's role in improving the natural environment, was also built entirely around sustainability. These firms included, in the United States, the outdoor clothing company Patagonia, founded in 1973 by Yvon Chouinard; by 2003 it had become a $500 million company committed to five key stakeholders: "owners, workers, customers, communities, and nature."[64] A second example is the US organic food retailer Whole Foods Market, which now has revenues of $9 billion. Its co-founder and chief executive, John Mackey, who had studied philosophy and religion at the University of Texas before starting his organic food retailing business in Texas in the 1980s, made the case for a "conscious capitalism" in which business is responsible for creating "value and well-being" for all stakeholders: "financial, intellectual, physical, ecological, social, cultural, emotional, ethical, and even spiritual."[65] A third example is Natura, the Brazilian direct selling beauty company founded in 1969, which by 2013 had revenues of $3 billion, employed over a million sales representatives, and ranked as one of the world's twenty largest beauty companies. The company's three co-founders embraced a radical view of corporate responsibility for social justice, ethical standards, and sustainability.[66] One of the co-founders, Guilherme Leal, was the vice-presidential candidate for the

Green Party in the elections in Brazil in 2010; his party lost, but secured over 19 per cent of the popular vote.

The New Liberal Era and Contemporary Globalization

Recent decades have seen several paradoxes. The pursuit of the wider corporate roles in society fell away in Western economies beginning in the 1980s as investors acquired shorter time horizons, finance theory followed Michael Jensen's strictures on agency costs, and globalization weakened the connection between firms and communities. Yet this did not mean that firms stopped talking about responsibility. Instead, corporate social responsibility became institutionalized as CSR, which grew as a virtual industry in itself. Mainstream corporations pursued CSR programs for multiple reasons, including enhancing their reputations, building legitimacy, and even gaining competitive advantage.[67]

The 2000s saw a return of more radical ideas. Although there was no single driver, a series of shocks undermined the legitimacy of global capitalism. The United States passed through a dismal decade of corporate wrongdoing that included the Enron accounting fraud, the Madoff investment scandal, and the Galleon Group hedge fund scandal, which also involved insider trading accusations against Rajat Gupta, the Indian-born Harvard MBA who had reached the pinnacle of corporate America as managing partner of McKinsey & Co between 1994 and 2003, as well as a director at Goldman Sachs Group and Procter & Gamble. It was hard to find a country where some major corporate misdeed was not revealed. Low points of corporate behaviour included the News Corporation phone-hacking scandal in Britain, the Satyam Computer Services fraud in India, and Olympus in Japan. Meanwhile the 2008 financial crisis, which caused such widespread economic and social dislocation in many parts of the world, was widely (and correctly) perceived to have been caused by systemic failures in the global financial system, including a wilful lack of corporate responsibility in matters such as subprime lending and derivatives trading.

The result is an ongoing re-evaluation of the responsibility of capitalism by leading management thinkers, especially in the United States. Rosabeth Moss Kanter's *SuperCorp* imagines a company of the future using actual examples from today, including IBM and Procter & Gamble, as well as non-US companies such as the Mexican-owned cement corporation, CEMEX. Kanter, who had been Levitt's successor as editor of the *Harvard Business Review*, terms such firms "vanguard companies" that are both progressive and successful in business and that also pay attention to community and social needs. In contrast to what she perceives as traditional CSR, this attention to societal needs enhances financial performance, rather than distracts from it.[68]

A second stream of work is associated with Michael Porter, another Harvard Business School faculty, and his concept of "Shared Value." In a co-authored article published in 2011, Mark Kramer and Porter argue that capitalism is "under siege," blamed for being "a major cause of social, environmental, and economic problems." In response they call for a reinvention of capitalism. The starting point of their analysis is the view that not all profit should be regarded as equal. Instead, they argue, profits serving a social purpose should be seen as more important than other sources of profit. An underlying assumption of this model is that conventional CSR is not sufficient – indeed, it is more of a problem for firms than the solution. Kramer and Porter argue that firms need to get beyond the view that social issues are at the periphery of a business, and instead see them at its core. The authors define the concept of shared value as "creating economic value in a way that also creates value for society by addressing its needs and challenges." They see societal needs, not just conventional economic needs, as defining markets. Social weaknesses create internal costs for firms, such as costly accidents or the need for remedial training to compensate for inadequate policies in education. Shared value is seen as not redistributing economic wealth, but as expanding the total pool of social value.[69]

The shared-value concept, in particular, strongly echoes Shibusawa's view that business activities which increase the public good are the most important virtue. The significance of these recent contributions, then, lies more in the status of the authors and their institutions. The evidence showing how many corporations have pursued such wider concepts of responsibility in recent years remains unclear. A key challenge is disentangling the now near-universal rhetoric of corporate responsibility from what is actually happening. It appears that, in the Western world, there is a spectrum of strategies, with a small minority of corporations actively implementing very broad concepts of corporate responsibility, a majority aiming to conform to regulatory and societal requirements and expectations, and some employing rhetoric cynically as a pure public relations device. A further challenge has been that the concept of CSR remains ill-defined, and evidently is interpreted in different ways in different countries, even within a single region such as Europe.[70] An even more serious issue is whether the evidence from the case studies of Kramer and Porter and Kanter that corporations can combine making profits and benefiting society is generalizable. It has proved very hard to demonstrate a positive correlation between corporate profitability and corporate social responsibility, at least in the United States.[71]

A striking feature of contemporary globalization is that some of the most radical strategies are found beyond the West and Japan. Given the historical evidence of Bajaj, Sekem, and others, this should be no surprise, but as a recent study of the extensive implementation of CSR by local companies in Mexico has noted, CSR research has focused almost entirely so far on developed countries.[72] Anecdotal evidence, however, suggests considerable innovation in Latin America, with corporations active in market-based solutions to poverty and environmental problems.[73]

Concluding Observations

Looking over the past one hundred and fifty years, a striking phenomenon has been the diffusion and globalization of the belief in corporate responsibility, broadly defined. Since the nineteenth century, there have been powerful prophets of responsibility in the business world, including Andrew Carnegie, Jamnalal Bajaj, Paul Rijkens, Robert Anderson, Ibrahim Abouleish, and Inamori Kazuo, as well as educators such as Wallace Donham and Donald David. Shibusawa Eiichi stands out as one of the pioneer thinkers about the challenges of realizing the public good by accumulating private wealth. He and the others were not prophets crying in the wilderness, but neither were they representative of general practice. It was only during the late twentieth century, and especially after 2000, that the rhetoric of corporate responsibility became globalized. By 2017 there was hardly a large corporation anywhere in the world that claimed in its published annual report that its primary purpose was to maximize the wealth of its shareholders.

Four factors seem to have driven the belief that corporations have responsibilities beyond making money for their owners. The first factor, especially until recently, is spirituality. Many of the most forceful exponents of responsibility have had strong religious or spiritual values. They did not accept the arguments of Adam Smith, Ted Levitt, and Milton Friedman that they should set aside these values in the sphere of business and simply take on trust that self-interest and profit maximization would automatically deliver public benefits. Shibusawa's primarily secular justification for business responsibility was quite unusual for its time, and reflected Confucian philosophy. It might be seen, as a result, as a precursor to the present day, when the case for business responsibility is more regularly framed in secular terms, even if individuals hold strong religious views themselves.

A second driver is self-interest. Early American corporate philanthropists were making investments in shaping the future. Less grandiosely, CSR and philanthropy could be interpreted as reflecting the desire of business leaders to secure legitimacy for themselves and their firms. In some cases, as in the peacemaking adventures of Henry Ford and T.J. Watson, we see strategies emerging from self-delusional egos. Although Shibusawa enjoyed the personal status he earned from his actions, his primary motivation lay in the desire to elevate the entire business community and capitalism.

The remaining two drivers are related to government. In the United States, in particular, there are fears of government intervention if business is perceived to be acting badly or responsible for social woes. This was important in the inter-war years, and remains so today. Finally, and more altruistically, some entrepreneurs have not been especially afraid of government, but have concluded that government is both unwilling and unable to address major social and environmental issues. Shibusawa, despite his period of government service, can also be regarded as falling into this category. This perception has been the driver of much of the most substantive corporate responsibility thought and action over the past decade, especially in areas experiencing fast economic growth but with weaker governmental structures, such as Latin America.

The global significance of Shibusawa Eiichi and *gapponshugi* is that he laid out many of the challenges of combining capitalism and societal responsibility, and suggested solutions that are still relevant today. There remain wide variations as to what responsibility means, and even wider variations in the relationship between rhetoric and practice, but Shibusawa stands out as a pioneer who helped start the journey towards making capitalism sustainable.

NOTES

I would like to thank my fellow members of the *Gapponshugi* research project for their many helpful comments on this paper. Special thanks are due to Chris Marquis and Tanaka Kazuhiro.

1 Max Weber, *The Protestant Ethic and the Spirit of Capitalism* (Oxford: Oxford University Press, [1905] 2011).

2 Quoted in B.W. Young, "Christianity, Secularization and Political Economy," in *Religion, Business and Wealth on Modern Britain,* ed. David J. Jeremy (London: Routledge, 1998), 43.

3 Reuven S. Avi-Yonah, "The Cyclical Transformations of the Corporate Form: A Historical Perspective on Corporate Social Responsibility," *Delaware Journal of Corporate Law* 30, no. 3 (2005): 767–818.

4 Howard F. Gospel, *Markets, Firms, and the Management of Labour in Modern Britain* (Cambridge: Cambridge University Press, 1992), 27–8.

5 Stuart D. Brandes, *American Welfare Capitalism: 1880–1940* (Chicago: University of Chicago Press, 1976).

6 D.J. Jeremy, "The Enlightened Paternalist in Action: William Hesketh Lever at Port Sunlight before 1914," *Business History* 33, no. 1 (1991): 58–81.

7 A.G. Gardiner, *Life of George Cadbury* (London: Cassell, 1923).

8 Charles Dellheim, "The Creation of a Company Culture: Cadburys, 1861–1931," *American Historical Review* 92, no. 1 (1987): 13–44.

9 Hardy Green, *The Company Town: The Industrial Edens and Satanic Mills that Shaped the American Economy* (New York: Basic Books, 2010).

10 Cited in Archie B. Carroll et al., *Corporate Responsibility: The American Experience* (Cambridge: Cambridge University Press, 2012), 81.

11 Oliver Zunz, *Philanthropy in America: A History* (Princeton, NJ: Princeton University Press, 2011), 1.

12 Carroll et al., *Corporate Responsibility*, 85–7; Zunz, *Philanthropy in America*, 23.

13 Zunz, *Philanthropy in America*, 22.

14 Ibid., 296.

15 Christine M. Rosen, "Businessmen against Pollution in Late Nineteenth Century Chicago," *Business History Review* 69, no. 3 (1995): 351–97; Carroll et al., *Corporate Responsibility*, 107–9.

16 Samuel Fromartz, *Organic, Inc.* (New York: Harcourt, 2006), 153–5; Frank Murray and Jon Tarr, *More than One Slingshot: How the Health Food Industry Is Changing America* (Richmond, VA: Marlborough House, 1984), 13–14.

17 Gustav Ranis, "The Community-Centered Entrepreneur in Japanese Development," *Explorations in Entrepreneurial History* 8, no. 2 (1955): 80–98; Yamamura Kōzō, "A Re-Examination of Entrepreneurship in Meiji Japan (1868–1912)," *Economic History Review* 21, no. 1 (1968): 144–58.

18 Werner von Siemens, *Lebenserinnerungen*, 3rd ed. (Berlin: Julius Springer, 1908).

19 Wilfried Feldenkirchen, *Werner von Siemens, Inventor and International Entrepreneur* (Columbus: Ohio State University Press, 1994), 146.

20 Rakesh Khurana, *From Higher Aims to Hired Hands: The Social Transformation of American Business Schools and the Unfilled Promise of Management as a Profession* (Princeton, NJ: Princeton University Press, 2007).

21 Carroll et al., *Corporate Responsibility*, 132–4.

22 Wallace B. Donham, "The Social Significance of Business," *Harvard Business School Alumni Bulletin*, July 1927.

23 Wallace B. Donham, "The Failure of Business Leadership and the Responsibility of the Universities," *Harvard Business Review* 11, no. 4 (1933): 423; Carroll et al., *Corporate Responsibility*, 179.

24 Adolf A. Berle and Gardiner C. Means, *The Modern Corporation and Private Property* (New York: Macmillan, 1932).

25 Ibid.; Carroll et al., *Corporate Responsibility*, 169–71.

26 Charles Howard Hopkins, *History of the Y.M.C.A. in North America* (New York: Association Press, 1951); Sophia A. Muirhead, *Corporate Contributions: The View from 50 Years*, Report 1249–99-RR (New York: Conference Board, 1999).

27 D.J. Jeremy, "Ethics, Religion, and Business in Twentieth Century Britain," in *Business in Britain in the Twentieth Century: Decline and Renaissance?* ed. Richard Coopey and Peter Lath (Oxford: Oxford University Press, 2009), 365–6.

28 John F. Wilson and Andrew Thomson, *The Making of Modern Management: British Management in Historical Perspective* (Oxford: Oxford University Press, 2006), 180.

29 Oliver Sheldon, *The Philosophy of Management* (London: Pitman, 1923).

30 Geoffrey Jones and Adrian Brown, "Thomas J. Watson, IBM, and Nazi Germany," Harvard Business School Case 807-133 (June 2007; revised May 2015).

31 Elisabeth Köll, *From Cotton Mill to Business Empire: The Emergence of Regional Enterprises in Modern China* (Cambridge, MA: Harvard University Press, 2003), 230–47.

32 Ashok Desai, "The Origins of Parsi Entrepreneurship," *Indian Economic and Social History Review* 5, no. 4 (1968): 307–18; Dwijendra Tripathi, *Oxford History of Indian Business* (New Delhi: Oxford University Press, 2004).

33 Tata Group, "Tata Corporate Social Responsibility: A Century of Trust," available online at http://www.slideshare.net/Odishadevelopment/tata-corporate-social-responsibility-a-century-of-trust, accessed November 2012.

34 Omar Goswami, "Then Came the Marwaris: Some Aspects of the Changes in the Pattern of Industrial Control in Eastern India," *Indian Economic and Social History Review* 22, no. 3 (1985): 225–49.

35 B.R. Nanda, *In Gandhi's Footsteps: The Life and Times of Jamnalal Bajaj* (Delhi: Oxford University Press, 1990).

36 Geoffrey Jones, Kerry Herman, and Prabakar Kothandaraman, "Jamnalal Bajaj, Mahatma Gandhi, and the Struggle for Indian Independence," Harvard Business School Case 807–028 (August 2006; revised May 2015).

37 Roland Marchand, *Creating the Corporate Soul: The Rise of Public Relations and Corporate Imagery in American Big Business* (Berkeley: University of California Press, 1998).

38 Adolf A. Berle, *The Twentieth Century Capitalist Revolution* (New York: Harcourt, Brace, 1954); Carroll et al., *Corporate Responsibility*, 199.

39 Bert Spector, "'Business Responsibilities in a Divided World': The Cold War Roots of the Corporate Social Responsibility Movement," *Enterprise & Society* 9, no. 2 (2008): 318.

40 Donald K. David, "Business Responsibilities in an Uncertain World," *Harvard Business Review* 27, no. 3 (1949): 1–8. See also Spector, "'Business Responsibilities in a Divided World,'" 329; and Carroll et al., *Corporate Responsibility*, 210–11.

41 Howard Rothmann Bowen, *Social Responsibilities of the Businessman* (New York: Harper, 1953); Carroll et al., *Corporate Responsibility*, 212–14.

42 Carroll et al., *Corporate Responsibility*, 217–19; Morrell Heald, *The Social Responsibilities of Business, Company, and Community 1900–1960* (Cleveland: Case Western Reserve University Press, 1970).

43 Carroll et al., *Corporate Responsibility*, 246–8, 250–1.

44 Tom Nicholas and Laura G. Singleton, "Control Data Corporation and the Urban Crisis," Harvard Business School Case 9–808–096 (2011); Carroll et al., *Corporate Responsibility*, 248–9.

45 Theodore Levitt, "The Dangers of Social Responsibility," *Harvard Business Review* 36, no. 5 (1958): 41–50.

46 Milton Friedman, "The Social Responsibility of Business Is to Increase Its Profits," *New York Times Magazine*, 13 September 1970.

47 Marta Rey-Garcia and Nuria Puig-Raposo, "Globalisation and the Organisation of Family Philanthropy: A Case of Isomorphism?" *Business History* 55, no. 6 (2013): 1019–46.

48 Keetie Sluyterman, "Corporate Social Responsibility of Dutch Entrepreneurs in the 20th Century," *Enterprise & Society* 13, no. 2 (2012): 313–49.

49 Geoffrey Jones, *Renewing Unilever: Transformation and Tradition* (Oxford: Oxford University Press, 2005), 247–8.

50 Pieter Kuin, *Management is méér: De sociale verantwoordelijkheid van de ondernemer* [Management is more: The social responsibility of the entrepreneur] (Amsterdam: Elsevier, 1977).

51 Sluyterman, "Corporate Social Responsibility," 328.
52 Jones, *Renewing Unilever*, 249.
53 Ibid., 173, 175.
54 See Geoffrey Jones, *Profits and Sustainability: A History of Green Entrepreneurship* (Oxford: Oxford University Press, 2017).
55 John Bloom, "Doing What Comes Naturally … Made Frank Ford Healthy and Wealthy," *Texas Monthly* (June 1979): 86.
56 Ibrahim Abouleish and Helmy Abouleish, "Garden in the Desert: Sekem Makes Comprehensive Sustainable Development a Reality in Egypt," *Innovations: Technology, Governance, Globalization* 3, no. 3 (2008): 21–48. On the influence of religion generally, see Geoffrey Jones, "Entrepreneurship in the Natural Food and Beauty Categories before 2000: Global Visions and Local Expressions," Harvard Business School Working Paper 13–024 (Boston: Harvard Business School, August 2012).
57 Sharp Global, "Sharp History," available online at http://sharp-world.com/corporate/info/his/h_company/1962/index.html; see also Sharp Corporation, *Opening New Frontiers: Annual Report 2009* (Osaka, 2009), available online at http://www.sharp-world.com/corporate/ir/library/annual/pdf/annual_2009.pdf.
58 Bob Johnston, *Switching to Solar: What We Can Learn from Germany's Success in Harnessing Clean Energy* (Amherst, NY: Prometheus Books, 2011), 125–6.
59 Interview of Inamori Kazuo by Geoffrey Jones, 27 May 2010, cited in Geoffrey Jones and Loubna Bouamane, "'Power from Sunshine': A Business History of Solar Energy," Harvard Business School Working Paper 12–105 (Boston: Harvard Business School, May 2012).
60 Inamori Kazuo, *A Compass to Fulfilment* (New York: McGraw-Hill, 2009), preface. I owe Tanaka Kazuhiro for this reference.
61 Ibid., 32.
62 Kenneth Harris, *The Wildcatter: A Portrait of Robert O. Anderson* (New York: Weidenfeld and Nicholson, 1987), 165.
63 Ion Bogdan Vasi, *Winds of Change: The Environmental Movement and the Global Development of the Wind Energy Industry* (Oxford: Oxford University Press, 2011); Wesley D. Sine and Brandon H. Lee, "Tilting at Windmills? The Environmental Movement and the Emergence of the US Wind Energy Sector," *Administrative Science Quarterly* 54, no. 1 (2009): 123–55.
64 Yvon Chouinard and Vincent Stanley, *The Responsible Company* (Ventura, CA: Patagonia Books, 2012).
65 John Mackey and Raj Sisoda, *Conscious Capitalism* (Boston: Harvard Business School Press, 2013).
66 Geoffrey Jones and Ricardo Reisen de Pinho, "Natura: Global Beauty Made in Brazil," Harvard Business School Case 807–029 (August 2006, revised

October 2012); Geoffrey Jones, "The Growth Opportunity that Lies Next Door," *Harvard Business Review* 90, nos. 7–8 (2012): 141–5.

67 Carroll et al., *Corporate Responsibility*, chap. 10. On the history of CSR, see Archie B. Carroll, "A History of Corporate Social Responsibility: Concepts and Practices," in *The Oxford Handbook of Corporate Social Responsibility*, ed. Andrew Crane, Abagail McWilliams, Dirk Matten, Jeremy Moon, and Donald S. Siegel, 19–46 (Oxford: Oxford University Press, 2008).

68 Rosabeth Moss Kanter, *SuperCorp: How Vanguard Companies Create Innovation, Profits, Growth, and Social Good* (New York: Crown, 2009).

69 Michael E. Porter and Mark R. Kramer, "Creating Shared Value," *Harvard Business Review* 89, nos. 1–2 (2011): 62–77.

70 André Habisch et al., eds., *Corporate Social Responsibility across Europe* (New York: Springer, 2005).

71 Joshua D. Margolis and James P. Walsh, "'Misery Loves Companies': Rethinking Social Initiatives by Business," *Administrative Science Quarterly* 48, no. 2 (2003): 268–305.

72 Alan Muller and Ans Kok, "CSR Performance in Emerging Markets: Evidence from Mexico," *Journal of Business Ethics* 8, supp. 2 (2009): 325–37.

73 See "Latin America: Social enterprise & philanthropy," *Financial Times*, 16 October 2012.

8 The Crisis of Capitalism and the *Gapponshugi* of Shibusawa Eiichi

KIKKAWA TAKEO

In this chapter I examine the contributions of Shibusawa Eiichi from a human resource development perspective, and I re-evaluate the concept of *gapponshugi*, which Shibusawa espoused, and seek to clarify the current significance of *gapponshugi* in the context of what has been termed the "crisis of capitalism."

During Shibusawa's roughly ninety years of life (1840–1931), Japan experienced the end of the Edo period and the opening of its ports, the Meiji Restoration, an industrial revolution, urbanization and electrification, and the development of heavy and chemical industries. Through this process of modernization, Japan managed to bridge the gap between its local context and the global economy. In doing so, Japan, like other latecomers, faced pressures from global markets for the first time in its history. To become a part of the international environment and to compete with the more advanced economies, Japan had to mobilize its human resources and to secure funds. In these efforts, Shibusawa played a significant role. He introduced the concept of *gapponshugi* to describe a specific type of corporation based on manpower, capital, technology, information, and intellectual networks. This concept guided him to pursue social entrepreneurship and to conduct business activities. During his life, he established 470 companies and founded the Japanese banking system.

Shibusawa's concept of *gapponshugi* was a unique contribution based on a particular philosophy of capitalism, which advanced the modernization of Japan's economy and society. During his travels to Europe he was impressed by the economic model he found there, which sought to garner both large and small investments to pursue entrepreneurial activities. Upon his return to Japan, he devised a more sophisticated concept of business development and entrepreneurial activity, reflected in the idea of *gapponshugi*: the assembly of competent people and the raising of funds from a wide variety of sources in order to realize business profits while enhancing public welfare.

Although many studies have focused on Shibusawa's role in the introduction of new mechanisms of acquiring capital, here I analyse his actions to promote human resources, the second economic function of *gapponshugi*. Shibusawa strongly supported education, especially recognizing the importance of both business studies and women's education. He was involved in the establishment of many privately financed educational institutions, and participated actively in their administration, often as a director or as president.

Japan's Industrialization Process

Industrialization often begins with handicraft industries before the introduction of machine systems, so it cannot be said that no signs of a move towards industrialization were seen in Edo Japan. By the mid-nineteenth century, wholesale domestic industries, mainly in the textile weaving industry, showed considerable progress. Some of these used manufacturing (factory handicraft) management systems, equating to "proto-industrialization,"[1] the phase just preceding industrialization. Japan did not commence full-fledged industrialization until it came into contact with global capitalism as a result of the opening of its ports at the end of the Edo period.

The process began with the arrival of a US naval squadron commanded by Matthew C. Perry in 1853, followed by the conclusion of the Treaty of Peace and Amity between the United States and Japan in 1854 and the Treaty of Amity and Commerce between the two nations in 1858. As a result the Tokugawa shogunate was forced to abandon its self-isolation policy, and Japan found itself confronted by global capitalism and overwhelmed by the gap in economic and military strength between itself and major Western powers – particularly Britain, "the world's factory." Japan thus had no choice but to accept the violation of its judicial independence (its one-sided consular jurisdiction) and the forfeiture of its customs autonomy (its conventional tariff system) in the treaties of amity and commerce it signed with major Western powers. The latter "fixed Japan as a rare practitioner of the principle of free trade and deprived it of its freedom to adopt protective tariffs as an instrument of industrial policy."[2] Japan did not come close to recovering its customs autonomy until the conclusion of the New Treaty of Commerce and Navigation between Japan and the United States in 1911.

The opening of the ports in the last days of the Edo period triggered movements of nationalistic reverence for the emperor and for the expulsion of foreigners. This led to the collapse of the Tokugawa regime and the end of Japan's feudalism. Opening the ports also accelerated the primitive accumulation of the two necessary elements of capitalism, capital and labour. This trend continued after the Meiji Restoration and entered its final stage with the rapid disappearance of feudalism during the wild waves of inflation and deflation brought about by the Ōkuma and Matsukata fiscal administrations.³ The establishment of the Bank of Japan in 1882 symbolized the temporary achievement of the accumulation of funds through primitive accumulation.

Around this time, leading companies began to be established in the form of joint-stock corporations, among them Tokio Marine Insurance Company (1879), Nippon Railway (1881), and Osaka Spinning Company (1882). The success of these pioneering cases boosted confidence in the stock corporation system, and from 1886 to 1889 there was a boom in the establishment of new stock corporations, including in the insurance, railway, and textile sectors. Although the 1890 depression brought this rise to an abrupt end, Japan was moving undeniably towards full-fledged industrialization.

The 1890 depression signalled that capitalist production had entered full swing in Japan. If the establishment of capitalism in a country is an industrial revolution, Japan's began in the 1880s, trailing Britain's by more than a century. In industrial revolutions among latecomers such as Japan, advanced technology developed by pioneering countries is readily available, but import pressure from those countries presents a challenge to industrialization. Labour costs tend to be lower in the latecomers, which mitigates this import pressure to some extent in labour-intensive light industries. In capital-intensive heavy industries, however, the pressure is severe. Accordingly, for a latecomer country to achieve an industrial revolution successfully, it needs to (1) establish factory production based on machine systems in light industries such as textiles and either (2) guarantee the stable import of heavy industrial products by inducing light industries to become export industries or (3) solidify the prospects for production by domestic heavy industries. In Japan, the Osaka Spinning Company's 1883 startup of a large factory with 10,500 spindles was a groundbreaking event in relation to (1). Regarding (2), the export volume of cotton yarn overtook its import volume in 1897, and exports of raw silk surged during the period from

1900 to 1905. With respect to (3), blast furnaces started full-scale operation at the government-owned Yawata Iron and Steel Works in 1904, and self-sufficient production systems were established in industries such as shipbuilding and armaments production in the latter half of the first decade of the twentieth century.

As Japan's industrial revolution advanced, the country fought wars with China (1894–95) and Russia (1904–05). The scale of central and local public finance in Japan was boosted after the wars, and government funds were spent in various sectors. Programs put in place after the Sino-Japanese War included military expansion, the Navigation Encouragement Act and the Shipbuilding Encouragement Act (both in 1896), the establishment of government-owned iron and steel plants (Yawata was chosen as the location of a government iron and steel works in 1897), the expansion of telecommunication and telephone businesses, and the establishment of special banks – Nippon Kangyo Bank (1897), prefectural Noko banks (1898–1900), Hokkaido Takushoku Bank (1900), and Industrial Bank of Japan (1902). In 1897, using massive reparations obtained from China that built up Japan's gold reserves, Japan adopted the gold standard. These programs were followed after the Russo-Japanese War by further military expansion, the nationalization of the railways, the establishment of the South Manchuria Railway, and the expansion of government iron and steel plants and telecommunication and telephone businesses. In addition, through the colonization of Formosa (Taiwan) in 1895 and South Sakhalin in 1905, and the annexation of Korea in 1910, Japan's colonial administration began in earnest.

By the end of the Russo-Japanese War, Japan's industrial revolution was essentially complete. A post-war depression then began in 1907 and continued for several years. Around 1910 there was a "temporary prosperity," driven mainly by the electricity industry, which took advantage of a hydroelectricity boom, but the overall pace of economic activity continued to languish and Japan's balance of payments worsened. The First World War, however, saw a dramatic change in Japan's economy. Joining the war on the side of Britain, France, and Russia (but essentially a non-combatant far removed from the battlefields), Japan experienced a sharp expansion of exports of military supplies and food to its European allies. As European exports to other Asian countries ceased as a result of the war, new business opportunities for Japan opened up there, while a wartime economic boom in the United States increased exports of Japanese raw silk to that country. At home, domestic production increased in heavy industries that previously had depended highly on European imports, helping Japan pull itself out of its balance-of-payments crisis. As a result of the war and the immediate post-war reconstruction demand, Japan's economic growth surged. The war also caused the gold standard system to cease functioning globally – indeed, Japan left the gold standard in 1917 when it prohibited the export of gold.

The economic boom caused by war and reconstruction could not last, however, and depression ensued in 1920. Thereafter the Japanese economy faced an era of chronic economic downturns: the earthquake depression of 1923, the financial depression of 1927, and the Showa Depression of 1929–31, which was linked to the world economic crisis that originated in the United States. Balance-of-payment difficulties again deepened, and Japan struggled to revert to the gold standard. Finance Minister Inoue Jyunnosuke repealed the gold embargo through austere fiscal policy, and in January 1930 Japan finally went back on the gold standard. Meanwhile, in 1930 and 1931, Japanese nominal national income plummeted.

It is worth noting, however, that Japan's economic growth rate during the 1920s was not necessarily low from a global perspective. From the 1910s through the 1920s, the growth of Japan's gross domestic product, in terms of both total and per capita amounts, slightly exceeded that of the United States, which was a leader in world economic development at that time.[4] What enabled Japan to achieve such growth, despite the deepening mood of recession, was the expansion of its domestic market, primarily attributable to the advancement of urbanization and electrification. Miwa Ryōichi considers that "the Japanese economy evolved to move onto the next stage in terms of the size of the economy, triggered by World War I." He posits that, "since the 1920s, the beginnings of a movement toward a mass consumption society began in Japan, accompanied by change in consumption practices in the direction toward westernization."[5]

Throughout this process of industrialization, many entrepreneurs played important roles. They can largely be divided into three types: owner managers such as Iwasaki Yatarō, salaried managers such as Nakamigawa Hikojirō, and investor managers such as Shibusawa Eiichi.

Three Types of Top Managers

The difference between owner managers and investor managers is clearly shown in the opposing portrayal of individualism versus *gapponshugi*. Those who espoused the former thought they owned their company, whereas those who promoted the latter thought that many shareholders owned their company. As well, salaried managers became top managers not through investment, but purely by specialized knowledge,[6] whereas owner managers became top managers based on investment.

Owner managers as typified by Iwasaki Yatarō

Iwasaki Yatarō, founder of the Mitsubishi *zaibatsu*, is often discussed in contrast to Shibusawa Eiichi. This distinction is well represented by comparing Iwasaki the individualist to Shibusawa the practitioner of *gapponshugi*.[7] In fact, Iwasaki and Shibusawa were engaged in fierce competition through their companies in the shipping industry.

In 1870 Iwasaki, a low-ranking warrior of the Tosa clan, launched a marine transportation business; the company adopted the name Mitsubishi Shokai in 1873. After the Meiji Restoration, Iwasaki had great success as a shipping agent upon winning a competition with Nipponkoku Yūbin Jōkisen Kaisha, a government-owned marine transportation company. In 1877, when the Satsuma Rebellion broke out, Yūbin Kisen Mitsubishi Kaisha undertook military transportation for the Meiji government, which aided the establishment of mixed cargo shipping associations in many parts of Japan and concluded exclusive cargo shipping agreements with them. With a political change in 1881, however, the Meiji government chose to regulate the activities of Yūbin Kisen Mitsubishi Kaisha, thereby igniting fierce competition between that company and a new, government-sponsored shipping company, Kyōdō Unyu Kaisha (literally, "joint transportation company"). The predecessor of the new company was Tokyo Fuhansen Kaisha, one of whose key founding members was Shibusawa Eiichi.

Upon the death of Iwasaki Yatarō in 1885, both Kyōdō Unyu Kaisha and Yūbin Kisen Mitsubishi Kaisha moved towards a compromise, merging that year to establish Nippon Yūsen Kaisha. Iwasaki's younger brother, Iwasaki Yanosuke, succeeded him in managing the businesses of Mitsubishi, and the *zaibatsu* began diversifying in earnest, with "development from the sea to shore."

Iwasaki Yatarō represents the type of entrepreneur, common in the early days of Japan's industrialization, who both owned his company and took part in its management. Other examples of owner managers include Yasuda Zenjirō, founder of the Yasuda *zaibatsu* (also called a *kinyū zaibatsu*, or financial conglomerate), and Asano Sōichirō and Furukawa Ichibei, who founded the Asano and Furukawa *zaibatsu*, respectively (examples of *sangyō zaibatsu*, or industrial conglomerates).

Born in Toyama Prefecture, Yasuda Zenjirō moved to Edo (later Tokyo) and opened a money exchange store called Yasuda Shōten in 1866. During the chaotic transition period from the end of the Edo period to the Meiji period, Yasuda served both the Tokugawa shogunate and the Meiji government. Taking the money made during this period, he set up Yasuda Bank in 1880. He then put banks all over the country under his control, and in 1912 established Gōmeigaisha Hozensha (later renamed Yasuda Hozensha) as a holding company to oversee the entire Yasuda *zaibatsu*.

Asano Sōichirō was also from Toyama. After repeated failures, he succeeded in acquiring a government grant for a government cement plant in 1884, and set it on the right track. Subsequently, Asano made his foray into the coal and shipping businesses, which were intrinsically connected with the cement business. He was also actively involved in land reclamation in the Keihin Industrial Zone. On the reclaimed ground, Nippon Kōkan, Asano Shipbuilding, and other affiliates of the Asano *zaibatsu* constructed their plants. In 1918 the Asano Dōzoku Kabushikikaisha (Asano Affiliated Corporation) was established as a holding company. The Asano *zaibatsu* had a funding problem, so financial support, mainly from Shibusawa Eiichi and hometown compatriot Yasuda Zenjirō, was essential.

Another owner manager was Kyoto native Furukawa Ichibei, who purchased the Ashio Copper Mine in 1877, followed in 1885 by the purchase of both the Innai Mine and the Ani Mine. Furukawa himself focused on the mining business, and was not particularly aggressive about entering other fields, except for electrolytic copper refining and copper wire manufacturing. After his death, however, the Furukawa *zaibatsu* strengthened its business diversification approach. In 1911 Furukawa Gōmei was established with the goal of becoming a comprehensive *zaibatsu*.[8] Both the Furukawa and Asano *zaibatsu* benefited from the financial support of Shibusawa Eiichi.

Salaried managers as typified by Nakamigawa Hikojirō

Before the Second World War, salaried managers who were not owner managers were more common in *zaibatsu*-affiliated companies than in those not so affiliated. The reason is that, "in Japan's *zaibatsu*, the relationships between a family or its kinship and the head office of the company that is capitalized by the family, and the relationships between the head office and its directly affiliated companies, worked as a dual containment of ownership."[9] This was a system in which "family property was not allowed to be divided and freedom of disposal, the original characteristic of private property, was not allowed for any member of the family."[10] This worked to constrain ownership; in addition, in the relationship between the head office and its directly affiliated companies, the former played the role of the latter's stable shareholder. Reflecting the penetration of salaried managers mainly in *zaibatsu*-affiliated companies, the weight of salaried managers on the boards of directors of large companies (including non-*zaibatsu*-affiliated companies) steadily increased until 1930.

One such salaried manager was Nakamigawa Hikojirō, an impressive figure who was a pioneer in that role in a *zaibatsu*-affiliated company. In 1891 Nakamigawa was assigned to the post of managing director of Mitsui Bank; the following year he assumed the office of deputy chief. At that time Mitsui Bank was undergoing a dire financial crisis with an accumulation of bad debts caused by its corporate structure, reflecting its privileged position in government – Mitsui Bank had been *acting as a central bank* until the establishment of the Bank of Japan in 1882. Nakamigawa tackled the bank's restructuring by introducing and promoting a series of reforms, including the settlement of non-performing loans, the development of various industries by means such as investment and financing – providing support to, among others, – and the mass hiring of salaried managers.[11] Nakamigawa had studied at the Keio School (now Keio University), and invited many graduates of the school to join the Mitsui family's businesses, including Asabuki Eiji, who moved from Mitsubishi and later became the chairman of Oji Paper; Fujiyama Raita, managing director of Oji Paper and president of Dai-Nippon Sugar; Muto Sanji, president of Kanegafuchi Spinning; Wada Toyoji, president of Fuji-Gas Spinning; Ikeda Seihin, director of both Mitsui Bank and Mitsui Gōmei Kaisha, governor of the Bank of Japan, and minister of finance; Hibi Ōsuke, chairman of Mitsukoshi; Fujiwara Ginjirō, president of Oji Paper; and Kobayashi Ichizō, president of Hankyū Railway, president of Tokyo Dentō Kabushiki Gaisha, and minister of communications. All became representative salaried managers before the Second World War.

The Mitsubishi *zaibatsu* also made use of salaried managers, a proactive stance taken by owner managers Iwasaki Yatarō and Iwasaki Yanosuke. Those who joined Mitsubishi included Keio School graduates Shōda Heigorō, chief manager of the head office of Mitsubishi Joint Stock Company; Yoshikawa Taijirō, president of Nippon Yūsen

Kabushiki Kaisha; Toyokawa Ryōhei, manager of the Banking Department of Mitsubishi Joint Stock Company; Asabuki Eiji, mentioned previously; and Yamamoto Tatsuo, governor of the Bank of Japan. Salaried managers who were graduates of the University of Tokyo included Kondō Renpei, president of Nippon Yūsen Kabushiki Kaisha; Suenobu Michishige, chairman of Tokio Marine Insurance; Katō Takaaki, prime minister; and Isono Kei, founder of Meidi-Ya.

Investor managers as typified by Shibusawa Eiichi

Shibusawa Eiichi was neither an owner manager like Iwasaki Yatarō nor a salaried manager like Nakamigawa Hikojirō. Shimada Masakazu, who has conducted an in-depth examination of Shibusawa's entrepreneurial activities, argues, rather, that he was an investor manager.[12]

In 1873 Shibusawa became the general office director of Dai-Ichi Kokuritsu Ginko (First National Bank). Two years later, in 1875, he became the bank's president. Using this as a solid platform, he chaired various stock corporations from the 1890s through the early 1900s, including Tokyo Gas; Nihon Renga Seizō; Tokyo Rope; textile company Kyoto Orimono; Tokyo Jinzō Hiryō; Tokyo Iishikawajima Zōsenjo; the Imperial Hotel; Oji Paper; Iwaki Coal Mine; Hiroshima Suiryoku Denki; and Sapporo Beer. He was also involved in the establishment of large companies that paved the way for Japan's industrialization and modernization – including the Osaka Spinning Company, Nippon Railway, Tokio Marine Insurance, and Nippon Yūsen Kaisha – and played active roles as an officer of these companies. An investor manager who can be cited as having similar characteristics to those of Shibusawa was Godai Tomoatsu, who was mainly active in Osaka. The two men were positioned together as "Shibusawa Eiichi of the east, Godai Tomoatsu of the west."

The economic thinking that formed the basis of Shibusawa's distinguished work as a private entrepreneur was *gapponshugi*. This was the concept that *gappon-hō* (the *gappon* system) was the only way to make the entire society rich based on a value system that "not only an individual but society as a whole needs to grow wealthy."[13] According to Shimada, Shibusawa's entrepreneurial activities had two aspects: (1) simultaneously establishing many modern companies, and (2) setting industries related to infrastructure and those essential for modernization on the right track, since both require long-term involvement. Crucial to the first was the mechanism of stock price formation, leading to securing funds through partial sales of shares, and using the funds as starter capital for the next company. At the heart of the second aspect was the "utilization of extensive networks of entrepreneurs who have financial power."[14]

Shimada also classifies the roles Shibusawa performed in general shareholders' meetings after the establishment of the companies in which he was involved into three categories: (1) involvement as a large shareholder, (2) involvement as an outside board member, and (3) support of mergers outside general shareholders' meetings. Shimada concludes that, "in each of the above cases, the function expected of Shibusawa was the role of adjusting conflicts of interest among relevant parties and trying to achieve resolutions through arbitration and intermediation."[15]

Shibusawa's contribution to human resource development

If a latecomer country is to industrialize and progress economically as an emerging country, it must not only employ funds, but also secure human resources. Indeed, Shibusawa Eiichi's *gapponshugi* held that human resource development was as equally important as raising funds. To illustrate the importance Shibusawa attached to this function, Table 8.1 shows donations he made by area over his lifetime; it clearly indicates that the largest donation area in terms of both the amount of money and the number of cases was education/academics.

Implications for the industrialization of latecomer countries

What were the relationships among the three types of entrepreneurs who took active roles in Japan's industrialization process, and what are the implications of these relationships for the industrialization of latecomer countries?

Owner managers, through the expansion of the scale of their businesses and diversification, became unable to manage their businesses solely with their own resources and needed the assistance of salaried managers. Typical examples are Iwasaki Yatarō and Iwasaki Yanosuke, who formed the Mitsubishi *zaibatsu* and proactively hired such managers. Among owner managers, those with insufficient access to capital established stock companies in the early stages of their businesses or relied on bank lending. In such cases, they had no choice but to draw on the power of investor managers such as Shibusawa Eiichi, who was

Table 8.1 Donations by Shibusawa Eiichi, by Area

Donation area	Amount (¥)	Percentage of total (%)	Number of cases	Amount per case (¥)
Education/academics	638,557,623	34.7	190	3,360,830
Social work/welfare	341,143,724	18.5	64	5,330,371
Domestic relief	94,715,461	5.1	36	2,630,985
Overseas relief	13,477,591	0.7	15	898,506
International activities	72,633,972	3.9	65	1,117,446
Religion	141,990,098	7.7	57	2,491,054
Military affairs/imperial rule assistance	107,172,570	5.8	39	2,748,015
Awards, etc.	37,843,405	2.1	25	1,513,736
Tokugawa family	69,086,803	3.8	8	8,635,850
Economic/industrial promotion	7,952,569	0.4	9	883,619
Kinship	144,566,256	7.9	12	12,047,188
Hometown/public works	17,108,884	0.9	14	1,222,063
Support for private organizations	119,414,568	6.5	60	1,990,243
Others	34,133,959	1.9	29	1,177,033
Total	1,839,797,483	100.0	623	2,953,126

Note: Amounts have been adjusted to the equivalent value in 2006.

Source: Compiled by the Shibusawa Eiichi Memorial Foundation.

a mastermind at establishing stock companies. In Shibusawa's case, he also supported owner managers through bank lending in his role as president of Dai-Ichi Bank. Asano Sōichirō and Furukawa Ichibei are typical examples of owner managers who benefited from Shibusawa's help. As an investor manager, Shibusawa also focused on entrepreneurial education, and established and supported the development of many institutes of higher learning, including the Tokyo Higher Commercial School (now Hitotsubashi University). In the latter half of the Meiji period, graduates of the Tokyo Higher Commercial School joined Mitsui and many other large companies and grew into active salaried managers.[16] In this case, investor managers supported the source of salaried managers.

Looking back on Japan's industrialization process, the fact that salaried managers were given opportunities to play active roles represented an important lever: owner managers proactively hired salaried managers, and investor managers supported the development of salaried managers. In the early stages of their businesses, salaried managers' use of the owner managers' funds for industrialization, and investor managers' use of society's money for introducing stock corporations represented important financial levers. (Shibusawa Eiichi also advanced the employment of society's money in the form of bank deposits.) The complementary actions of the three types of entrepreneurs thus led to the effective use of scarce human capital and funds, a mechanism that is likely applicable to the industrialization of latecomer countries in general.

Global Capitalism at a Crossroads

To this point I have sought to illuminate the contributions of Shibusawa Eiichi, who aided the formation of modern Japan, from a human resource development perspective. I now address the concept of *gapponshugi*, as espoused by Shibusawa, to clarify its current significance in the light of what has been termed the "crisis of capitalism."

The idea of a "crisis of capitalism" was sparked by the collapse of Lehman Brothers in September 2008. The global recession that followed this "Lehman Shock" was called a "once-in-a-century economic crisis," prompting comparisons with the worldwide Great Depression that began in 1929. Considering, however, first, that the recent global recession rippled outward from the United States to the rest of the world extremely rapidly against the backdrop of the globalization of markets and, second, that its spread was accompanied by substantial turmoil in the financial system, one could argue that it was even more serious than the Great Depression.[17] Of these two points, the first resulted from the leading role that newly developing countries – including the so-called BRICs (Brazil, Russia, India, and China) – played during the global economy's expansionary phase prior to the collapse of Lehman Brothers, and their use of exports to advanced countries (particularly the United States) as an engine of economic growth. Consequently, if the global economy is to follow a stable growth path in the future, newly developing countries, which will continue to play a key role, will have to move away from export-dependence to an economic growth model that is led by domestic demand. The second point – turmoil in global financial markets – on the other hand, was an inevitable result of what Ronald Dore has called "financialization," and it is a problem with deep roots. Despite the collapse of Lehman Brothers, financialization is expected to continue – indeed, in 2011, Europe faced a grave financial crisis triggered by the fiscal plight of Greece. Moreover, once a financial system plunges into chaos, a considerable length of time is required to achieve a recovery. That is clear from Japan's recent experience as well: the country required approximately ten years to emerge from the "Heisei financial crisis" that began in 1997.

Ronald Dore's Stock Market Capitalism

Ronald Dore uses the word "financialization" in his book *Stock Market Capitalism: Welfare Capitalism – Japan and Germany versus the Anglo-Saxons*.[18] According to Dore, financialization is where "shareholder value comes to be preached as the sole proper objective of corporate managers," and aims in the "direction of putting people who make money in a dominant position over people who make things, causing speculative instability in the economy and bringing uneasiness to people's lives."[19] Dore sees financialization, which originated in the so-called Anglo-Saxon countries, the birthplace of "stock market capitalism," spreading to Germany and Japan, which had adopted the opposing mechanism of "welfare capitalism," and continuing on to dominate the capitalist world. Although Dore is scathingly critical of financialization, he views the process as no longer stoppable.

According to Dore, Japan forged a distinctive economic system unlike the Anglo-Saxon model. In short, it is an economy characterized by "long-term commitment" and is the product of unique corporate structures and management roles – including employment relationships in the form of lifetime employment and low labour mobility, and shareholders who prefer long-term commitment over short-term earnings – as well as business relationships with long-term suppliers (the subcontractor system), moderate relationships among competitors, and a government role that might be described as that of "referee." Two factors enabled these elements to be constituted as a unique system – namely, interdependent relationships among the various elements, and the coincidence of motivations in terms of long-term commitment, altruism, and productivism. Dore deems the breakdown of this unique system in Japan to be inevitable in the face of the advance of financialization.[20]

Among the elements Dore specifies as constituting Japan's economic system, lifetime employment,[21] low labour mobility, and the development of the subcontractor system[22] are thought to have formed during the post-war period of rapid economic growth between 1956 and 1973. The characteristics of Japanese shareholders, the development of moderate relationships among competitors, and the role of government as referee, however, can be said to have put down roots prior to the Second World War, and are related to *gapponshugi* and the philosophy of Shibusawa Eiichi. Although some of these elements and the interdependent relationships among them did not develop until after Shibusawa's lifetime, the coincidence of motivations does overlap with *gapponshugi*.

"Peopleism" and "companyism"

One criticism of the current prevailing capitalist view is the humanistic argument of Itami Hiroyuki, who characterizes the Japanese enterprise system following the Second World War as *jinpon shugi kigyō* ("peopleism"). He asserts that, "while capitalism regards money as the most fundamental and scarce resource in economic activities, and assumes that the corporate system is built around the providers of that resource, peopleism highlights people as the most fundamental and scarce resource in economic activities, and essentially seeks the formation of a corporate system shaped as a network of providers of that resource."[23] Itami argues against the approach of owner-driven corporate governance based on the predominant capitalistic view, and proposes instead the establishment of the "sovereignty of employees," including managers.[24] On this basis Itami points out that the peopleist corporate system has four advantages: highly motivated participation, facilitation of cooperation, possession of a long-term perspective, and enhancement of informational efficiency.[25] In the context of this argument, it is possible to claim that these advantages bore fruit during Japan's periods of high growth (1956–73) and stable growth (1974–85).

A theory that is quite close to Itami's "peopleism" is Baba Hiroji's *kaisha shugi* ("companyism"), developed by the University of Tokyo's Institute of Social Science as part of a research project on modern

Japanese society conducted during the late 1980s and early 1990s. Baba, who was central to the study, characterizes companyism as follows:

> Companyism is an exquisite combination of capitalistic competition and communal or socialistic relationships, and for that reason it proved to be an extremely effective mechanism for the development of production capacity following the establishment of the heavy and chemical industries. With regard to its characteristics as a mechanism for the development of production capacity, the communal aspects should be underscored when dealing with Western countries, while the competitive aspect should be highlighted when facing China and the Soviet Union.[26]

According to Baba, as a result of the combination of competitive and communal aspects, company-centred enterprises in post-war Japan had four distinct characteristics: weak control by owners, few gaps and little alienation among employee groups, the predominance of workplace decisions, and long-term business relationships. These characteristics contributed to the expansion of productive capacity in Japan from the mid-1950s to the mid-1980s.[27]

As Japan's economy reached the end of its period of stable growth, however, and began showing aspects of a protracted economic recession, the influence of both peopleism and companyism waned. The distinctive management system in Japanese enterprises that embodied peopleism and companyism was subjected to heavy attack. In response to the economic phase that followed the collapse of the bubble economy, Itami presented arguments for "peopleism overrun" and the "need to shift to digital peopleism."[28] Although his insistence that Japanese firms should continue to hold fast to peopleism as a fundamental principle is in itself worth listening to,[29] it also is true that the implications of the crucial central concepts of "peopleism overrun" and "digital peopleism" (especially their historical positioning) are vague. Itami's recognition of a phase during which the deterioration of corporate operating results, not peopleism, was the problem,[30] immediately prompted a counterargument that the cause of the deterioration of corporate results could be found in none other than peopleism. For their part, adherents of companyism, affected perhaps by the collapse of socialism in Europe, were sapped of energy. The University of Tokyo's Institute of Social Sciences, which earlier had advocated companyism, turned in the 1990s to research on "twentieth-century systems," and for the most part has never re-examined companyism as part of that effort.[31]

Rebuilding Capitalism

In this chapter I have tried to emphasize that, in Shibusawa's *gappons-hugi* capitalist view, both money and people are valued, and if one takes the theories of peopleism and companyism into account, the capitalist view in which people are valued can be thought to have made post-war Japanese management successful. The collapse of the bubble economy, however, exposed Japanese management to strong headwinds. How should we understand this situation? Moreover, how should we now proceed to rebuild capitalism? What lessons does *gapponshugi* hold for confronting the current crisis of global capitalism and the process of financialization? Is financialization truly irreversible, as Dore asserts? If it is not, what alternatives might exist? I am convinced that Shibusawa's perspectives on human resource development will lead to the answers to these questions, and that capitalism that emphasizes money can be replaced by capitalism that emphasizes people. Shibusawa's contributions, indeed, offer a significant hint about how to change capitalism's current emphasis on ranking lenders of money above individuals. Simply put, *the extensive fostering of the human resources required for modernization in an open format* is of decisive importance – not only for newly industrializing countries, but also for advanced countries currently suffering from the worldwide economic crisis.

In the balance of this chapter, I look at the past, present, and future of Japanese management, and discuss the modern significance of *gapponshugi*.

Three types of Japanese firms

To develop a proper discussion of Japanese management, one should begin by clarifying what it is. One should also note that not all Japanese firms have practised "Japanese management."

Like those in other advanced economies, Japanese companies can be categorized broadly as small, medium-sized, or large-scale firms. They can also be divided into managerial enterprises, where salaried managers wield more power than owners (rare among small and medium-sized firms), and capitalist enterprises, where owners (or owners concurrently acting as managers) have greater power than salaried managers. In other words, the three types of firms that exist in Japan are (a) large-scale firms that are managerial enterprises, (b) large-scale firms that are capitalist enterprises, and (c) small and medium-sized firms that are capitalist enterprises.

If, prior to the collapse of the bubble economy, one had asked in Japan, "to whom does a company belong?" the answers for types (a) and (c) would have been "the employees" and "the owners," respectively, while the answer for type (b) would have been either "the employees" or "the owners," depending on the case. The answers, moreover, would not have differed greatly if the respondent had been a manager or an employee. In countries in which stock market capitalism holds sway, in contrast, the answer is always, "a company belongs to the owners (shareholders)." Therefore, during the period before the collapse of the bubble economy, Japan's distinctive management style – that is, Japanese management conducted in its model form – was practised only in type (a) firms, at which the response would have been "the company belongs to its employees." Even in Japan, "Japanese management" was always a limited phenomenon.

The essence of "Japanese management"

What is "Japanese management"? One must recall here the "three sacred treasures" of lifetime employment, the seniority system, and enterprise labour unions. That all three are matters related to labour-management relations is indicative of the importance of such relations to Japanese management. One can thus say that Japanese management is management that seeks to maximize employee benefits based on cooperative labour relations.

Among Japanese firms, managerial enterprises were a small minority prior to the Second World War, but had become the most common type by the mid-1950s, when Japan launched into its period of rapid economic growth. If, during the decades that followed, these type (a) firms were said to belong to their employees (including managers), in the United States such large-scale enterprises belong to shareholders, while in the Soviet Union they were said to belong to "the workers."

At many shareholder-owned US firms, specialist managers cannot take their eyes off the singular pursuit of short-term profits, and are unable to adopt a long-term perspective because their overarching imperative is to increase their company's share price. Compelled to make dividend-focused appropriations of earnings, they have little incentive to use internal reserves for future investment. At Soviet firms, workers opposed increases in their numbers because they feared this would reduce their per capita share. Moreover, because competition among Soviet firms was non-existent, there was a strong propensity to resist the introduction of new technologies. In contrast, type (a) large-scale Japanese firms that "belong" to employees are free of such factors that hamper business growth. Because Japanese management deterred – through means such as stockholder stabilization as a result of cross-shareholding – the "shareholder counterrevolution"[32] that occurred in the United States from the 1960s onward, and avoided Soviet-style organized competition among employees, it allowed Japanese managerial enterprises to make growth-oriented decisions and the Japanese economy to achieve a high growth rate relative to most other economies during the period from the mid-1950s to the mid-1980s.

Although they were in the minority, type (b) large-scale Japanese firms that are capitalist enterprises – typified by companies such as Toyota Motor, Matsushita Electric, Idemitsu Kosan, Suntory, Ajinomoto, Bridgestone Tire, Canon, SANYO, Hayakawa Electric, Sony, and Honda – also played a prominent role during the Japanese economy's period of rapid growth. Supporters of groundbreaking entrepreneurial activities, these firms achieved growth that rivalled or surpassed that of the type (a) managerial enterprises. As well, at type (b) capitalist enterprises, specialist managers accounted for an ever-larger share of top management as their firms grew, heightening the belief that such companies, like type (a) firms, belonged to their employees. Consistent decision-making to maximize the benefits to employees while supporting a strong sense of unity among workers and managers: this was the characteristic approach to management that had become entrenched in both type (a) and type (b) large-scale Japanese corporations by the end of the period of rapid economic growth.

The formation of Japanese-style labour relations

Researchers disagree on when the cooperative labour relations that characterize Japanese management were formed, but it is clear that such relations played a key role in Japan's rapid post-war economic growth. With the "three sacred treasures" of lifetime employment, the seniority system, and enterprise labour unions in place, one could argue that, by the early 1960s, Japanese workers had begun to become actively involved in efficient production management, "total quality control," and "quality control circles."[33] This occurred against the backdrop of a growing number of operating crises and changes in competitive conditions faced by many key firms – for example, the liberalization of trade and capital for Komatsu, the maturation of the domestic market for Matsushita Electric, defeat in the "First BC War" (Bluebird–Corona War) for Toyota, and defeat in the "Second BC War" for Nissan.

"Japanese management" and technological innovation

"Japanese management" was well-suited to incremental (cumulative) technological innovation.[34] After the Second World War, Japanese firms achieved broad-ranging results through the development of applied technology. This strong technological development capacity was intimately related both to the system of relationships among firms and to the internal systems of firms, including the setting of business objectives from a long-term perspective; horizontal, flexible organizational structures; and employment practices such as long-term employment, internal transfers among divisions, and a system of internal promotions.

Setting business objectives from a long-term perspective enabled investment related to technological developments that were not expected to yield immediate results. Firms were also able to maintain continuity and stability in research and development without being buffeted by short-term fluctuations in earnings. Horizontal, flexible organizational structures ensured smooth "sideways" flows of information within firms. Maintaining close communications among internal divisions – including research, design, production, and sales – and keeping the necessary information flowing freely were also extremely important for achieving results from applied research, new product development, and production technology development. Long-term employment and a system of internal promotions lowered resistance to the introduction of new technologies, something that has been a problem in US and European firms. They also had the effect of increasing the incentive of both labour and management to engage in in-house education and training centred on on-the-job training). In addition, internal transfers among a firm's divisions made for a smooth "sideways" flow of information.

As a system among Japanese firms for promoting technology development, long-term business relationships were critical. Such relationships allowed firms to exchange both goods and information and frequently to form cooperative relations between the parties to transactions. This, in turn, elicited valuable information concerning customers' demands, to which Japanese firms excelled at responding and pursuing timely product development. Such exchanges of information over many years also led to production technology enhancements and greater production efficiency between assembly manufacturers and parts suppliers. Thus, by promoting technological innovation through the enlargement of production facilities, the proliferation of automation, advances in the materials revolution, and the successive introduction of new products, Japanese management contributed to Japan's rapid economic growth.

"Japanese management" and economic growth

The relationship between "Japanese management" and Japan's economic growth is, however, a complex issue. As we have seen, by the end of the period of rapid economic growth, large-scale Japanese enterprises overwhelmingly were thought of as belonging to their employees, and mechanisms that achieved incremental technological innovations from production sites, premised on cooperative labour relations, were at work. Although it is possible to deem such mechanisms to have been the product of Japanese management, sometimes Japanese management resulted in economic growth – let me call this the "A aspects" – and times when economic growth influenced Japanese management (the "B aspects"). Furthermore, the relationship between Japanese management and economic growth is thought to have changed over time.[35] During the first half of the period of Japan's rapid economic growth, from the latter half of the 1950s through the first half of the 1960s, the "B aspects" worked strongly – that is, economic growth influenced Japanese management. During the latter half of the period of rapid growth, from the latter half of the 1960s through the beginning of the 1970s, the two aspects acted mutually to amplify each another. Then, during the period of stable growth from the mid-1970s through the first half of the 1980s, the "A aspects" came to the fore – that is, Japanese management influenced the country's economic growth. This understanding is consistent with research results in the field of labour history, which assume that the cooperative management-labour relations that are characteristic of Japanese management were formed in the 1960s.

Dysfunctions of "Japanese management"

When the asset-inflated bubble burst and Japan entered the 1990s, however, the conditions in which Japanese management and the Japanese economy functioned were utterly changed. As the recession following the collapse of the economic bubble grew prolonged and problem loans accumulated, a financial crisis arose, leading to a string of institutional failures in 1997 and 1998, including those of Hokkaido Takushoku Bank, Yamaichi Securities, Long-Term Credit Bank of Japan, and Nippon Credit Bank.

Against the backdrop of these circumstances, a "systemic fatigue" theory rapidly gained a following. The theory severely criticized Japanese enterprise, including the rigidity of the employment and promotions systems, an excessive reliance on financial institutions from a financing perspective and slipshod fund management, the closed nature of transactions between firms, and over-regulation. The perception of "Japanese management" took a 180-degree turn, from an object of praise to an object of scorn.

Without doubt, Japanese management led to dysfunction after the bubble economy collapsed. What caused Japanese management to lose its vigour was a complete loss of self-confidence at large-scale, type (a) managerial enterprises that, until the 1980s, had been its core supporters. This, in turn, led them to push "shareholder-oriented management" to the fore. Let me avoid any misunderstanding by stating that this shift was not in itself incorrect. As a result of the expansion of Japan's capital markets and globalization from a financial perspective, both of which progressed rapidly beginning in the second half of the 1980s, firms were required to raise capital from capital markets, and for that they had to adopt a shareholder-oriented attitude. The problem was the thinking that equated shareholder-oriented management with the pursuit of short-term profits.[36] Many managerial enterprise-type large-scale firms completely forgot to maintain the long-term perspective that is a strength of Japanese management.

After Japan's bubble economy collapsed, managerial enterprise-type large-scale firms aggressively pursued a shift to US-style corporate management emphasizing return on assets (ROA) and return on equity (ROE). In the United States, which enjoyed a "New Economy" in the 1990s, firms invested aggressively and adopted strategies to realize a higher ROA and ROE by expanding their assets and equity and, with even greater vigour, boosting their returns. In contrast to this, many managerial enterprise-type large-scale firms in Japan restricted investment and attempted to increase their returns by reducing both assets and equity. Thus, although they had the same objective of increasing returns on assets and equity, Japanese and US firms adopted totally opposing attitudes towards investment. In Japan, what might be called "investment control mechanisms" were at work after the economic bubble collapsed, with extremely grave results. Atrophied managers unable to undertake the investments that are the original duty of a firm, and employees who cooperated actively with the survival of their firm as a result of investment controls, were observed at managerial enterprise-type Japanese firms. The Japanese management strength of maintaining a long-term perspective and accurately undertaking necessary investments had disappeared.

After the collapse of the economic bubble, it was capitalist enterprises whose owners held management leadership – the type (b) capitalist enterprises – that took up the tasks of maintaining the long-term view and undertaking necessary investment. One can say that, as part of the Japanese economy's transition from growth to stagnation, the main supporters of Japanese management underwent a shift from managerial enterprises to capitalist enterprises. Managerial enterprises, however, not capitalist enterprises, have always accounted for the majority of large enterprises in Japan. At managerial enterprises the investment control mechanism has prevailed, and so long as necessary investments are not made from a long-term standpoint, the rejuvenation of Japan's entire economy will remain precarious. In that sense, rebuilding Japanese management at managerial enterprises will be the key to the revival of Japan's economy.

The Revival of Japan's Economy and the "New Japanese Management"

As I have explained elsewhere,[37] the revival of the Japanese economy, which has been in a slump since the 1990s, will require the successful implementation of five scenarios:

- the acquisition of equity finance know-how by operating companies;
- progress in financial business reform with the establishment of (i) internationally competitive universal banks and (ii) superior regional banks that demonstrate detailed monitoring capabilities;
- an increase in international specialization in manufacturing, tied to efforts to provide greater added value;
- the achievement of new combinations of manufacturing and services; and
- the development of service businesses and logistics businesses that will actualize the private sector demand that is latent in the market.

Finally, to accomplish this, managerial enterprises will need to reject their investment control mechanisms, rebuild "Japanese management," and invest from a long-term perspective.

To rebuild Japanese management, it will be critical to develop a growth strategy along the lines of the five scenarios outlined above and to ensure that, over the medium to long term, shareholders' interests (higher share prices) and employees' interests (enhancements to working conditions) are aligned. The two sets of interests need not be in conflict – successful investments and growing firms will achieve both simultaneously. Although it has been argued that a strategy of growth will be difficult to adopt in a Japan where the population has begun to decline, such a strategy is quite possible if firms broaden their gaze to encompass the entire world and develop their businesses globally.

The rebuilding of Japanese management, however, should not be a mere return to the old form. While maintaining the tradition of long-term employment, reforms such as fundamentally reviewing the seniority system and introducing a merit system will have to be carried out resolutely. The "old Japanese management" of long-term employment and the seniority system must be transformed into a "new Japanese management" that emphasizes long-term employment without emphasizing the seniority system. In short, Japan's economy will revive when managerial enterprises adopt the "new Japanese management" and make intelligent investments from a long-term viewpoint and develop their businesses globally.

The modern significance of Shibusawa Eiichi's gapponshugi

Such a strategy for rebuilding "Japanese management" actually has much in common with the *gapponshugi* of Shibusawa Eiichi. By focusing on long-term employment, "new Japanese management" would give employees a sense of security, which relates to Shibusawa's ideal of capitalism that values people. By adopting the merit system, "new Japanese management" would put to work the principle of competition among employees, which overlaps with Shibusawa's emphasis on the use of open market mechanisms. Finally, by taking a long-term viewpoint, "new Japanese management" would conform to Shibusawa's frequent call for long-term participation in firms that invest in their shareholders.

A memo prepared in January 2012 for the *Gapponshugi* Project, managed by the Shibusawa Eiichi Memorial Foundation, notes that, although Shibusawa's *gapponshugi* overlaps normal capitalism on several points – including the aim to create an open economic system that uses market mechanisms, compared with the closed economic system formed by industrial conglomerates, and a limited role for government and a private sector-led economic management orientation – it is distinct from the normal outlook of capitalism on several points, including requiring the long-term participation of all of a firm's stakeholders (including shareholders), emphasizing an ethical viewpoint and warning against self-serving conduct when managing stakeholders (shareholders or managers), and demanding a certain amount of order in competition among firms.[38] If these *gapponshugi* characteristics can be systematized, it might be possible to create a new view of capitalism – one that challenges the pessimistic capitalist outlook of Ronald Dore that the wave of financialization can no longer be stopped. Those of us who are investigating Shibusawa Eiichi's contribution to human resource development based upon *gapponshugi* are resolved to play a role in that challenge.

NOTES

1 Proto-industrialization (in Japanese, *genkiteki kōgyōka*) is a concept proposed by Franklin Mendels based on a case study of the Flanders region in the eighteenth century; see Franklin F. Mendels, *Industrialization and Population Pressure in Eighteenth-Century Flanders* (New York: Arno Press, 1981).
2 Miwa Ryōichi, *Gaisetsu Nippon keizaishi: Kingendai* [Introduction to Japanese economic history: Modern history] (Tokyo: University of Tokyo Press, 1993), 23.
3 Ōkuma Shigenobu and Matsukata Masayoshi took the post of lord of treasury in 1873 and 1881, respectively. Inflation emerged under the Ōkuma fiscal administration, while deflation progressed under the Matsukawa administration.
4 Ando Yoshio, ed., *Kindai Nippon keizaishi yōran* [Handbook of modern Japanese economic history], 2nd ed. (Tokyo: University of Tokyo Press, 1979).
5 Miwa, *Gaisetsu Nippon keizaishi*, 100.
6 Salaried managers often became equity holders by acquiring treasury shares as they climbed the career ladder in their company. However, their career success was purely attributable to their specialized knowledge, and becoming equity holders was only a result of their career success.
7 For example, such a perspective is also taken in *Yūki dōdō* [Heroic drive and boundless energy] (published under the original title *Kantō* [Cold

light] in 1971), a novel by Shiroyama Saburō that depicts Shibusawa Eiichi.

8 The Furukawa *zaibatsu*'s movement for becoming a comprehensive *zaibatsu* suffered a setback, however, due to the failure of Furukawa Shoji in 1921, triggered by a soybean speculation failure known as the Dalian Incident.

9 Kikkawa Takeo, *Nippon no kigyō shūdan* [Company groups in Japan] (Tokyo: Yuhikaku, 1996), 231; author's translation.

10 Takeda Haruhito, *Takakuteki jigyō bumon no teichaku to kontsern soshiki no seibi* [The establishment of diversified departments and the development of conglomerate organizations] (Tokyo: Hosei University, Center for Business and Industrial Research, 1992); and Hashimoto Jyurō and Takeda Haruhito, eds., *Nippon keizai no hatten to kigyō shūdan* [Development of the Japanese economy and enterprise groups] (Tokyo: University of Tokyo Press, 1922), 78.

11 However, the industrialization policy promoted by Nakamigawa Hikojirō led to an earnings deterioration over the short term, which led to criticism of his reforms within Mitsui. This is one reason he died young, at the age of forty-seven, in 1901. He never saw the results of his reforms.

12 Shimada Masakazu, *Shibusawa Eiichi no kigyōsha katsudō no kenkyū: Senzenki kigyō shisutemu no sōshutsu to shusshisha keieisha no yakuwari* [The entrepreneurial activities of Shibusawa Eiichi: The creation of a joint-stock company system in the pre-war period and the role of the investor-executive] (Tokyo: Nihon Keizai Hyoronsha, 2007).

13 Kenjō Teiji, *Hyōden Nippon no keizai shiso: Shibusawa Eiichi* [Biography of Japanese economic thoughts: Shibusawa Eiichi] (Tokyo: Nihon Keizai Hyoronsha, 2008), 63.

14 See Shimada, *Shibusawa Eiichi no kigyōsha katsudō no kenkyū*, chap. 1.

15 Ibid., chap. 3.

16 A joint study by the Shibusawa Eiichi Memorial Foundation and Hitotsubashi University is currently underway to gain further insight into Shibusawa's contributions to human resource development.

17 For the characteristics of the global slump triggered by the Lehman Brothers bankruptcy and the path to breaking out of the recession, see Kikkawa Takeo, *Chiiki keizai kasseika to koyō sōshutsu: Gurōkarizeishon no konnichiteki igi* [Revitalization of regional economies and job creation: The modern significance of glocalization], CCIJ Report 63 (Tokyo: Consumer Co-operative Institute of Japan, 2009).

18 Ronald Dore, *Stock Market Capitalism: Welfare Capitalism – Japan and Germany versus the Anglo-Saxons* (Oxford: Oxford University Press, 2000).

19 The Japanese translation of Dore's *Stock Market Capitalism* is *Nihongata shihonshugi to shijōshugi no shōtotsu* [The collision of Japanese-style capitalism and market capitalism], trans. Fujii Mahito (Tokyo: Toyo Keizai, 2001), vi–vii, 5.

20 Ibid., 31–66.

21 See, for example, Nitta Michio, *Rōshi kankei no henyō to "futatsu no moderu"* [The transformation of labour relationships and the "two models"], in *20 seiki shihon shugi I: Gijutsu kakushin to seisan shisutemu* [20th century capitalism I: Technical innovation and production systems], ed. Hashimoto Jyurō (Tokyo: University of Tokyo Press, 1995).

22 See, for example, Ueda Hiroshi, "Shitauke to keiretsu" [Subcontractors and corporate groups], in *Ke-subukku: Nihon kigyō no keiei kōdō 1: Nihonteki keiei no seisei to hatten* [Case book: Managerial behaviour of Japanese companies 1: Formation and development of Japanese management], ed. Itami Hiroyuki, Kagono Tadao, Miyamoto Matao, and Yonekura Seiichirō (Tokyo: Yuhikaku, 1998).

23 Itami Hiroyuki, *Jinpon shugi kigyō* [Humanism enterprise] (Tokyo: Chikumashobo, 1987), 29–30.

24 Ibid., 37.

25 Ibid., 99.

26 Baba Hiroji, "Gendai sekai to nihon kaisha shugi" [The modern world and Japanese companyism], in *Gendai nihon shakai 1: Kadai to shikaku* [Modern Japanese society 1: Issues and viewpoints], ed. University of Tokyo, Institute of Social Sciences (Tokyo: University of Tokyo Press, 1991): 71–2.

27 Ibid., 72–3.

28 Itami Hiroyuki, *Keiei no mirai wo miayamaru na Dejitaru jinpon shugi e no michi* [Do not misread future management: The path to digital peopleism] (Tokyo: Nihon Keizai Shimbunsha, 2000).

29 This author's thinking on this matter is based on an evaluation that, even during the period of the so-called lost decade in the 1990s, Japan's production system remained fundamentally sound. See Kikkawa Takeo, "Gendai nihon kigyō ga chokumen suru mondai to sono kaiketu hōkō" [Problems confronting Japanese companies, and directions toward their solution], in *Gendai nihon kigyō Dai 2 kan* (The contemporary Japanese enterprise, vol. 2), ed. Kudō Akira, Kikkawa Takeo, and Glenn D. Hook (Tokyo: Yuhikaku Publishing, 2005).

30 Itami, *Keiei no mirai wo miayamaru*, 369.

31 University of Tokyo, Institute of Social Science, ed., *20 seiki shisutemu* [The 20th century global system], 6 v. (Tokyo: University of Tokyo Press, 1998).

32 "Shareholder counterrevolution" refers to owners retaking control of corporate management from managers, as opposed to a "managerial revolution," when managers seize control of corporate management from a firm's
owners.

33 Udagawa Masaru et al., *Nihon kigyō no hinshitu kanri* [Quality control
at Japanese firms], ed. Hosei University, Industrial Information Center
(Tokyo: Yuhikaku Publishing, 1995). "Total quality control" (TQC) means
quality control activities in which every employee participates. "Quality
control circles" (QC circles) are small groups that perform quality control activities in the workplace. Following the Second World War, Japanese firms imported a variety of control methodologies from the United
States, most of which did not take root in their original form but became
entrenched in a "Japanized" form. The transformation of quality control
based on statistical methods imported from the United States into TQC
and QC circles and the establishment of these methods at Japanese firms
was a typical example.

34 "Incremental technological innovation" is cumulative, continuous technological innovation, as contrasted with radical technological innovation.

35 For more on this view, see Kikkawa Takeo, "Nihon no kigyō shisutemu to
kōdo seichō" [The Japanese corporate system and rapid economic growth],
in Hashimoto, *20 seiki shihon shugi I*, 163.

36 Certainly there is a tendency to equate a shareholder orientation with the
pursuit of short-term profit. In fact, because US firms over the period of
the 1960s through the 1980s also took this view, they neglected necessary
investment and, as a result, fell behind Japanese firms when Japan and
the United States "traded places." In the 1990s, however, US firms turned
to investing aggressively with a long-term perspective while maintaining
their shareholder-oriented stance, leading Japan and the United States to
"trade places" again.

37 Kikkawa Takeo, "Nihon keizai to nihon kigyō ga chokumen suru mondai"
[The problems confronting Japan's economy and Japanese firms], in *Nihon
keieishi (shinpan) – Edo jidai kara 21 seiki e* [Japanese business history (new
edition) – From the Edo period to the 21st century], ed. Miyamoto Matao
et al. (Tokyo: Yuhikaku Publishing, 2007).

38 Shibusawa Eiichi Memorial Foundation, *Gapponshugi* Project: Meeting
at the Shibusawa Eiichi Memorial Foundation, Tokyo, 5 January 2012.
The Shibusawa Eiichi Memorial Foundation's *Gapponshugi* Project was
launched in 2011 and, as of January 2012, had defined the characteristics of
gapponshugi. These are interim findings; the project's work is ongoing.

Bibliography

Abe E. "Shibusawa, Eiichi." In *International Encyclopedia of Business and Management*. Edited by M. Warner. London; New York: Routledge, 1996.

Abend, Gabriel. *The Moral Background: An Inquiry into the History of Business Ethics*. Princeton, NJ: Princeton University Press, 2014.

Abouleish, Ibrahim, and Helmy Abouleish. "Garden in the Desert: Sekem Makes Comprehensive Sustainable Development a Reality in Egypt." *Innovations: Technology, Governance, Globalization* 3, no. 3 (2008): 21–48.

Acquier, Aurélien, Jean-Pascal Gond, and Jean Pasquero. "Rediscovering Howard R. Bowen's Legacy: The Unachieved Agenda and Continuing Relevance of *Social Responsibilities of the Businessman*." *Business & Society* 50, no. 4 (2011): 607–46.

Ando Yoshio, ed. *Kindai Nippon keizaishi yōran* [Handbook of modern Japanese economic history], 2nd ed. Tokyo: University of Tokyo Press, 1979.

Anon. *Mercantile Morals: A Book for Young Men Entering upon the Duties of Active Life*. London: James Blackwood, 1861.

Arakawa Minoji. "Kaigai bōeki fushin no gen'in oyobi shinsaku no hōhō" [Causes of inactivity in foreign trade and means of promoting it]. *Jitsugyō no Nihon* 1, no. 5 (October 1897).

Arima Hiromasa. "Shōgyō dōtoku" [Commercial morality]. In *Nihon shōnin shi* [History of merchants in Japan]. Edited by Nihon Rekishi Chiri Gakkai. Tokyo: Nihon Gakujutsu Fukyūkai, 1935.

Arisawa Hiromi, ed. *Showa keizaishi* [Economic history of the Showa period]. Tokyo: Nikkei, 1994.

Asano S. *Nihon no kindaika to keiei rinen* [Japanese modernization and management philosophy]. Tokyo: Nihon Keizai Hyoronsha, 1991.

Asano Sōichirō. "Kaigai bōeki kakuchō saku" [Strategy for expanding overseas trade]. *Jitsugyō no Nihon* 4, no. 22 (1900).

Avi-Yonah, Reuven S. "The Cyclical Transformations of the Corporate Form: A Historical Perspective on Corporate Social Responsibility." *Delaware Journal of Corporate Law* 30, no. 3 (2005): 767–818.

Baba Hiroji. "Gendai sekai to nihon kaisha shugi" [The modern world and Japanese companyism]. In *Gendai nihon shakai 1 Kadai to shikaku* [Modern Japanese society 1: Issues and viewpoints], edited by University of Tokyo, Institute of Social Sciences. Tokyo: University of Tokyo Press, 1991.

Bartrum, Edward. *Wanderings, West and East*. London: S.W. Partridge, 1899.

Bayard, Françoise, Patrick Fridenson, and Albert Rigaudière, eds. *Genèse des marchés*. Paris: Comité pour l'histoire économique et financière de la France, 2015.

Bezançon, Xavier. "Histoire du droit concessionnaire en France." *Entreprises et Histoire* 14, no. 38 (2005): 24–54.

Berle, Adolf A. *The Twentieth Century Capitalist Revolution*. New York: Harcourt, Brace, 1954.

Berle, Adolf A., and Gardiner C. Means. *The Modern Corporation and Private Property*. New York: Macmillan, 1932.

Bloom, John. "Doing What Comes Naturally ... Made Frank Ford Healthy and Wealthy." *Texas Monthly*, June 1979.

Blumental, Tuvia. "The Practice of Amakudari within the Japanese Employment System." *Asian Survey* 25, no. 3 (1985): 310–21.

Bowen, Howard Rothmann. *Social Responsibilities of the Businessman*. New York: Harper, 1953.

Brandes, Stuart D. *American Welfare Capitalism: 1880–1940*. Chicago: University of Chicago Press, 1976.

Calder, Kent E. "Elites in an Equalizing Role: Ex-bureaucrats as Coordinators and Intermediaries in the Japanese Government-Business Relationship." *Comparative Politics* 21, no. 4 (1989): 379–403.

Calder, Kent E. *Strategic Capitalism: Private Business and Public Purpose in Japanese Industrial Finance*. Princeton, NJ: Princeton University Press, 1993.

Carroll, Archie B. "A History of Corporate Social Responsibility: Concepts and Practices." In *The Oxford Handbook of Corporate Social Responsibility*. Edited by Andrew Crane, Abagail McWilliams, Dirk Matten, Jeremy Moon, and Donald S. Siegal, 19–46. Oxford: Oxford University Press, 2008.

Carroll, Archie B., Kenneth J. Lipartito, James E. Post, and Patricia H. Wehane. *Corporate Responsibility: The American Experience*. Cambridge: Cambridge University Press, 2012.

Chagnollaud, Dominique. "Du pantouflage ou 'la descente du ciel.'" *Pouvoirs* 80 (January 1997): 77–88.

Charle, Christophe. "Le pantouflage en France (vers 1880–vers 1980)." *Annales: Économies, Sociétés, Civilisations* 42, no. 5 (1987): 1115–37.

Chouinard, Yvon, and Vincent Stanley. *The Responsible Company.* Ventura, CA: Patagonia Books, 2012.

Colignon, Richard A., and Chikako Usui. *Amakudari: The Hidden Fabric of Japan's Economy.* Ithaca, NY: Cornell University Press, 2003.

Confucius. "Analects, 8/13." Translated by B. Watson. In *The Analects of Confucius.* New York: Columbia University Press, 2007.

Confucius. "Analects, 4/5." Translated by R.T. Ames and H. Rosemont, Jr. In *The Analects of Confucius: A Philosophical Translation.* New York: Ballantine Books, 1998.

Confucius. "Analects, 6/28." Translated by J. Legge. In *Confucian Analects: The Great Learning and The Doctrine of the Mean.* New York: Dover Publications, [1893] 1971.

Cruikshank, Jeffrey L. *A Delicate Experiment: The Harvard Business School, 1908–1945.* Boston: Harvard Business School Press, 1987.

David, Donald K. "Business Responsibilities in an Uncertain World." *Harvard Business Review* 27, no. 3 (1949): 1–8.

Dellheim, Charles. "The Creation of a Company Culture: Cadburys, 1861–1931." *American Historical Review* 92, no. 1 (1987): 13–44.

Desai, Ashok. "The Origins of Parsi Entrepreneurship." *Indian Economic and Social History Review,* 5, no. 4 (1968): 307–18.

de Touchet, Elisabeth. *Quand les Français armaient le Japon: l'arsenal de Yokosuka 1865–1882.* Rennes, France: Presses Universitaires de Rennes, 2003.

Diosy, Arthur. *The New Far East,* 5th ed. London: Cassell, 1904.

Donham, Wallace B. "The Failure of Business Leadership and the Responsibility of the Universities." *Harvard Business Review* 11, no. 4 (1933): 418–35.

Donham, Wallace B. "The Social Significance of Business." *Harvard Business School Alumni Bulletin,* July 1927.

Donzé, Pierre-Yves. *L'ombre de César: les chirurgiens et la construction du système hospitalier vaudois (1840–1960).* Lausanne, Switzerland: Éditions BHMS, 2007.

Dore, Robert. *Nihongata shihonshugi to shijōshugi no shōtotsu* [The collision of Japanese-style capitalism and market capitalism]. Translated by Fujii Mahito. Tokyo: Toyo Keizai, 2001.

Dore, Robert. *Stock Market Capitalism: Welfare Capitalism – Japan and Germany versus the Anglo-Saxons.* Oxford: Oxford University Press, 2000.

Duguid, P. "Reading Registrations: An Overview of 100 Years of Trademark Registrations in France, the United Kingdom, and the United States." In

Trademarks, Brands and Competitiveness. Edited by Teresa da Silva Lopes and Paul Duguid, 9–30. New York; London: Routledge, 2010.

Ehrenburg, Richard. *Der Handel: Seine wirtschaftliche Bedeutung, seine nationalen Pflichten und sein Verhältnis zum Staate* [Trade: Its economic significance, its national obligations and its relationship with the state]. Jena, Germany: Verlag von Gustav Fischer, 1897.

Emery, Henry C. "Chinese Commercial Morality." *Harper's*, July 1923.

Feldenkirchen, Wilfried. *Werner von Siemens, Inventor and International Entrepreneur.* Columbus: Ohio State University Press, 1994.

France. Service historique de la Défense. Archives. *Catalogue général des manuscrits, 1672, lieutenant-colonel Léopold Villette, Rapports et lettres sur une mission au Japon.* Vincennes, France.

Fridenson, Patrick. "Authority Relations in German and French Enterprises, 1880–1914." In *Bourgeois Society in Nineteenth-Century Europe.* Edited by Jürgen Kocka and Allan Mitchell, 223–44. Oxford: Berg, 1993.

Friedman, Milton. "The Social Responsibility of Business is to Increase Its Profits." *New York Times Magazine,* 13 September 1970.

Fromartz, Samuel. *Organic, Inc.* New York: Harcourt, 2006.

Furubayashi K., ed. *Jitsugyōka jinmei jiten* [Biographical dictionary of businessmen]. Tokyo: Jitsugyō Tsūshin, 1911.

Gardiner, A.G. *Life of George Cadbury.* London: Cassell, 1923.

Gerschenkron, Alexander. *Economic Backwardness in Historical Perspective.* Cambridge, MA: Belknap Press of Harvard University Press, 1962.

Gisborne, Thomas. *An Enquiry into the Duties of Men in the Higher and Middle Classes of Society in Britain.* London: B. & J. White, 1795.

Gospel, Howard F. *Markets, Firms, and the Management of Labour in Modern Britain.* Cambridge: Cambridge University Press, 1992.

Goswami, Omar. "Then Came the Marwaris: Some Aspects of the Changes in the Pattern of Industrial Control in Eastern India." *Indian Economic and Social History Review* 22, no. 3 (1985): 225–49.

Green, Hardy. *The Company Town: The Industrial Edens and Satanic Mills that Shaped the American Economy.* New York: Basic Books, 2010.

Grelon, André. "Le patronat chrétien." In *Dictionnaire historique du patronat français.* Edited by Jean-Claude Daumas, 1055–60. Paris: Flammarion, 2010.

Gremillon, Joseph B. *The Catholic Movement of Employers and Managers: A Study of UNIAPAC.* Rome: Gregorian University Press, 1961.

Habisch, André, Jan Jonker, Martina Wegner, and René Schmidpeter, eds. *Corporate Social Responsibility across Europe.* New York: Springer, 2005.

Hamon, Claude. "Ethique et diplomatie chez Shibusawa Eiichi." *Ebisu* 34, no. 1 (2005): 149–62.

Hamon, Claude. *Shibusawa Eiichi (1840–1931), bâtisseur du capitalism*. Paris: Maisonneuve et Larose, 2007.

Hara Terushi. "Les facteurs psychologiques et culturels de la modernisation japonaise: le cas de Eiichi Shibusawa." In *Autour de Alain Peyrefitte*. Edited by Raymond Boudon and Pierre Chaunu. Paris: Éditions Odile Jacob, 1996.

Harris, Kenneth. *The Wildcatter: A Portrait of Robert O. Anderson*. New York: Weidenfeld and Nicholson, 1987.

Hartmann, Heinrich. *Organisation und Geschäft: Unternehmensorganisation in Frankreich und Deutschland, 1890–1914*. Göttingen, Germany: Vandenhoeck und Ruprecht, 2010.

Hashimoto Jyurō and Takeda Haruhito, eds. *Nippon keizai no hatten to kigyō shūdan* [Development of the Japanese economy and enterprise groups]. Tokyo: University of Tokyo Press, 1922.

Hatano Shōgorō. "Waga shōnin wa hatashite fushin'yō naru ya" [How our merchants end up untrustworthy]. *Jitsugyō no Nihon* 5, no. 2 (1901).

Hattori Yukimasa. *The Foreign Commerce of Japan since the Restoration, 1869–1900*. Baltimore: Johns Hopkins Press, 1904.

Heald, Morrell. *The Social Responsibilities of Business, Company, and Community 1900–1960*. Cleveland: Case Western Reserve University Press, 1970.

Heermance, Edgar L. *The Ethics of Business: A Study of Current Standards*. New York; London: Harper & Brothers, 1926.

Higgins, David. "Trademarks and Infringement in Britain, c.1875–c.1900." In *Trademarks, Brands and Competitiveness*. Edited by Teresa da Silva Lopes and Paul Duguid, 102–18. New York; London: Routledge, 2010.

Hilkey, Judy. *Character Is Capital: Success Manuals and Manhood in Gilded Age America*. Chapel Hill: University of North Carolina Press, 1997.

Hirschmeier, J. *Nihon ni okeru kigyōka seishin no keisei* [The origins of entrepreneurship in Meiji Japan]. Translated by Tsuchiya T. and Yui T. Tokyo: Toyo Keizai Shinposha, 1965.

Hō Risei. "Zannen nagara Nihonjin wa Shinjin yori shōbai ga kaku no gotoku heta de katsu sai nai" [Unfortunately Japanese are inferior to the Chinese when it comes to trade]. *Jitsugyō no sekai* 7, no. 7 (1910).

Hoare, J.E. *Japan's Treaty Ports and Foreign Settlements: The Uninvited Guests, 1858–1899*. London: RoutledgeCurzon, 1995.

Honjō, Yuki Allyson. *Japan's Early Experience of Contract Management in the Treaty Ports*. London: Routledge, 2003.

Hopkins, Charles Howard. *History of the Y.M.C.A. in North America*. New York: Association Press, 1951.

Horwitz, Morton J. "The History of the Public/Private Distinction." *University of Pennsylvania Law Review* 130 (1982): 1423–8.

Hunter, Janet. *"Deficient in Commercial Morality"? Japan in Global Debates on Business Ethics in the Late Nineteenth and Early Twentieth Centuries*. Basingstoke, UK: Palgrave Macmillan, 2016.

Inamori Kazuo. *A Compass to Fulfilment*. New York: McGraw-Hill, 2009.

Ishikawa Bungo. *Shōgyō Jūnikō* [Twelve lectures on commerce]. Tokyo: Shimizu Shoten, 1926.

Itami Hiroyuki. *Jinpon shugi kigyō* [Humanism enterprise]. Tokyo: Chikumashobo, 1987.

Itami Hiroyuki. *Keiei no mirai wo miayamaru na Dejitaru jinpon shugi he no michi* [Do not misread future management: The path to digital peopleism]. Tokyo: Nihon Keizai Shimbunsha, 2000.

Jeremy, D.J. "The Enlightened Paternalist in Action: William Hesketh Lever at Port Sunlight before 1914," *Business History* 33, no. 1 (1991): 58–81.

Jeremy, D.J. "Ethics, Religion, and Business in Twentieth Century Britain." In *Business in Britain in the Twentieth Century: Decline and Renaissance?* Edited by Richard Coopey and Peter Lath, 356–84. Oxford: Oxford University Press, 2009.

Johnson, Chalmers. *MITI and the Japanese Miracle: The Growth of Industrial Policy, 1925–1975*. Stanford, CA: Stanford University Press, 1982.

Johnson, Chalmers. "The Reemployment of Retired Government Bureaucrats in Japanese Big Business." *Asian Survey* 14, no. 11 (1974): 963–75.

Johnston, Bob. *Switching to Solar: What We Can Learn from Germany's Success in Harnessing Clean Energy*. Amherst, NY: Prometheus Books, 2011.

Joly, Hervé. *Diriger une grande entreprise au XXᵉ siècle: l'élite industrielle française*. Tours, France: Presses de l'Université François-Rabelais, 2013.

Joly, Hervé. "Grands corps et pantouflage: le vivier de l'Etat." In *Dictionnaire historique des patrons français*. Edited by Jean-Claude Daumas, 796–803. Paris: Flammarion, 2010.

Jones, Geoffrey. "Entrepreneurship in the Natural Food and Beauty Categories before 2000: Global Visions and Local Expressions." Harvard Business School Working Paper 13–024. Cambridge, MA: Harvard Business School, August 2012.

Jones, Geoffrey. "The Growth Opportunity that Lies Next Door." *Harvard Business Review* 90, no. 7–8 (2012): 141–5.

Jones, Geoffrey. *Profits and Sustainability: A History of Green Entrepreneurship*. Oxford: Oxford University Press, 2017.

Jones, Geoffrey. *Renewing Unilever: Transformation and Tradition*. Oxford: Oxford University Press, 2005.

Jones, Geoffrey, and Loubna Bouamane. "'Power from Sunshine': A Business History of Solar Energy." Harvard Business School Working Paper 12-105. Cambridge, MA: Harvard Business School, May 2012.

Jones, Geoffrey, and Adrian Brown. "Thomas J. Watson, IBM, and Nazi Germany." Harvard Business School Case 807-133. June 2007; revised May 2015.

Jones, Geoffrey, Kerry Herman, and Prabakar Kothandaraman. "Jamnalal Bajaj, Mahatma Gandhi, and the Struggle for Indian Independence." Harvard Business School Case 807-028. August 2006; revised May 2015.

Jones, Geoffrey, and Ricardo Reisen de Pinho. "Natura: Global Beauty Made in Brazil." Harvard Business School Case 807-029. August 2006; revised October 2012.

Kamata Eikichi. "Wagakuni no shōgyō dōtoku o takamuru saizen sairyō saku" [Best strategies for improving the standard of commercial morality in our country]. *Jitsugyō no sekai* 5, no. 1 (1908).

Kanji Ishii. "Seiritsu-ki Nihon teikokushugi no ichi danmen – shikin chikuseki to shihon yushutsu" [One aspect of Japanese imperialism in its formative period – the accumulation of funds and the export of capital]. *Rekishigaku Kenkyū* no. 383 (1972).

Kanno Watarō. *Zoku Osaka keizaishi kenkyū* [Sequel to the study on economic history of Osaka]. Tokyo: Seibundo Shuppan, [1935] 1982.

Kanter, Rosabeth Moss. *SuperCorp: How Vanguard Companies Create Innovation, Profits, Growth, and Social Good*. New York: Crown, 2009.

Kashima Shigeru. "Saint-Simon shugisha – Shibusawa Eiichi." *Shokun* 31, no. 8 (1999) through 36, no. 1 (2004).

Kashima Shigeru. *Shibusawa Eiichi I: Sorobanhen*. [Shibusawa Eiichi I: Abacus] Tokyo: Bungeishunju, 2011.

Katō Takaaki. "Gaikoku bōeki jō no shōgai" [Obstacles to foreign trade]. *Jitsugyō no Nihon* 4, no. 15 (1900).

Kenjō Teiji. *Hyōden Nippon no keizai shisō: Shibusawa Eiichi* [Biography of Japanese economic thoughts: Shibusawa Eiichi]. Tokyo: Nihon Keizai Hyoronsha, 2008.

Kenjō Teiji. *Shibusawa Eiichi – "Dōtoku" to keizai no aida*. Tokyo: Nihon Keizai Hyoronsha, 2008.

Khurana, Rakesh. *From Higher Aims to Hired Hands: The Social Transformation of American Business Schools and the Unfilled Promise of Management as a Profession*. Princeton, NJ: Princeton University Press, 2007.

Kikkawa Takeo. *Chiiki keizai kasseika to koyō sōshutsu: Gurōkarizeishon no konnichiteki igi* [Revitalization of regional economies and job creation: The modern significance of glocalization]. CCIJ Report 63. Tokyo: Consumer Cooperative Institute of Japan, 2009.

Kikkawa Takeo. "Gendai nihon kigyō ga chokumen suru mondai to sono kaiketu hōhō" [Problems confronting Japanese companies, and directions toward their solution]. In *Gendai nihon kigyō Dai 2 kan* [The contemporary

Japanese enterprise, vol. 2]. Edited by Akira Kudo, Kikkawa Takeo, and Glenn D. Hook. Tokyo: Yuhikaku Publishing, 2005.

Kikkawa Takeo. "Nihon Keizai to nihon kigyō ga chokumen suru mondai" [The problems confronting Japan's economy and Japanese firms]. In *Nihon keieishi (shinpan) – Edo jidai kara 21 seiki he* [Japanese business history (new edition) – From the Edo period to the 21st century]. Edited by Miyamoto Matao, Abe Takeshi, Udagawa Masaru, Sawai Minoru, and Kikkawa Takeo. Tokyo: Yuhikaku Publishing, 2007.

Kikkawa Takeo. "Nihon no kigyō shisutemu to kōdo seichō" [The Japanese corporate system and rapid economic growth]. In *20 seiki shihon shugi I: Gijutsu kakushin to seisan shisutemu* [20th century capitalism I: Technological innovation and production systems]. Edited by Hashimoto Jyurō. Tokyo: University of Tokyo Press, 1995.

Kikkawa Takeo. *Nippon no kigyō shūdan* [Company groups in Japan]. Tokyo: Yuhikaku, 1996.

Kikkawa Takeo and Patrick Fridenson, eds. *Gurōbaru shihonshugi no naka no Shibusawa Eiichi: Gappon kyapitarizumu to moraru* [Gappon capitalism: The economic and moral ideology of Shibusawa Eiichi in global perspective]. Tokyo: Toyo Keizai, 2014.

Kikkawa Takeo, Shimada Masakazu, and Tanaka Kazuhiro, eds. *Shibusawa Eiichi to hitozukuri* [Shibusawa Eiichi and building human capital]. Tokyo: Yuhikaku, 2013.

Kimura Masato. *Nichibei minkan keizai gaikō 1905–1911* [Japan-US private economic diplomacy: 1905–1911]. Tokyo: Keio Tsushin, 1989.

Kimura Masato. *Shibusawa Eiichi: Minkan keizai gaikō-no sōshisha* [Shibusawa Eiichi: Pioneer of private economic diplomacy]. Tokyo: Chuokoron-Sha, 1991.

Kimura Tsuyoshi and Waseda University Historical Archive, eds. *Ōkuma Shigenobu sōsho*, vol. 1, *Ōkuma Shigenobu wa kataru – Kokon tōzai jinbutsu hyōron* [Ōkuma Shigenobu series, vol. 1, Ōkuma Shigenobu speaks – Commentary on significant figures of the east and west, past and present]. Tokyo: Waseda University Press, 1969.

Kinoshita Eitarō. *The Past and Present of Japanese Commerce*. New York: Columbia University Press, 1902.

Kocka, Jürgen. "Family and Bureaucracy in German Industrial Management, 1850–1914: Siemens in Comparative Perspective." *Business History Review* 45, no. 2 (1971): 133–56.

Kocka, Jürgen. "Industrielles Management: Konzeptionen und Modelle in Deutschland vor 1914." *Vierteljahrschrift fur Sozial- und Wirtschaftsgeschichte* 56, no. 3 (1969): 332–72.

Kōda Rohan. "Kōtoku kōeki to shitoku shieki to" [Public morality, public benefit and personal morality, personal benefit]. *Jitsugyō no sekai* 10, no. 15 (1913).

Köll, Elisabeth. *From Cotton Mill to Business Empire: The Emergence of Regional Enterprises in Modern China*. Cambridge, MA: Harvard University Press, 2003.

Koyama Kenzō. "Shōgyō dōtoku kōryō" [Consideration of commercial morality]. *Jitsugyō no Nihon* 1, no. 13 (1898).

Kuin, Pieter. *Management is méér: De sociale verantwoordelijkheid van de ondernemer* [Management is more: The social responsibility of the entrepreneur]. Amsterdam: Elsevier, 1977.

L'Aoufir, Rachid. *La Prusse de 1815 à 1848: l'industrialisation comme processus de communication*. Paris: l'Harmattan, 2004.

Ladd, G.T. *Shōgyō dōtoku – Lectures of G.T. Ladd*. Translated by Moriya Tsunetaro. Tokyo: Tokyo Kōtō Shōgyō Gakkō/Hakubunkan, 1907.

Landes, David S., Joel Mokyr, and William J. Baumol, eds. *The Invention of Enterprise: Entrepreneurship from Ancient Mesopotamia to Modern Times*. Princeton, NJ: Princeton University Press, 2010.

Latz, Gil. "Back to the Future: The Intellectual Themes of the Second Shibusawa Seminar on Japanese Studies." In *Challenges for Japan: Democracy, Business, and Aging*, 5–28. Tokyo: International House of Japan, 2001.

Latz, Gil. "Introduction to Shibusawa Eiichi's Legacy." In *Challenges for Japan*. Edited by Gil Latz and Izumi Koide, vi–xi. Tokyo: International House of Japan, 2003.

Latz, Gil, ed. *Rediscovering Shibusawa in the 21st Century*. Tokyo: Shibusawa Eiichi Memorial Foundation, 2014.

Lay, A.H. "Report on Commercial Education in Japan." United Kingdom, British Parliamentary Papers, *Commercial and Consular Reports, Japan*, vol. 10. Shannon: Irish University Press, [1899] 1971.

Le Bret, Hervé. "The *Saint-Simonisme*: Doctrine and Practice of Management." In *Managerial Thought and Practice in France, 19th–21st Centuries: Assessment and Future Prospects*. Edited by Gilles Garel et al., 2011. Available online at http://mtpf.mlab-innovation.net/en/.

Lehmann, Jean-Pierre. *The Image of Japan: From Feudal Isolation to World Power, 1850–1905*. London: Routledge, [1978] 2011.

Levitt, Theodore. "The Dangers of Social Responsibility." *Harvard Business Review* 36, no. 5 (1958): 41–50.

Locke, Robert R. *The End of the Practical Man*. Greenwich, CT: JAI Press, 1984.

Longford, Joseph H. "The Commercial Morality of the Japanese." *Contemporary Review* 87 (January–June 1905): 705.

Mackey, John, and Raj Sisoda. *Conscious Capitalism*. Boston: Harvard Business School Press, 2013.

Marchand, Roland. *Creating the Corporate Soul: The Rise of Public Relations and Corporate Imagery in American Big Business*. Berkeley: University of California Press, 1998.

Margolis, Joshua D., and James P. Walsh. "'Misery Loves Companies': Rethinking Social Initiatives by Business." *Administrative Science Quarterly* 48, no. 2 (2003): 268–305.

Masuda Takashi. *Japan: Its Commercial Development and Prospects*. London: Sisley's, 1908.

Matsukawa K. "Kōdō no shishin toshite no Rongo" [The *Analects* of Confucius as a guide for action]. In *Shinjidai no Sōzō Kōeki no Tsuikyūsha Shibusawa Eiichi* [Creation of the new era: Shibusawa Eiichi – Proponent of the public good]. Edited by Shibusawa Kenkyūkai. Tokyo: Yamakawa Shuppansha, 1999.

Medzini, Meron. *French Policy in Japan during the Closing Years of the Tokugawa Regime*. Cambridge, MA: Harvard University, East Asian Research Center, 1971.

Mendels, Franklin F. *Industrialization and Population Pressure in Eighteenth-Century Flanders*. New York: Arno Press, 1981.

Millward, Robert. *The State and Business in the Major Powers: An Economic History, 1815–1939*. London: Routledge, 2013.

Mishima Chūshū. "Gi ri gōitsu ron" [On the inseparability of morality and profit]. *Tokyo Gakusikaiin Zasshi* 8, no. 5 (1886): 54.

Miwa Ryōichi. *Gaisetsu Nippon keizaishi: Kingendai* [Introduction to Japanese economic history: Modern history]. Tokyo: University of Tokyo Press, 1993.

Miyamoto Mataji. *Osaka shōnin taiheiki Taishōhen jō* [Record of Osaka-based merchants in the Taisho period, part I]. Tokyo: Sogensha, 1964.

Miyamoto Matao. "The Management Systems of Edo Period Merchant Houses." *Japanese Yearbook on Business History* 13 (1997): 97–142.

Miyamoto Matao. *Nihon no kindai 11: Kigyōkatachi no chōsen* [Modern Japan 11: The challenge of the entrepreneurs]. Tokyo: Chuo Koronsha, 1999.

Miyamoto Matao. "The Products and Market Strategies of the Osaka Cotton Spinning Company, 1883–1914." *Japanese Yearbook on Business History* 5 (1989): 117–59.

Miyamoto Matao. "Sangyōka to kaisha seido no hatten" [Japan's industrialization and the development of the company system]. In *Nihon Keizaishi 4: The Age of Industrialization*. Edited by Nishikawa Shunsaku and Abe Takeshi. Tokyo: Iwanami Shoten, 1990.

Miyamoto Matao, and Abe Takeshi. "The Corporate Governance of Japanese Firms at the Early Stage of Industrialization: Osaka Cotton Spinning and

Nippon Life Assurance." In *The Development of Corporate Governance in Japan and Britain*. Edited by Robert Fitzgerald and Abe Etsuo, 9–31. Burlington, VT: Ashgate, 2004.

Morikawa H. "Shibusawa Eiichi – Nihon kabushiki kaisha no sōritsusha" [Shibusawa Eiichi – Founder of the joint-stock company in Japan]. In *Nihon no kigyō to kokka* [Enterprises and the state in Japan]. Nihon rekishi koza, 4. Tokyo: Nihon Keizai Shimbunsha, 1976.

Morimura Ichizaemon. "Gyōdōtoku no kaizen wa daiyoku o kosui suru ni kagiru" [Improvement in business morality constrained by advocacy of greed]. *Jitsugyō no sekai* 5, no. 3 (1908).

Morimura Ichizaemon. "Jitsugyō rikkoku no hōshin" [How to build up our national business]. *Jitsugyō no Nihon* 3, no. 20 (1899).

Muirhead, Sophia A. *Corporate Contributions: The View from 50 Years*. Report 1249-99-RR. New York: Conference Board, 1999.

Muller, Alan, and Ans Kok. "CSR Performance in Emerging Markets: Evidence from Mexico." *Journal of Business Ethics* 8, supp. 2 (2009): 325–37.

Murphy, Kevin. *The American Merchant Experience in Nineteenth Century Japan*. London: RoutledgeCurzon, 2002.

Murray, Frank, and Jon Tarr. *More than One Slingshot: How the Health Food Industry Is Changing America*. Richmond, VA: Marlborough House, 1984.

Nakagawa Keiichirō. "Nihon no kōgyōka katei ni okeru soshikikasareta kigyōshakatsudō" [Organized entrepreneurship in the process of Japan's industrialization]. *Keieishigaku* 2, no. 2 (1967): 8–37.

Nakajima Rikizō. *Shōgyō dōtoku kyōkasho* [Commercial morality textbook]. Tokyo: Dobunkan, 1901.

Nanda, B.R. *In Gandhi's Footsteps: The Life and Times of Jamnalal Bajaj*. Delhi: Oxford University Press, 1990.

Nemoto Tadashi, "Honpō shōnin no heifū" [Evil practices of Japanese merchants], *Jitsugyō no Nihon* 2, no. 15 (1898): 13–15.

Nicholas, Tom, and Laura G. Singleton. "Control Data Corporation and the Urban Crisis." Harvard Business School Case 9-808-096, September 2011.

Nihon Ginkō hyakunenshi hensan'iinkai, ed. *Nihon Ginkō hyakunen shi* [100-year history of the Bank of Japan] 1 (1982): 3–31.

Nippon Life Insurance Company, ed. *The 100-year History of Nippon Life*. Osaka: Nippon Life Insurance Company, 1992.

Nitta Michio. "*Rōshi kankei no henyou to 'futatsu no moderu'*" [The transformation of labour relationships and the "two models"]. In *20 seiki shihon shugi I: Gijutsu kakushin to seisan shisutemu* [20th century capitalism I: Technical innovation and production systems]. Edited by Hashimoto Juro. Tokyo: University of Tokyo Press, 1995.

Oh Kaka. "Shibusawa Eiichi no *Rongo soroban* setsu to *Nihonteki na shihonshugi no seishin*" [Shibusawa Eiichi's *The Analects and the Abacus* and the Japanese spirit of capitalism]. In *Shibusawa kenkyū 7*. Edited by Shibusawa Kenkyūkai. Tokyo: Shibusawa Memorial Museum, 1994.

Okazaki Tetsuji and Okuno Masahiro, eds. *Gendai nihon keizai shisutemu no genryū* [The Japanese economic system and its historical origins]. Tokyo: Nihon Keizai Shimbun Shuppansha, 1993.

Ōshima Kiyoshi, Katō Toshihiko, and Ōuchi Tsutomu. *Jinbutsu – Nihon shihonsyugi: 3 Meiji shoki no kigyōka* [Personalities in Japanese capitalism: 3 entrepreneurs of the early Meiji period]. Tokyo: Tokyo University Press, 1976.

Pauer, Erich. "Deutsche Ingenieure in Japan, japanische Ingenieure in Deutschland in der Zwischenkriegszeit" [German engineers in Japan, Japanese engineers in Germany in the inter-war period]. In *Deutschland-Japan in der Zwischenkriegszeit* [Germany-Japan in the inter-war period]. Edited by J. Kreiner and R. Mathias, 309–11. Bonn, Germany: Bouvier Verlag, 1990.

Peaucelle, Jean-Louis. "Saint-Simon, aux origines de la pensée de Henri Fayol." *Entreprises et Histoire* 12, no. 34 (2003): 68–83.

Peaucell, Jean-Louis, and Cameron Guthrie. *Henri Fayol, the Manager*. London: Pickering and Chatto, 2015.

Peery, R.B. *Gist of Japan*. Edinburgh; London: Oliphant, 1897.

Picon, Antoine. *Les saint-simoniens: raison, imaginaire et utopie*. Paris: Belin, 2002.

Pilbeam, Pamela M. *Saint-Simonians in Nineteenth-Century France: From Free Love to Algeria*. Basingstoke, UK: Palgrave Macmillan, 2014.

Porter, Michael E., and Mark R. Kramer. "Creating Shared Value." *Harvard Business Review* 89, nos. 1–2 (2011): 62–77.

Prochasson, Christophe. *Saint-Simon ou l'anti-Marx*. Paris: Perrin, 2005.

Ranis, Gustav. "The Community-Centered Entrepreneur in Japanese Development." *Explorations in Entrepreneurial History* 8, no. 2 (1955): 80–98.

Rathgen, Karl. *Die Japaner in der Weltwirtschaft* [The Japanese in the world economy]. Leipzig: B.G. Teubner, 1911.

Rey-Garcia, Marta, and Nuria Puig-Raposo. "Globalisation and the Organisation of Family Philanthropy: A Case of Isomorphism?" *Business History* 55, no. 6 (2013): 1019–46.

Reynolds, John. *Ethics in Investment Banking*. With Edmund Newell. Basingstoke, UK: Palgrave Macmillan, 2011.

Rosen, Christine M. "Businessmen against Pollution in Late Nineteenth Century Chicago." *Business History Review* 69, no. 3 (1995): 351–97.

Ryūmonsha, ed. *Shibusawa Eiichi denki shiryō* [Shibusawa Eiichi biographical materials], 68 v. Tokyo: Shibusawa Eiichi denki shiryō kankōkai, 1955–71.

Saint-Simon, Henri de. *Œuvres completes*. 4 v. Paris: PUF, 2012.

Sakamoto Shinichi. *Shibusawa Eiichi no kesei saimin shisō* [Confucian politico-economic thought of Shibusawa Eiichi]. Tokyo: Nihon Keizai Hyoronsha, 2002.

Sakata Yasuo, ed. *Kokusai businessman-no tanjō: Nichibei keizaikankei no kaitaku-sha* [Emergence of international businesspeople: Pioneers of Japan-US economic relations]. Tokyo: Tokyodo Shuppan, 2009.

Scranton, Philip, and Patrick Fridenson. *Reimagining Business History*. Baltimore: Johns Hopkins University Press, 2013.

Segrestin, Blanche. "Le tournant fayolien: des révolutions industrielles à la naissance de l'entreprise moderne." *Entreprises et Histoire* 25, no. 83 (2016): 5–12.

Seoka M. "Shibusawa Eiichi niokeru ideorogi to kakushinsei" [Shibusawa Eiichi's ideology and progressiveness]. *Osaka daigaku keizaigaku* 26, nos. 1–2 (1976).

Seoka M. "Shibusawa Eiichi niokeru kakushinsei no keiseikatei" [The formation of Shibusawa Eiichi's progressive thought]. *Osaka Daigaku kejzajgaku* 26, nos. 3–4 (1977).

Sharp Corporation. *Opening New Frontiers: Annual Report 2009*. Osaka: Sharp Corporation, 2009. Available online at http://www.sharp-world.com/corporate/ir/library/annual/pdf/annual_2009.pdf.

Sheldon, Oliver. *The Philosophy of Management*. London: Pitman, 1923.

Shibusawa Eiichi. *Amayogatari: Shibusawa Eiichi jiden* [The autobiography of Shibusawa Eiichi]. Annotated by Chō Yukio. Tokyo: Iwanami Shoten, 1984.

Shibusawa Eiichi. "The Analects and the Abacus." *Modern Japanese*. Translated by Moriya Atsushi. Tokyo: Chikumashobo, 2010.

Shibusawa Eiichi. *The Autobiography of Shibusawa Eiichi: From Peasant to Entrepreneur*. Edited by Craig Teruko. Tokyo: University of Tokyo Press, 1994.

Shibusawa Eiichi. "Dōtoku keizai gōitsu setsu" [The doctrine of inseparability of morality and economy]. Radio broadcast, 13 June 1923. In *Seien-sensei enzetsu senshō*. Tokyo: Tokyo Ryūmonsha, 1937.

Shibusawa Eiichi. *Rikkai ryakusoku* [The elements of company formation]. Tokyo: Ministry of Finance, 1871.

Shibusawa Eiichi. *Rongo kōgi* [Lectures on *The Analects*] Tokyo: Meitoku Shuppan Sha, [1925] 1975.

Shibusawa Eiichi. *Rongo to soroban* [*The Analects* and the abacus]. Tokyo: Kokusho Kankōkai, [1916] 1985.

Shibusawa Eiichi. *Seien hyakuwa* [Seien's 100 stories]. Tokyo: Kokumin Kyōiku Kai, [1913] 1926.

Shibusawa Eiichi. "Seien-sensei kungen" [The precepts of Dr Seien], *Ryūmon Zasshi* 249, 1909.

Shibusawa Eiichi. *Shibusawa Eiichi jijoden* [Autobiography of Shibusawa Eiichi]. Tokyo: Ijin Resshiden Hensanjo, 1937.

Shibusawa Eiichi Kinen Zaidan, ed. *Shibusawa Eiichi o shiru jiten* [A dictionary of Shibusawa Eiichi]. Tokyo: Tokyodo, 2012.

Shibusawa Eiichi Memorial Foundation. Gapponshugi Project: Meeting at the Shibusawa Eiichi Memorial Foundation, 5 January 2012.

Shibusawa Memorial Museum, ed. *Shibusawa Eiichi America e iku: Hyakunen nae no minkan keizai gaikō* [Shibusawa Eiichi goes to the United States: Private economic diplomacy of 100 years ago]. Tokyo: Shibusawa Eiichi Memorial Foundation, 2009.

Shibusawa Hideo. *Shibusawa Eiichi*. Tokyo: Shibusawa Seien Kinen Zaidan, 1956.

Shimada Masakazu. "Eiichi Shibusawa, Industrialist, as Viewed through the Financial Documents of the Shibusawa Family." *Bunkyo Women's University Keiei Ronshū* 7, no. 1 (1997): 19–40.

Shimada Masakazu. "The Entrepreneurial Activities of Shibusawa Eiichi: The Creation of a Joint Stock Company System in the Prewar Period and the Role of the Investor-Executive." *Japanese Research in Business History* 25 (2008): 93–114.

Shimada Masakazu. "How Shibusawa Eiichi Offered Models of Investment and Management to Introduce Modern Business Practice into Japan." *Japanese Yearbook on Business History* 19 (2002): 9–31.

Shimada Masakazu. "Senzenki nihon no shōgyō kyōiku seido no hatten – Tokyo no shiritsu shōgyō gakkō to Shibusawa Eiichi" [The development of the commercial school system in prewar Japan – The support from Shibusawa Eiichi to the private commercial school in Tokyo]. *Business Review Faculty of Business Administration* (Bunkyo Gakuin University) 19, no. 1 (2009).

Shimada Masakazu. *Shibusawa Eiichi no kigyōsha katsudō no kenkyū: Senzenki kigyō shisutemu no sōshutsu to shusshisha keieisha no yakuwari* [The entrepreneurial activities of Shibusawa Eiichi: The creation of a joint-stock company system in the pre-war period and the role of the investor-executive]. Tokyo: Nihon Keizai Hyoronsha, 2007.

Shimada Masakazu. *Shibusawa Eiichi: Shakai kigyōka no senkusha* [Shibusawa Eiichi: The pioneer of the social enterprise]. Tokyo: Iwanami Shoten, 2011.

Siemens, Werner von. *Lebenserinnerungen*, 3rd ed. Berlin: Julius Springer, 1908.

Sine, Wesley D., and Brandon H. Lee. "Tilting at Windmills? The Environmental Movement and the Emergence of the US Wind Energy Sector." *Administrative Science Quarterly* 54, no. 1 (2009): 123–55.

Sluyterman, Keetie. "Corporate Social Responsibility of Dutch Entrepreneurs in the 20th Century." *Enterprise & Society* 13, no. 2 (2012): 313–49.

Smith, Adam. *An Inquiry into the Nature and Causes of the Wealth of Nations.* New York: Modern Library, [1776] 1937. Translated by Ōuchi Hyōe and Matsukawa Shichirō. Tokyo: Iwanami Shoten, 1959.

Smith, Adam. *The Theory of Moral Sentiments.* Indianapolis, IN: Liberty Fund, [1790] 1982.

Sonoda Kōkichi. "Shōgyō dōtoku yōsei no hitsuyō" [Need to cultivate commercial morality]. *Jitsugyō no Nihon* 4, no. 1 (1900).

Spector, Bert. "'Business Responsibilities in a Divided World': The Cold War Roots of the Corporate Social Responsibility Movement." *Enterprise & Society* 9, no. 2 (2008): 314–36.

Stigler, George. "The Theory of Economic Regulation." *Bell Journal of Economics and Management Science* 2, no. 1 (1971): 3–21.

Sugiyama Kazuo. "Kabushikikaishaseido no hatten" [The development of the joint-stock company system]. In *The Studies of Japanese Business History*, vol. 1. Edited by Kobayashi Masaaki et al. Tokyo: Yuhikaku, 1976.

Suire, Yannis. *Le Marais poitevin: une écohistoire du XVIᵉ à l'aube du XXᵉ siècle.* La Roche sur Yon, France: Centre vendéen de recherches historiques, 2006.

Suzuki Tsuneo. "Meiji-ki no kaisha oyobi keieisha no kenkyū – Nihon zenkoku kaisha yakuinroku (Meiji 31-nenban) no bunseki" [Research on corporations and managers in the Meiji period – An analysis of the 1898 National List of Directors of Japanese companies]. *Sangyō keizai kenkyū kiyō* (Chubu University) 9 (1999).

Suzuki Tsuneo, Kobayakawa Yōichi, and Wada Kazuo, eds. *Kigyōka nettowaku no keisei to tenkai: Detabesu karamita Nihon no chiiki Keizai* [The formation and development of business networks: A database study of regional economics in modern Japan]. Aichi: University of Nagoya Press, 2009.

Takamura Naosuke. *Kaisha no tanjō* [The birth of the corporation]. Tokyo: Yoshikawa Kobunkan, 1996.

Takeda Haruhito. *Takakuteki jigyō bumon no teichaku to kontsern soshiki no seibi* [The establishment of diversified departments and the development of conglomerate organizations]. Tokyo: Hosei University, Center for Business and Industrial Research, 1992.

Tanaka Kazuhiro. "Dōtoku keizai gōitsu setsu no Shin'i" [Real meaning of the idea of the unity of morality and economy]. In *Shibusawa Eiichi to Hitozukuri* [Shibusawa Eiichi and building human capital]. Edited by Kikkawa Takeo, Shimada Masakazu, and Tanaka Kazuhiro. Tokyo: Yuhikaku, 2013.

Tata Group. "Tata Corporate Social Responsibility: A Century of Trust." Available online at http://www.slideshare.net/Odishadevelopment/tata-corporate-social-responsibility-a-century-of-trust, accessed November 2012.

Tateishi Sajirō. *Japan's Internationale Handelsbeziehungen, mit besonderer Rücksichtigung der Gegenwart* [Japan's international trading relations, with special regard to the present]. Halle, Germany: Hofbuch Druckerei von C.A. Kaemmerer, 1902.

Teramoto Noriko. *Lettres de Léopold Villette à Akitake Tokugawa: de l'Exposition universelle de Paris en 1867 à la Guerre russo-japonaise.* Tokyo: Hitotsubashi University, Center for Historical Social Science Literature, 2009.

Teranishi Jūrō. *Nihon no keizai shisutemu* [The Japanese economic system]. Tokyo: Iwanami Shoten, 2003.

Thomas, Joseph Llewellyn. *Journeys among the Gentle Japs in the Summer of 1895.* London: Sampson Low, 1897.

Tōyō Bōseki Kabushikikaisha. *Hyakunenshi Toyobo* [100 years' history of Toyobo]. Osaka: Tōyō Bōseki, 1986.

Toyosaki Zennosuke. "Shōtorihikijō ni okeru shinyō no kachi" [Value of trust in commercial dealings]. *Jitsugyō no sekai* 10, no. 21 (1913).

Tripathi, Dwijendra. *Oxford History of Indian Business.* New Delhi: Oxford University Press, 2004.

Tsuchiya Takao. *Nihon keiei rinen shi* [The history of Japanese philosophy of management]. Kashiwa, Japan: Reitaku Daigaku Shuppan Kai, 2002.

Tsuchiya Takao. *Nihon shjhonsyugi-ō no shidōsyatachi* [Leaders in the history of Japanese capitalism]. Tokyo: Iwanami Shoten, 1939.

Tsugai Yoshio. *Nihon shihonsyugi no gunzō* [Figures in Japanese capitalism]. Tokyo: Kyōikusha, 1980.

Udagawa Masaru, Satō Hiroki, Nakamura Keisuke, and Nonaka Izumi. *Nihon kigyō no hinshitu kanri* [Quality control at Japanese firms]. Edited by Hosei University, Industrial Information Center. Tokyo: Yuhikaku Publishing, 1995.

Ueda Hiroshi. "Shitauke to keiretsu" [Subcontractors and corporate groups]. In *Ke-subukku: Nihon kigyō no keiei kōdō 1: Nihonteki keiei no seisei to hatten* [Case book: Managerial behaviour of Japanese companies 1: Formation and development of Japanese management]. Edited by Itami Hiroyuki, Kagono Tadao, Miyamoto Matao, and Yonekura Seiichiro. Tokyo: Yuhikaku, 1998.

Umezu J. "Shijō no rinritreki kiso wo motomete – Fukuzawa Yukichi to Shibusawa Eiichi" [Toward an ethical basis for the market economy – Yukichi Fukuzawa and Shibusawa Eiichi]. In *Jiyū keizai to rinri* [The liberal economy and ethics]. Edited by Katō Hirotaka. Tokyo: Seibundo, 1995.

University of Tokyo. Institute of Social Science, ed. *20 seiki shisutemu* [The 20th century global system]. 6 v. Tokyo: University of Tokyo Press, 1998.

Uno Yonekichi, ed. *Yamanobe Takeo-kun shōden* [Short biography of Mr Yamanobe Takeo]. Osaka: Bōsekizasshisha, 1918.

Vasi, Ion Bogdan. *Winds of Change: The Environmental Movement and the Global Development of the Wind Energy Industry*. Oxford: Oxford University Press, 2011.

Weber, Max. *The Protestant Ethic and the Spirit of Capitalism*. Oxford: Oxford University Press, [1905] 2011.

Weintraub, Jeff. "The Theory and Politics of the Public/Private Distinction." In *Public and Private in Thought and Practice*. Edited by Jeff Weintraub and Krishan Kumar, 1–42. Chicago: University of Chicago Press, 1997.

Williams, Melissa S. "Moral Foundations of Politics and the Harmony of Ideas." In *Rediscovering Shibusawa Eiichi in the 21st Century*. Edited by Gil Latz, 250–2. Tokyo: International House of Japan, 2003.

Wilson, John F., and Andrew Thomson. *The Making of Modern Management: British Management in Historical Perspective*. Oxford: Oxford University Press, 2006.

Yago Kazuhiko. "Introduction of French Managerial Thought and Practices in Japan." *Managerial Thought and Practice in France, 19th–21st Centuries: Assessment and Future Prospects*. Edited by Gilles Garel et al., 2011. Available online at http://mtpf.mlab-innovation.net/en/.

Yamafuji Ryūtarō. "Chūtō shōgyō kyōiku no fukyū to kōritsu shōgyō gakkō" [Spread of commercial education at middle schools and public commercial schools]. In *Shibusawa Eiichi to hitozukuri* [Shibusawa Eiichi and building human capital]. Edited by Kikkawa Takeo, Shimada Masakazu, and Tanaka Kazuhiro. Tokyo: Yuhikaku, 2013.

Yamamura Kōzō. "A Re-Examination of Entrepreneurship in Meiji Japan (1868–1912)." *Economic History Review* 21, no. 1 (1968): 144–58.

Yamanobe Takeo. "Bōseki-gyō kōchaku shihon shōkyaku oyobi son'eki keisan ni kansuru shisetsu" [My opinion on the depreciation of fixed capital in the spinning industry and the profit and loss account]. *Bōseki rengō geppō* 2. 1889.

Young, B.W. "Christianity, Secularization and Political Economy." In *Religion, Business and Wealth on Modern Britain*. Edited by David J. Jeremy. London: Routledge, 1998.

Zopf, Eva-Maria. *Amakudari: Descent from Heaven and Its Implications on Doing Business in Japan*. Saarbrücken, Germany: Verlag Dr. Müller, 2009.

Zunz, Oliver. *Philanthropy in America: A History*. Princeton, NJ: Princeton University Press, 2011.

Contributors

Patrick Fridenson, PhD, University Paris VIII, is Professor Emeritus of International Business History at the École des hautes études en sciences sociales, Paris. He has published many monographs and articles, including *Reimagining Business History*, with Philip Scranton (Johns Hopkins University Press, 2013); *Beyond Mass Distribution: Distribution, Market and Consumers*, co-editor with Tsunehiko Yui (Japan Business History Institute, 2012); and *The Automobile Revolution*, co-author (University of North Carolina Press, 1982).

Janet Hunter, PhD, University of Oxford, is Professor of Economic History at the London School of Economics and Political Science. She has published many monographs and articles, including *The Historical Consumer: Consumption and Everyday Life in Japan, 1850-2000*, co-edited with Penelope Francks (Palgrave, 2012; Japanese edition Hosei University Press, 2016) and *"Deficient in Commercial Morality"? Japan in Global Debates on Business Ethics in the Late Nineteenth and Early Twentieth Centuries* (Palgrave, 2016).

Geoffrey Jones, PhD, Cambridge University, is Professor of Business History, Harvard Business School. He has published many monographs and articles, including *Beauty Imagined: A History of the Global Beauty Industry* (Oxford University Press, 2010) and *Entrepreneurship and Multinationals: Global Business and the Making of the Modern World* (Edward Elgar, 2013).

Kikkawa Takeo, PhD, University of Tokyo, is Professor of Business History at the Graduate School of Innovation Studies, Tokyo University of Science. He has published many monographs and articles, including *Policies for Competitiveness: Comparing Business-Government Relationships in the "Golden Age of Capitalism,"* co-edited with Miyajima Hideaki and Takashi Hikino (Oxford University Press, 1999); *Shibusawa Eiichi to hitodukuri,* co-edited with Shimada Masakazu and Tanaka Kazuhiro (Yuhikaku, 2013); and *Nippon no enerugi mondai* (NTT Shuppan, 2013).

Kimura Masato, PhD, Keio University, is Senior Director of the Shibusawa Eiichi Memorial Foundation. He has published numerous monographs and articles on US-Japanese relations, including *Zaikai Networks and US-Japan Diplomatic Relations* (Yamakawa shuppansha, 1997, in Japanese) and *Tumultuous Decade: Empire, Society, and Diplomacy in 1930s Japan,* edited by Masato Kimura and Tosh Minohara (University of Toronto Press, 2013).

Miyamoto Matao, PhD, Osaka University, is Professor Emeritus, Osaka University. He has published many monographs and articles in Japanese, including *Kinsei Nihon no shijōkeizai* (Yuhikaku, 1988) and *Kigyōkatachi no chōsen* (Chuokoronshinsha, 2013).

Shimada Masakazu, PhD, Meiji University, is Professor of Japanese Business History at the Graduate School and Faculty of Business Administration, Bunkyo Gakuin University, Tokyo. He has published numerous monographs and articles, including "The Entrepreneurial Activities of Eiichi Shibusawa," *Japanese Yearbook on Business History* (2008) and *Shibusawa Eiichi: The Pioneer of the Social Entrepreneur* (Iwanami Shoten, 2011).

Tanaka Kazuhiro, PhD, Hitotsubashi University, is Professor of Philosophy of Management at the Graduate School of Commerce and Management, Hitotsubashi University, Tokyo. Among his monographs and articles are *Thinking about Corporate Governance from the Perspective of Conscience* (Toyo Keizai, 2014) and "Perceived Development and Unperceived Decline of Corporate Governance in Japan," in *Japanese Management in Change: The Impact of Globalization and Market Principles,* edited by Kambayashi N. (Springer, 2014).

Japan and Global Society

Printed and bound by CPI Group (UK) Ltd, Croydon, CR0 4YY

14/04/2025

14656916-0001